*Public Policy*
*toward General Aviation*

*Studies in the Regulation of Economic Activity*

Studies in the Regulation of Economic Activity

# Public Policy toward General Aviation

JEREMY J. WARFORD

The Brookings Institution / Washington, D.C.

*Copyright © 1971 by*

THE BROOKINGS INSTITUTION

*1775 Massachusetts Avenue, N.W., Washington, D.C. 20036*

*ISBN 0-8157-9226-3*

*Library of Congress Catalog Card Number 70-161598*

*1 2 3 4 5 6 7 8 9*

**THE BROOKINGS INSTITUTION** is an independent organization devoted to nonpartisan research, education, and publication in economics, government, foreign policy, and the social sciences generally. Its principal purposes are to aid in the development of sound public policies and to promote public understanding of issues of national importance.

The Institution was founded on December 8, 1927, to merge the activities of the Institute for Government Research, founded in 1916, the Institute of Economics, founded in 1922, and the Robert Brookings Graduate School of Economics and Government, founded in 1924.

The general administration of the Institution is the responsibility of a Board of Trustees charged with maintaining the independence of the staff and fostering the most favorable conditions for creative research and education. The immediate direction of the policies, program, and staff of the Institution is vested in the President, assisted by an advisory committee of the officers and staff.

In publishing a study, the Institution presents it as a competent treatment of a subject worthy of public consideration. The interpretations and conclusions in such publications are those of the author or authors and do not necessarily reflect the views of the other staff members, officers, or trustees of the Brookings Institution.

# Foreword

FEW PEOPLE appreciate that the aircraft flown by commercial airlines constitute only a small fraction of the total number of aircraft that use the nation's airways. Only 2 percent of all civil aircraft registered in the United States belong to the airlines; the remaining 98 percent are used in general aviation by business firms and individuals for such activities as business and personal transportation, air taxi services, and instructional and recreational flying. The aircraft in general aviation make three-quarters of the landings and takeoffs recorded by control towers operated by the Federal Aviation Administration and account for 75 percent more mileage than the commercial carriers. Air traffic is already heavy in practically every major airport in the country, and general aviation—which is growing much more rapidly than commercial aviation—is helping to make the airways system increasingly difficult to manage.

In this study, Jeremy J. Warford focuses attention on the burden placed by general aviation on the nation's airports and airways system, and examines critically the methods employed by public authorities to deal with the problem. The major objective of the study is to suggest methods of allocating a fair share of the costs of operating the nation's airways system to general aviation, preferably by methods that will at the same time bring about more efficient utilization of aviation facilities. To achieve these objectives, Mr. Warford proposes substantial increases in the taxes on aviation fuel, but also suggests that greater reliance be placed on landing fees as a method of allocating airport capacity and terminal airspace. He recommends that landing fees be flexible, so that additional charges can be imposed where competing demands for terminal areas lead to congestion and delays.

Mr. Warford, now an economist at the International Bank for Reconstruction and Development, conducted the study while he was a member of the staff of the Brookings Institution. It is one of a series of Brookings Studies in the Regulation of Economic Activity, which are devoted to analysis of the issues of public concern in the field of economic regulation. Supported by a grant from the Ford Foundation, this research is directed by Joseph A. Pechman, who heads the Brookings Economic Studies Program, with the assistance of Roger G. Noll of the economics staff.

The author wishes to express his gratitude to several of the Brookings staff as well as to many members of the industry and of the Federal Aviation Administration for their helpful comments and advice during the preparation of the book. He is particularly grateful to Henry J. Aaron, Gary Fromm, Milton Iyoha, Gerald R. Jantscher, George Lanka, and John E. Tilton, Jr. His greatest debt, however, is to Charles L. Schultze, senior fellow at Brookings, who first proposed that this study be carried out and provided constant help and advice throughout. The author also acknowleges the research assistance of Betty Cooper and Nancy C. Wilson, the secretarial help of Diane H. Burke, and the diligent checking of statistical material by Evelyn P. Fisher. The manuscript was edited by Ruth Kaufman; the index was prepared by Joan C. Culver.

The views expressed in this book are those of the author and do not necessarily represent the opinions of the trustees, officers, or other staff members of the Brookings Institution or of the Ford Foundation.

KERMIT GORDON
*President*

*October 1971*
*Washington, D.C.*

# Contents

Text Tables

Appendix Tables

## Appendix Figures

# CHAPTER ONE

# *Introduction*

GENERAL AVIATION in the United States includes all civil aircraft not legally classified as air carriers or, more loosely, the commercial airlines. General aviation aircraft range widely in size and technical sophistication and are used for a variety of activities, including transporting company executives, salesmen, and other personnel for business purposes, air taxi services, crop dusting, surveying, advertising, photography, and recreational and instructional flying.

Although this study is of public policy toward general aviation, it is important to bear in mind that the competing demands of various types of aircraft for space and facilities frequently mean that a given policy for general aviation automatically has implications for policy toward military aircraft and commercial airlines. Consequently, public policy toward general aviation cannot be discussed without frequent reference to the treatment of other categories of aviation.

To go even further, the distinction between general aviation and air carriers is often completely arbitrary and, furthermore, is the source of much confusion about how public authorities should treat the various segments of aviation. Nevertheless, sufficient reason to concentrate on the treatment of general aviation is that a distinction, however false, is made between general aviation and air carriers. Moreover, while the activities of the commercial airlines have been the subject of a considerable amount of economic analysis, general aviation has been almost entirely ignored by economists other than those employed by the manufacturers of general aviation aircraft or by the Federal Aviation Administration (FAA).

The lack of scholarly attention to general aviation is rather surprising when one considers its importance. This importance is substantiated by any conceivable measure one cares to make, whether number of aircraft, mileage or hours flown, passengers carried, landings and takeoffs, or rate of growth.

Although general aviation aircraft are found in ever increasing numbers in other countries of the world, nowhere has the rapid growth in general aviation activity matched that in the United States. The United States now has more operational civil aircraft than the rest of the world combined, and about 98 percent of U.S. operational aircraft come within the general aviation category. For that reason, this study deals solely with general aviation in the United States,[1] although similar problems may be encountered elsewhere in the world as private flying (indeed all flying) grows in importance. Perhaps this analysis of the situation in the United States will be of value in helping others to avoid some of the pitfalls into which aviation administrators in this country have fallen.

General aviation organizations have been very successful in maintaining the special economic status of users of private aircraft and have, therefore, contributed greatly to its increasing importance. Reversal of this trend now, in view of the influence of general aviation groups, may be extremely difficult. This situation in particular is one that other countries would do well to avoid by establishing from the beginning efficient policies of cost recovery for all users of airport and airway facilities.

The book contains ten chapters. Chapter 2 outlines the development and current role of general aviation, describing the fleet and the types of organizations, individuals, and interest groups manufacturing and operating general aviation aircraft. This chapter also outlines the division of responsibility for public regulation of and assistance to the industry, and briefly describes some of the problems now confronting public authorities.

Chapter 3 summarizes the theoretical principles that should serve as a guide to tackling these problems. The study is an exercise in applied welfare economics, and the analytical chapter is a very important part of the book. The approach is very pragmatic. In the following pages, policies are recommended that diverge considerably from the theoretical ideal, but this is inevitable if a practicable solution is to be proposed. Since the methods currently employed to deal with the problems of general aviation are so inefficient, we can afford to be unconcerned with some of the

1. This work concentrates on domestic operations of the U.S. general aviation fleet. Very little research has been done on international general aviation activity, a notable exception being found in Gary Fromm, "Aviation User Charges," in *Economic Analysis and the Efficiency of Government,* Hearings before the Subcommittee on Economy in Government of the Joint Economic Committee, 91 Cong. 1 sess. (1970), Pt. 2, pp. 518–85.

finer points of economic theory. The worst aspects of present policy can certainly be vastly improved by implementing a rough approximation to the pricing and investment principles outlined in Chapter 3.

The major part of the book is concerned with federal policy. Most federal expenditures for civil aviation are on the airways system, a complex network of navigational aids and air traffic control facilities. This is described in Chapter 4, along with the methods used by the FAA to allocate the costs of the system among the various categories of aviation and the forms of cost recovery (or user charges) that are employed. Rough estimates are made of the extent to which general aviation is subsidized by these practices.

In the light of the theory outlined earlier, Chapter 5 delves more deeply into the problem of user charges for the federal airways system. Present policy is characterized by heavy subsidization of general aviation and economically inefficient methods of cost recovery. A proposed alternative is that direct charges, in the form of landing fees, be levied with respect to facilities located at terminal areas, with indirect charges, such as a fuel tax, being used for the remainder of the airways system. Practical problems of implementation are discussed at some length.

The discussion at this stage ignores the financing of facilities complementary to the federal airways system, such as airport runways and terminal buildings. Certain theoretical complications arise as a result, but this approach recognizes the practical difficulties involved in laying down pricing and investment rules where responsibility for the operation of aviation facilities is split between the federal government on the one hand and state and local authorities on the other.

In the absence of appropriate action at the state and local level, landing fees levied by the federal government could include peak hour "congestion charges," reflecting the delay costs imposed by airport users on each other. But since congestion is due in large measure to the cost of expanding the capacity of state and local facilities, detailed discussion of the application of such a policy is left until state and local airport pricing and investment policies enter the analysis.

The arguments that have been voiced by general aviation interests against FAA cost-recovery proposals form a useful framework within which possible modifications, both of FAA user charges policy and the suggested alternative, may be examined. Such a discussion is found in Chapter 6. The user charges controversy is a useful peg on which to hang the whole question of what contribution general aviation makes to the well-being of the community and what costs the community should and does bear in maintaining it. This introduces, among other things, particularly interesting problems relating to the "external" benefits and costs that may result from general aviation activity.

Chapter 7 outlines the various methods used by state and local authorities to finance airport construction and operation. A rough estimate is made of the extent to which general aviation is the beneficiary of subsidies resulting from such policies, as well as of direct subsidies to public airport authorities from the federal government. The arguments used to justify local subsidization of general aviation activity are also briefly discussed.

The subject of airport pricing is continued in Chapter 8, which is concerned with the phenomenon of airport congestion and the consequent delays suffered by air travelers. The case for congestion charges and an estimate of the delay costs imposed on the commercial airlines by general aviation receive detailed treatment.

Chapter 9 then summarizes and makes more explicit the implications of previous chapters as they relate to airport pricing and investment strategies. The ideal situation, in which the division of responsibility between federal, state, and local authorities can be ignored, is the framework within which optimal pricing and investment rules for the terminal area are outlined. The chapter contains a summary of the appropriate rules to be followed under a variety of assumptions concerning the presence of congestion, delays, and the types of aircraft involved. Although for expositional purposes the discussion builds up gradually from the simplest to the most complicated case, the general reader may wish to bypass this short chapter altogether and proceed directly to the conclusion. This can be done without loss of continuity.

Two major aspects of public policy toward general aviation are dealt with throughout the book: the question of subsidization on the one hand and efficiency in resource allocation on the other. Chapter 10 brings them together and suggests that in practice the elimination of subsidy, conservatively estimated at $640 million annually, or $3,500 per annum per aircraft, need not be inconsistent with the introduction of efficient pricing and investment policies for aviation-related facilities. It also suggests, however, that such theoretical problems are small compared with institutional and political obstacles to reform.

# CHAPTER TWO

# General Aviation

CIVIL AIRCRAFT registered in the United States are normally classified as belonging to either of two categories: air carriers (or the commercial airlines) and general aviation. In turn, the air carriers are divided into three major groups. By far the most important of these groups is the certificated route air carriers. They hold certificates of public convenience and necessity, issued by the Civil Aeronautics Board (CAB), and are authorized to operate scheduled flights, carrying passengers, mail, and other cargo over specified routes, and a limited number of nonscheduled flights. Some 90 percent of the aircraft in the United States air carrier fleet are in this category.

The second group consists of the supplemental air carriers. These are required to hold (temporary) CAB certificates of public convenience and necessity, and their main function is to operate charter flights for passengers and cargo. Supplemental air carriers may also obtain temporary or limited authority from the CAB to perform scheduled passenger or cargo operations.

The distinguishing feature of the third and smallest group, the commercial operators, is that its members operate on a strictly private, for-hire basis; it lacks the common or public carrier status of the other two groups. Nevertheless, a commercial operator certificate, issued by the Federal Aviation Administration, is necessary for private transportation of passengers or cargo for compensation.

All other civil aviation activity is lumped together and referred to as general aviation. In consequence, in marked contrast to the relative homogeneity of the air carrier group, general aviation operations encompass a tremendously wide range of activity. The aircraft are used for purposes ranging from purely recreational flying to air taxi service and corporate-owned executive transportation, and as a result the types of aircraft found in this category form a most heterogeneous group. As an indication of the variety of aircraft employed, in 1970 seventeen U.S. manufacturers among them produced 106 different models of general aviation aircraft, ranging from a fully equipped two-seater single-piston-engined aircraft selling for about $8,000 to a jet aircraft costing almost $3 million.

In contrast to the interest shown in the activities of the commercial airlines,[1] general aviation has been largely ignored by economists. Several very good reasons account for the preoccupation with the airlines. Obvious contributory factors are the glamour attached to the industry and the fact that the layman's contact with aviation is normally as an airline passenger. General aviation to most people, including most economists, is an unknown quantity altogether. A further reason, which applies particularly to the U.S. domestic airlines, is the form that official regulation of the industry has taken.

Regulation by the CAB of fares and routes, and the administration of a subsidy program, require an abundance of statistical data to be supplied by the airlines. As a consequence, masses of information on prices and costs, as well as physical operating data, are freely available to the researcher in a way that is almost unique to this industry.[2] To the economist who yearns for usable microeconomic data, the activities of the U.S. domestic airlines present a golden opportunity to test textbook theory, for the effects of regulatory changes on both the demand and the supply sides of commercial air transport are open to his inspection. Moreover, the exogenous determination of routes and fares has afforded endless opportunity for speculation as to the likely results of permitting airlines to indulge in price competition.

None of this applies to general aviation. Since most general aviation aircraft are normally smaller, slower, less sophisticated—and, it may be added, quieter—they lack the glamour of their airline counterparts. In addition, general aviation has never been subject to the degree of economic regulation that the airlines have, and "economic" information has therefore been collected less assiduously. Moreover, general aviation interests, particularly sensitive at the present to threats of government restriction of their activities, are often unwilling to divulge information to outsiders. These factors obviously help to explain the relative neglect of general aviation by economists other than those employed either by the

1. For an outstanding contribution, see Richard E. Caves, *Air Transport and Its Regulators* (Harvard University Press, 1962).

2. See, for example, U.S. Civil Aeronautics Board, *Handbook of Airline Statistics,* various issues.

appropriate governmental agency (the Federal Aviation Administration) or within the industry itself. Indeed, partly as a result, the outsider may be tempted to assert that general aviation activity is not a very important subject when compared with that of the commercial airlines. In this he would be gravely mistaken, as the following examples demonstrate.

**Table 2-1. U.S. Eligible Registered Aircraft on Record with FAA, January 1, Selected Years, 1954–69**

| | | | General aviation | | | | | |
| | | | Fixed-wing aircraft | | | | | |
| | | | | | Single-engine | | | |
| Year | Total | Air carrier[a] | Total | Multi-engine | 4-place and over | 3-place and less | Rotor-craft | Other |
|---|---|---|---|---|---|---|---|---|
| 1954 | 55,505 | 1,615 | 53,890 | n.a. | n.a. | n.a. | n.a. | n.a. |
| 1956 | 60,432 | 1,642 | 58,790 | 3,342 | 19,240 | 35,740 | 237 | 231 |
| 1958 | 67,153 | 1,864 | 65,289 | 5,036 | 23,751 | 35,898 | 344 | 260 |
| 1960[b] | 70,747 | 2,020 | 68,727 | 6,034 | 27,301 | 34,543 | 525 | 324 |
| 1962 | 82,853 | 2,221 | 80,632 | 8,401 | 38,206 | 32,800 | 798 | 427 |
| 1964 | 87,267 | 2,179 | 85,088 | 9,695 | 42,657 | 30,977 | 1,171 | 588 |
| 1966 | 97,741 | 2,299 | 95,442 | 11,977 | 49,789 | 31,364 | 1,503 | 809 |
| 1968 | 116,781 | 2,595 | 114,186 | 14,651 | 56,865 | 39,675 | 1,899 | 1,096 |
| 1969 | 127,164 | 2,927 | 124,237 | 16,760 | 60,977 | 42,830 | 2,350 | 1,320 |

Source: U.S. Federal Aviation Agency, *FAA Statistical Handbook of Aviation, 1965*, p. 55, and *1969*, p. 180.
n.a. Not available.
a. Registered but not necessarily in operation. Includes helicopters.
b. Excludes approximately 4,000 unclassified active aircraft.

## The Importance of General Aviation

Of the number of eligible civil aircraft registered in the United States,[3] general aviation forms the bulk, and the fastest growing portion, of the civil aviation fleet as shown in Table 2-1. In 1969 it accounted for 98 percent of all civil aircraft registered in the United States. It more than doubled in size between 1956 and 1969, rising from 58,790 to 124,237 aircraft. It will be observed that the increase in the number of general

3. An eligible aircraft is defined as one with a current FAA air-worthiness certificate (that is, one obtained or renewed within the previous twelve months).

aviation aircraft has been due almost entirely to the growth in the number of the larger aircraft. The number of multi-engine and single-engine aircraft with four or more seats increased by roughly 400 percent and 215 percent, respectively.

Other useful measures of the importance of general aviation are mileage, passengers carried, and the use made of airports and facilities provided by the FAA. The FAA estimates that in 1968, 3,700 million aircraft miles were flown by general aviation,[4] whereas the certificated route air carriers flew 2,146 million revenue aircraft miles in the same year. It is also estimated that general aviation is responsible for the carriage of roughly one-third of all domestic air passengers.[5] As for the use of facilities supplied by the FAA, in 1968 general aviation aircraft, despite their ability often to make use of landing strips with no FAA facilities at all, made three-quarters of the landings and takeoffs recorded by FAA-operated control towers.

Even more surprising to those who believe that high air traffic density is confined to the large air carrier airports such as Chicago (O'Hare), Los Angeles, and New York (John F. Kennedy International) will be the information supplied in Table 2-2, which lists the leading FAA-operated air traffic control towers in rank order of total operations for 1968, and compares this with the rankings when other measures are used.

Table 2-2 highlights how little is known about general aviation, for few people would place Van Nuys, California, in such a high position among the great airports. The high rankings of Van Nuys, Opa Locka, Fort Lauderdale, Santa Ana and Long Beach, all of which have more total operations than Kennedy International, are due entirely to the volume of general aviation activity at these airports.

The difference between columns 1 and 2 of Table 2-2 derives from two types of operation defined by the FAA. Local operations are performed by aircraft that operate in the local traffic pattern or within sight of the airport traffic control tower, *or* are known to be departing for, or arriving from, flight in local practice areas located within a 20-mile radius of the control tower, *or* are executing simulated instrument approaches or low passes at the airport. Itinerant operations are all aircraft arrivals and departures other than local operations. Consequently, airports catering largely to general aviation, in which local operations can be ex-

4. The FAA estimates miles, hours flown, and so on, from Aircraft Use and Inspection Reports (FAA Form AC8320-3), annual receipt of which is necessary for aircraft certification.

5. See U.S. Federal Aviation Agency, Air Traffic Service, "General Aviation Occupant Load Factor" (FAA, 1966; processed), p. 6.

**Table 2-2. Twenty-five Leading FAA-Operated Air Traffic Control Towers in Rank Order of Number of Operations, 1968**

| | (1) Total operations | | (2) Total itinerant operations[a] | | (3) Air carrier operations[a] | | (4) General aviation itinerant operations[a] | |
|---|---|---|---|---|---|---|---|---|
| Airport | Rank | Number | Rank | Number | Rank | Number | Rank | Number |
| Chicago, Illinois (O'Hare) | 1 | 690,810 | 1 | 689,925 | 1 | 628,632 | — | — |
| Los Angeles, California | 2 | 594,486 | 2 | 577,193 | 2 | 438,386 | — | — |
| Van Nuys, California | 3 | 567,973 | 11 | 326,198 | — | — | 1 | 317,816 |
| Opa Locka, Florida | 4 | 563,618 | 13 | 308,176 | — | — | 2 | 301,610 |
| Fort Lauderdale, Florida | 5 | 517,848 | 19 | 286,226 | — | — | 4 | 245,099 |
| Santa Ana, California | 6 | 512,973 | — | — | — | — | 5 | 214,043 |
| Long Beach, California | 7 | 496,917 | 16 | 294,302 | — | — | 3 | 280,513 |
| New York, N.Y. (John F. Kennedy International) | 8 | 465,120 | 3 | 464,916 | 3 | 398,466 | — | — |
| Minneapolis, Minnesota (Flying Cloud) | 9 | 446,198 | — | — | — | — | 19 | 148,158 |
| Tamiami, Florida | 10 | 438,916 | — | — | — | — | — | — |
| Miami, Florida | 11 | 431,802 | 9 | 340,127 | 6 | 256,400 | — | — |
| Torrance, California (Municipal) | 12 | 428,127 | — | — | — | — | 16 | 158,240 |
| Oakland, California | 13 | 420,049 | — | — | — | — | 11 | 176,084 |
| San Jose, California (Municipal) | 14 | 411,753 | — | — | — | — | 8 | 192,483 |
| Atlanta, Georgia (Municipal) | 15 | 400,445 | 5 | 384,259 | 4 | 312,912 | — | — |
| Denver, Colorado | 16 | 395,120 | 10 | 327,466 | 17 | 148,383 | 9 | 178,121 |
| Dallas, Texas (Love Field) | 17 | 394,040 | 4 | 391,341 | 8 | 242,650 | 21 | 145,794 |
| Seattle, Washington (Boeing) | 18 | 386,203 | — | — | — | — | 6 | 198,201 |
| Columbus, Ohio (International) | 19 | 373,720 | 24 | 251,515 | — | — | 10 | 176,720 |
| New York, N.Y. (La Guardia) | 20 | 357,382 | 6 | 356,912 | 7 | 251,026 | — | — |
| Hollywood, Florida | 21 | 357,162 | — | — | — | — | — | — |
| Phoenix, Arizona | 22 | 353,376 | 21 | 279,962 | — | — | 7 | 196,015 |
| San Francisco, California | 23 | 353,255 | 7 | 352,417 | 5 | 297,588 | — | — |
| Santa Monica, California | 24 | 351,190 | — | — | — | — | 14 | 161,945 |
| Concord, California | 25 | 348,885 | — | — | — | — | — | — |

Source: U.S. Federal Aviation Administration, *FAA Statistical Handbook of Aviation, 1969*, pp. 27–30.
a. Dashes signify that the airport did not rank among the first twenty-five for this type of operation.

pected to be relatively more important than at air carrier airports, are ranked lower in column 2 than in column 1.

So much for this brief introduction to the current importance of general aviation. What of the future? The FAA has made estimates of the probable growth in aviation of all kinds up to 1980.[6] The estimated number of active aircraft by type is shown in Table 2-3. The predicted increase of 60 percent in the number of general aviation aircraft between 1970 and 1980 compares with an estimated increase of 30 percent for the air carrier fleet. Noticeable changes are expected in the size and type of aircraft to be produced during the period, as reflected in part by the relatively faster growth predicted for turbine-powered than for piston-en-

6. Federal Aviation Administration, Office of Policy Development, "Aviation Forecasts, Fiscal Years 1969–1980" (FAA, 1969; processed).

**Table 2-3. Active Aircraft by Type: Forecasts for Selected Years, January 1, 1970–80**

| Year | Air carrier[a] | General aviation | | | | | |
|------|------|------|------|------|------|------|------|
| | | | Piston | | | | |
| | | Total | Single-engine | Multi-engine | Turbine | Other |
| 1970 | 2,746 | 131,000 | 109,700 | 15,600 | 2,050 | 3,650 |
| 1971 | 2,790 | 139,000 | 116,000 | 16,600 | 2,450 | 3,950 |
| 1972 | 2,860 | 147,000 | 122,050 | 17,800 | 2,900 | 4,250 |
| 1973 | 2,960 | 155,000 | 128,150 | 19,000 | 3,350 | 4,500 |
| 1974 | 3,050 | 162,000 | 133,400 | 20,000 | 3,850 | 4,750 |
| 1979 | 3,480 | 205,000 | 166,200 | 25,500 | 7,000 | 6,300 |
| 1980 | 3,600 | 214,000 | 173,000 | 26,650 | 7,800 | 6,550 |

Source: Federal Aviation Administration, Office of Policy Development, "Aviation Forecasts, Fiscal Years 1969–1980" (FAA, 1969; processed), pp. 25, 28.
a. Includes only aircraft actually in service.

gined general aviation aircraft. The assumptions underlying FAA forecasts of future aviation activity are discussed later in this chapter; suffice to say now that, although the predictions may be reasonably accurate, whether or not the level of activity predicted is economically desirable is another matter altogether.

## The Aircraft

In terms of the number of aircraft produced, the general aviation manufacturing industry in the United States has in recent years been dominated by two firms, Cessna Aircraft Company and Piper Aircraft Corporation. As Table 2-4 demonstrates, this has been a feature of the industry since the early 1950s; in 1952, after the effects of the war years (including an artificial postwar boom) had subsided, these two firms produced about 83 percent of all fixed-wing general aviation aircraft manufactured in the United States. In 1970 their share amounted to 73 percent.

No such dominance is observed when the value of aircraft sales is used as a measure of market share. Because Cessna and Piper have manufactured primarily smaller, less expensive general aviation aircraft, their share of the market has always been smaller in value terms than in number of aircraft sold.

## Table 2-4. Production of General Aviation Aircraft by Selected Manufacturers, Selected Years, 1947-70

| Year | Total | Beech | Cessna | Lear | Lock-heed | Mooney[a] | North American Rockwell[b] | Piper | Other |
|------|-------|-------|--------|------|-----------|-----------|---------------------------|-------|-------|
| 1947 | 15,764 | 1,288 | 2,390 | — | — | — | — | 3,634 | 8,452 |
| 1952 | 3,058 | 414 | 1,373 | — | — | 49 | 39 | 1,161 | 22 |
| 1956 | 6,738 | 724 | 3,235 | — | — | 79 | 154 | 2,329 | 217 |
| 1960 | 7,588 | 962 | 3,720 | — | — | 172 | 155 | 2,313 | 266 |
| 1964 | 9,371 | 1,103 | 4,188 | 3 | 6 | 650 | 109 | 3,196 | 116 |
| 1965 | 11,967 | 1,192 | 5,629 | 80 | 18 | 775 | 110 | 3,776 | 387 |
| 1966 | 15,747 | 1,535 | 7,888 | 51 | 24 | 917 | 354 | 4,437 | 541 |
| 1967 | 13,577 | 1,260 | 6,233 | 34 | 19 | 642 | 386 | 4,490 | 513 |
| 1968 | 13,698 | 1,347 | 6,578 | 41 | 16 | 579 | 471 | 4,228 | 438 |
| 1969 | 12,456 | 1,061 | 5,887 | 61 | 14 | 376 | 344 | 3,951 | 762 |
| 1970 | 7,391 | 793 | 3,730 | 35 | 2 | c | 450 | 1,675 | 706 |

Sources: Aerospace Industries Association of America, *Aerospace Facts and Figures, 1970* (1970), p. 33; *Aviation Week and Space Technology*, Vol. 94 (March 8, 1971), pp. 154–55.
a. Includes production of Imco.
b. Includes production of Aero Commanders through 1969, and of Aerostars in 1970.
c. Consolidated with a manufacturer included in "other".

Owing to nonreporting by some manufacturers, data on the value of sales are less reliable for most years than those on the number of aircraft produced. In 1952, the leading manufacturer of general aviation aircraft, measured by value of sales, was Beech Aircraft Corporation. Beech's sales of $9.85 million represented 38 percent of the total; Cessna followed closely with sales of $9.22 million (35 percent), with Piper next, having sales of $4.89 million representing 19 percent of the market. The picture for 1970 is summarized in Table 2-5. Cessna leads not only in the number of aircraft sold, but also in value of sales; Beech is in second place by value, with Grumman and Piper about evenly matched for third place.

As noted above, a feature of the recent development of general aviation is that the growth in the number of aircraft has been almost entirely confined to multi-engined aircraft and single-engined aircraft of four places and over. In varying degrees, Beech, Piper, and Cessna have all accommodated themselves, and contributed, to this trend in demand. The most recent development is the introduction of turbine-powered aircraft, constructed specifically for general aviation purposes. Beech has produced turboprop aircraft for several years. Fairchild Hiller and Mitsubishi also produce turboprop aircraft, while North American Rockwell produces both turboprop and turbojet aircraft specifically designed

**Table 2-5. Shipments of General Aviation Aircraft
by Selected Manufacturers, 1970**

| Manufacturer | Number of units | Percentage of total | Value of sales[a] (thousands of dollars) | Percentage of total |
|---|---|---|---|---|
| Aerostar | 238 | 3 | 9,588 | 3 |
| Beech | 793 | 11 | 80,689 | 22 |
| Cessna | 3,730 | 50 | 97,423 | 27 |
| Gates Learjet | 35 | b | 26,890 | 7 |
| Grumman | 111 | 2 | 47,825 | 13 |
| Lockheed | 2 | b | 3,500 | 1 |
| North American Rockwell | 212 | 3 | 29,187 | 8 |
| Piper | 1,675 | 23 | 48,530 | 14 |
| Others | 595 | 8 | 15,578 | 4 |
| Total | 7,391 | 100 | 359,210 | 100 |

Source: *Aviation Week and Space Technology*, Vol. 94 (March 8, 1970), pp. 154–55. Percentages do not total 100 because of rounding.

a. Data for Grumman, two Lockheed craft, and seven North American Rockwell craft are estimates, based on list prices of basic aircraft minus interiors, avionics, and other customer options. See Appendix Table A-1, note d, for the normal range of additional cost for electronic equipment, by broad aircraft categories.

b. Less than 0.5 percent.

for the general aviation market. As Table 2-3 shows, the FAA expects the number of turbine-powered aircraft to increase at a much faster rate than other elements of the general aviation fleet.

For the reader interested in the composition of the general aviation fleet there are a number of excellent descriptions.[7] A tabulation of some of the basic characteristics of representative models of general aviation aircraft produced by U.S. manufacturers in 1970 is given in Appendix Table A-1.

## Uses of General Aviation[8]

The FAA publishes annual estimates of hours and miles flown in various types of general aviation activity. These are categorized by use, such

7. See, for example, Federal Aviation Agency, Office of Policy Development, *General Aviation: A Study and Forecast of the Fleet and Its Use in 1975* (1966). For descriptions of the aircraft themselves, see John W. R. Taylor (ed.), *Jane's All the World's Aircraft, 1970–71* (McGraw-Hill, 1970), and *The 1970 Aerospace Year Book* (Aerospace Industries Association of America, 1970).

8. Probably the best available description of the uses of the general aviation fleet is to be found in FAA, *General Aviation: A Study and Forecast of the Fleet and Its Use in 1975*.

as (a) business, (b) commercial, (c) instructional, and (d) personal, and are summarized for the year 1968 in Table 2-6. Data in this form, estimated by the FAA from annual Aircraft Use and Inspection Reports, are particularly useful as a framework within which the nature of the general aviation community may be described. Although there are significant overlaps, the categories are sufficiently distinct to encompass groups of aircraft users who often differ considerably from each other with respect to reasons for aircraft operation, the type of aircraft flown, pilot qualifications, and attitudes toward official airport and airways policies and user charges. In addition, an interest group structure has emerged in

**Table 2-6. Hours and Miles Flown in General Aviation, by Type of Flying, 1968**

| Type of flying | Hours flown (thousands) | Percentage of total | Miles flown (millions) | Percentage of total |
|---|---|---|---|---|
| Business | 6,976 | 29 | 1,406 | 38 |
| Commercial | 4,810 | 20 | 666 | 18 |
| Instructional | 6,494 | 27 | 814 | 22 |
| Personal | 5,532 | 23 | 777 | 21 |
| Other | 241 | 1 | 37 | 1 |
| Total | 24,053 | 100 | 3,701 | 100 |

Source: Federal Aviation Administration, *FAA Statistical Handbook of Aviation, 1969*, pp. 207–08. Figures are rounded and may not add to totals.

which different organizations tend to polarize around at least three of the four categories listed above.

The disparate nature of general aviation activity explains much of the conflict among the various groups, and it is rare that the industry speaks with one voice. At the instigation of an association of manufacturers,[9] attempts have recently been made to unite the industry in the face of proposals by the federal government to impose increased taxes on general aviation. Although moderately successful, complete unity is frustrated by certain fundamental conflicts, inherent in the heterogeneous nature of general aviation, among various categories of users.

9. Prior to December 1969, the Aerospace Industries Association, and now known as the General Aviation Manufacturers Association, its members are Avco, Beech, Bendix, Cessna, Collins Radio, Edo-Aire, Garrett, Gates Lear Jet, Grumman, King Radio, Narco Scientific Industries, North American Rockwell, Piper, RCA, Sperry Rand, Swearingen, Teledyne Continental Motors, and United Aircraft.

*Business Use*

Business use is defined by the FAA to include any use of aircraft by individuals or firms in the course of their business, excluding the operation of aircraft for compensation or hire. The FAA makes a distinction, within this category, between executive or corporate transportation and other business transportation. The distinction is somewhat blurred, but inclusion in the former category is restricted to aircraft owned and used by corporations, and flown by professional pilots, while other business transportation refers to aircraft owned and piloted by individuals in connection with their occupation or business.

Table 2-6 indicates that business use, whether measured in aircraft miles or hours flown, represented the most important category of use in 1968. It also shows that the average speed of aircraft employed for business purposes is greater than the average speed of those employed in other forms of general aviation activity. The business category also leads the field with respect to the size and sophistication of the aircraft employed. Table 2-7 provides a breakdown of aircraft according to primary use, and shows that turbojet and turboprop aircraft form a much higher proportion of the corporate fleet than of any other category, although in terms of absolute numbers more are to be found in the "other business" group.

**Table 2-7. Eligible General Aviation Aircraft, by Type of Aircraft and Primary Use, 1968**

| | | Primary Use | | | | | | | |
| | | Business | | Commercial | | | | | |
| Type of aircraft | Total number of aircraft | Executive transportation | Other | Air taxi | Aerial application | Industrial special | Instructional | Personal | Other[a] |
|---|---|---|---|---|---|---|---|---|---|
| Single-engine, piston powered | | | | | | | | | |
|   1–3 places | 42,806 | 51 | 1,691 | 397 | 4,634 | 90 | 9,187 | 24,752 | 2,004 |
|   4 places and over | 60,929 | 245 | 11,735 | 2,538 | 531 | 83 | 4,778 | 38,544 | 2,475 |
| Multi-engine piston powered | | | | | | | | | |
|   Under 12,500 pounds | 13,856 | 1,058 | 6,976 | 1,996 | 46 | 35 | 409 | 2,725 | 611 |
|   12,500 pounds and over | 1,143 | 266 | 430 | 15 | 95 | 46 | 8 | 77 | 206 |
| Turboprop | 1,034 | 374 | 413 | 102 | — | 1 | 7 | 33 | 104 |
| Turbojet | 799 | 282 | 292 | 28 | — | 1 | 3 | 123 | 70 |
| Rotorcraft | 2,350 | 85 | 293 | 438 | 286 | 109 | 155 | 623 | 361 |

Source: Federal Aviation Administration, *FAA Statistical Handbook of Aviation, 1969*, p. 204.
a. Including aircraft whose use was not reported.

There is no need to dwell on the motives for corporate aircraft ownership. An abundance of literature in the aviation journals and elsewhere[10]
explains the advantages aircraft ownership has for a company. Numerous
examples of "typical" traveling schedules purport to demonstrate the advantages of the private aircraft over use of the commercial airlines. The
monetary-equivalent savings in terms of executives' time which would
otherwise be spent in traveling to and from air carrier airports and in
waiting for scheduled air carrier flights, loom large on the benefit side of
such calculations. Normally unquantified are the advantages of flexibility
and prestige (which may or may not bring about pecuniary benefits) and
of the fact that private meetings may be held in privately owned aircraft.

Although ownership of business aircraft is apparently dominated by
small companies,[11] a survey published in 1966 showed that all of the top
10 companies in *Fortune*'s 500 owned turbojet or turboprop airplanes,
while 85 out of the top 100 owned aircraft.[12] However, in 1963, only 1.5
percent of the active corporations in the United States owned their own
aircraft. More than half the fleet was owned by firms in transportation,
communications, and public utilities; retailing; and manufacturing (20.2
percent, 19.3 percent, and 15.4 percent, respectively); 48 percent of all
aircraft were owned by air-oriented firms, such as aircraft manufacturers
and dealers, noncertificated airlines, flying schools, and so forth.[13]

The aviation interests of companies owning and operating their own
aircraft for business purposes other than for hire are represented by the
National Business Aircraft Association (NBAA). The NBAA speaks for
about 750 companies, owning over 2,000 aircraft; 95 of the top 100 corporations listed in *Fortune*'s annual directory of the 500 largest industrials
are claimed as members.[14] Because of the stature of its members, NBAA
is a very influential part of the general aviation community.

10. See, for example, Henry W. Ryan, "Economics of Business Aircraft" (New
York: Society of Automotive Engineers, 1966; processed); National Business
Aircraft Association, *Business Flying: Historical Statistical Operational Informa-
tion*, Special Report 68-8 (Washington: NBAA, 1968); and Michigan Aeronautics
Commission, Department of Commerce, "Aviation and Economic Development"
(The Commission, revised 1969; processed).

11. Those with annual business receipts of less than $500,000, and employing
fewer than 20 people, owned 90 percent of business aircraft in 1963. See Tri-State
Transportation Committee, "General Aviation: The Nation's Business Aircraft
Fleet" (New York: The Committee, 1965), p. 3.

12. National Business Aircraft Association, *Business Flying*, p. 2.

13. Tri-State Transportation Committee, "General Aviation: The Nation's
Business Fleet," pp. 12, 19. Use by noncertificated airlines, flying schools, and so
on, obviously does not fall within the FAA's definition of corporate use.

14. National Business Aircraft Association, *Business Flying*, pp. 2, 5.

General aviation aircraft are also used by doctors, lawyers, farmers, engineers, and others in the course of their business. Typically, such persons use their aircraft partly for business and partly for pleasure. But, as Table 2-7 shows, they differ substantially from the purely private flier with respect to the type of aircraft employed: for example, single-engined piston aircraft constitute a much higher proportion of the aircraft used primarily for personal flying than of those used mainly for noncorporate business transportation. A number of organizations represent the interests of the noncorporate business flier; by far the most important is the Aircraft Owners and Pilots Association (AOPA), which is also the spokesman for the personal flier and which will be briefly described in the section dealing with that group.

### Commercial Use

The FAA defines three subcategories of commercial general aviation activity: air taxi operation, aerial application, and industrial/special usage. The distinction between commercial general aviation and commercial and other air carrier activity is somewhat arbitrary. This is particularly so with regard to air taxis and commercial air carriers. Roughly speaking, air taxi operations are the transportation of passengers, freight, or mail by aircraft whose maximum takeoff weight is 12,500 pounds or less. The exceptions to this rule are not sufficiently important to concern us here.[15]

Air taxis are licensed by the FAA, their operation requiring the possession of an air taxi/commercial operator's (ATCO) certificate, but they are not subject to CAB control over routes and fares in the same way as are the airlines. All air taxi operators have to register annually with the CAB, at which time they must produce a certificate of compliance with a rule requiring them to carry liability insurance. In 1968, air taxi operations were responsible for more than half of the commercial hours flown, claiming, by primary use, 48 percent of the aircraft used for commercial purposes. These in turn represented about 5 percent of all general aviation aircraft.

The term "air taxi" covers various forms of activity, including scheduled and nonscheduled operations, which may in turn include the on-call

---

15. The regulations are to be found in Office of the Federal Register, *Code of Federal Regulations* (1969), Title 14, Ch. 1, Pt. 135, and Civil Aeronautics Board, Regulation No. ER-574, Economic Regulations, Pt. 298.

air taxi, as well as aircraft leasing and charters. Scheduled air taxi operators sometimes make flights on a scheduled basis; nonscheduled never
do. The CAB in 1969 designated a further subcategory to be known as
the commuter air carrier: any air taxi operator flying at least five round
trips weekly on published schedules between any two points. Because of
their importance to the nation's overall transportation system, these operators are required to file quarterly reports on traffic data and to supply
details, including fares, of scheduled flights.[16] In 1969, 101 commuter
air carriers served 359 cities (171 with populations of less than 25,000),
110 of which were not served by air carrier.[17]

The commercial airlines have for some time recognized the importance of the scheduled air taxi as a "feeder" service. Recent "fly all the
way" campaigns have been accompanied by agreements between commercial airlines and air taxi operators that the latter should provide such
supplementary service. The willingness of airlines to issue a single ticket
covering a passenger's entire journey, including that part during which he
is conveyed by air taxi, has been a significant development in the history
of the scheduled air taxi.

Another important development has been the Post Office Department's
policy, introduced at the end of 1965, of permitting air taxis to carry mail.
So far this is a relatively small part of air taxi operators' total revenue,
representing roughly $8.5 million in fiscal year 1969. In mid-1969 there
were 151 mail routes, operated by 35 air taxi and commuter air carriers.[18]
A further stimulus has been provided by the CAB policy of taking into account the extent to which a route is already served by air taxis in deciding
on whether that route should be awarded to a feeder airline.[19]

These influences have contributed to a phenomenal rate of increase in
scheduled air taxi operations. For example, the number of scheduled air
taxi operators grew from 12, operating 72 aircraft, at the beginning of
1964, to 240, operating 1,272 aircraft, in November 1968.[20] As one
might expect, fewer data are available on nonscheduled air taxis, but it

16. Civil Aeronautics Board, Regulation No. ER-574, amendment to Part 298
of the Economic Regulations, effective July 1, 1969.

17. *Aviation Facilities Maintenance and Development,* Hearings before the
House Committee on Interstate and Foreign Commerce, 91 Cong. 1 sess. (1969),
Pt. 2, p. 494.

18. *Ibid.,* p. 495.

19. CAB Docket 16024, April 5, 1965.

20. Federal Aviation Administration, *FAA Statistical Handbook of Aviation,
1968,* p. 116, and *1969,* p. 210.

appears that the growth of this category has been less dramatic in the last two or three years: between 1964 and 1968 the total number of aircraft used primarily as nonscheduled air taxis rose from 5,267 to 5,514.[21]

The last detailed analysis, of 1966 operations, is, in the light of the foregoing, unsatisfactory as a guide to present circumstances, but it is of interest that in that year nonscheduled flights carried an estimated 3.3 million passengers, while scheduled flights carried 1.3 million.[22] It is probable that at present the numbers of passengers carried by scheduled and nonscheduled operators are roughly the same.

The on-call air taxi, charter, and leasing activities are lumped together and referred to as nonscheduled air taxi operations. Data adequately distinguishing them are not available; indeed, it is common to find an individual operator performing all these functions in addition to others. This is in contrast to the larger scheduled operators who normally specialize in this activity. The smaller ones, as well as the majority of nonscheduled operators of various kinds, usually also act as fixed base operators (FBOs). They supply a variety of support services essential to general aviation, including airport and aircraft maintenance and the sale of fuel and aircraft components. Many also act as aircraft dealers and distributors for the major manufacturers, often give flying lessons, and engage in such commercial activities as aerial application and industrial/special operations.

The great advantage of the on-call air taxi, also applicable to the leased or chartered aircraft, is its flexibility. A further advantage, claimed for the air taxi group as a whole, is that it enables small communities to be linked to major metropolitan areas when air carriers do not perform this service. Indeed, one community (Spencer, Iowa, population under 9,000) apparently values the air taxi service so highly that it has signed an agreement with Fleet Airlines guaranteeing to underwrite the air taxi's direct operating costs for daily service between Spencer and Minneapolis-St. Paul.[23]

Aerial application and industrial/special uses accounted for the remainder of commercial use, aerial application representing roughly one-third of total commercial hours flown in 1968. The major manufacturers

21. FAA, *General Aviation: A Study and Forecast of the Fleet and Its Use in 1975,* pp. 6, 40; FAA, *FAA Statistical Handbook of Aviation, 1969,* p. 194.

22. Federal Aviation Administration, "1966 Census of Air Taxi Operators" (FAA, 1968; processed).

23. *Aviation Facilities Maintenance and Development,* Hearings, Pt. 2, p. 495.

produce aircraft specially designed for crop spraying—usually single-engined piston aircraft, plus some rotorcraft. The industrial/special category includes aircraft used for a host of different purposes, among them advertising, photography, aerial surveying, highway and pipeline patrol, and a variety of emergency and rescue operations, including fire-fighting. In comparison with other general aviation activity, however, this category is relatively unimportant in terms of the number of aircraft employed and hours flown.

*Instructional Use*

Instructional flying includes any use of an aircraft for purposes of formal instruction, either with the instructor aboard or when the student is flying solo but is carrying out maneuvers according to the instructor's specifications. It is dominated by instruction leading to the private pilot's license. Among the aircraft commonly used for this purpose are the Cessna 150 Trainer and the Piper PA-28-140 Cherokee.

There are four major classes of certificated pilots.[24] Listed in ascending order of the degree of competence required, these are the holders of student, private, commercial, and airline transport licenses. Significantly smaller in number are pilots whose licenses limit them to flying helicopters or gliders or balloons. Since general aviation includes all activity other than airline transport, it is clear that the number of persons currently holding student, private, and commercial licenses is a minimum measure of the number of pilots currently qualified to fly general aviation aircraft, for those pilots with airline transport qualifications will also be licensed to fly most general aviation aircraft. In 1968 the number of pilots limited to general aviation operations formed about 70 percent of all persons licensed to fly.

Graduation from one pilot category to another is by means of written and practical examinations conducted by the FAA.[25] To obtain a student's license, an applicant must be at least sixteen years old, and have passed an FAA-approved medical examination within the previous two years. Thereafter, medical examinations are required biennially to maintain the validity of the license. This continues to be necessary after he has obtained his private pilot's license, which in turn also requires that he

24. See *Code of Federal Regulations,* Title 14, Ch. 1, Pt. 61.
25. Specific requirements are listed in *ibid.* Our brief survey does not include regulations concerning licenses to fly gliders, balloons, dirigibles, and blimps.

should be at least seventeen years of age and have passed the necessary proficiency tests, and had at least forty hours of flying experience. The number of hours spent flying with an FAA-approved instructor, as well as of solo flight, are specified in the regulations.

To obtain a commercial license the private pilot has to be at least eighteen years old and be able to demonstrate a higher level of proficiency in written and practical examinations. He must have had at least 200 hours of flying time, with a specified proportion of instructional and other experience. Finally, should he wish to become an airline transport pilot, it is necessary to pass still more stringent tests of proficiency and experience. The airline pilot certificate can be obtained at a minimum age of twenty-three years. Medical examinations for commercial and airline pilots are required annually and semiannually, respectively. Moreover, the examinations themselves become progressively more demanding as one moves from the private to the commercial to the airline transport grade.

The privileges and limitations applicable to each of the purely general aviation categories (student, private, and commercial) are laid down in the Federal Aviation Regulations[26] and are briefly summarized as follows:

*Student Pilots.* With some minor exceptions, a student pilot may not act as pilot in command of an aircraft that is carrying a passenger or is on an international flight or in the furtherance of a business. Neither may he pilot an aircraft for compensation or hire. The make and model of any aircraft he flies must be endorsed on his certificate by his certificated flight instructor.

*Private Pilots.* With certain minor exceptions, a private pilot may not act as a pilot in command of an aircraft that is carrying passengers or property for compensation or hire. He must have a type rating for the aircraft concerned which means, for example, that he cannot qualify in a single piston-engined aircraft and then fly a four-engined turbojet for general aviation purposes. At the end of 1968 this category accounted for roughly 60 percent of all qualified (that is, nonstudent) general aviation pilots.

*Commercial Pilots.* As long as he has a type rating for the aircraft, a commercial pilot's license entitles him to act as pilot in command of an aircraft that is carrying passengers or property for compensation or hire, and he may himself, for compensation or hire, act as pilot in command of an aircraft. Such a license therefore allows him to command any air-

26. *Ibid.*

craft other than an airliner (that is, one defined by the CAB as such). Commercial pilots are employed by corporations to fly their executive aircraft, and by air taxi operators and other companies engaging in the business of air transportation.

At the end of 1968 there were 2,035 FAA-approved pilot schools in the United States. Of these, 1,173 provided flight and ground training, 698 provided flight, and 164 ground training only. Flying schools are normally operated by fixed base operators as part of the regular sales, maintenance, and charter services available at local airports. A 1964 FAA report showed that over 80 percent of FAA-approved flight schools were operated by FBOs, the remainder being private schools operated exclusively as training institutions, or forming part of the curriculum of universities, colleges, or high schools.[27] In 1968 a TIME survey questionnaire, sent to 1,026 newly qualified pilots and student pilots, showed, on the basis of a 50.9 percent return, that 42 percent learned or were learning to fly by means of lessons from an airplane dealer, while 47 percent took lessons at other flying schools. (Both categories, dealers and flying schools, would be largely coincident with the FBO group.) The remainder learned to fly in the armed forces or were taught by (presumably FAA-approved) friends or independent instructors.[28]

General aviation aircraft manufacturers, understandably, have shown a keen interest in encouraging flight training. For example, Piper Aircraft Corporation in 1968 introduced a standardized system of flight training to be operated by authorized Piper dealers and other flight schools franchised by Piper. As described in an FBO trade journal,[29] the basic idea was that one aircraft (a Cherokee) would be used exclusively, and instructors would follow a standardized syllabus, so a student pilot could change instructors without severely damaging his training. This wa clearly aimed at reducing the high student dropout rate. Should the stu dent move from one part of the country to another, or not get along wi' his current instructor, he finds it relatively easy to complete his traini elsewhere. The franchised FBO gains in that he becomes identified w'

27. See *Report of the Aviation Human Resources Study Board on Manpo Requirements of the Civil Aviation Industry (Project Long Look)* (FAA, 19' pp. 65–66.

28. TIME Marketing Information, "Survey on Flying (Students and Pilots)" (TIME, Inc., no date; processed). Because of multiple mentions, the centages given in the survey add up to more than 100 percent; for examj small number of people may have received lessons from both dealers and flying schools.

29. *Airport Services Management,* Vol. 8 (December 1968), p. 38.

the Piper image and therefore obtains valuable advertisement. Similar plans are operated by other manufacturers; other schemes that have received some publicity include the $5.00 first lesson offered by some manufacturers through their dealers.[30]

The problem of dropouts, referred to above, does indeed trouble the industry. FAA statistics suggest that roughly one-third of all students fail to obtain a private pilot's license. Project Long Look identified the obvious causes of this situation, such as the high cost of learning to fly, attributable in part to the lack of accessible airports and of competent instructors. Charges for flying instruction appeared to be a particularly important deterrent. Initial flight training for the average pilot costs between $300 and $700, depending upon the type of aircraft and quality of instruction, while the total cost of acquiring a commercial license worked out at between $4,000 and $5,500.[31] More recently, the results of the 1968 TIME survey suggested that the average annual amount spent by students on flying lessons was something over $400.

One difficulty that the aircraft industry has had to contend with is the length of time needed to train flight instructors up to a level of competence that would be approved by the FAA. There has been ample demonstration that the supply of qualified flight instructors is slow to respond to changes in demand conditions. In late 1966, Cessna Aircraft was persuaded by its distributors to abandon a national advertising campaign because of lack of instructors and time to cater to the needs of new potential fliers.[32] However, the current emphasis on "learn to fly" advertising suggests that this bottleneck no longer presents such severe problems, although recent statistics on the number of qualified flight instructors are not available.

Instructional flying is unique in that in absolute terms it failed to show a steady increase after the war. Although since the early 1960s the number of hours and miles flown have continued to increase, its peak, in 1947, was at a level of use that vastly exceeds comparable measures for 1968. Its relative importance has also fluctuated: it grew from 28 percent

30. For a description of the Cessna Aircraft Company's scheme, see *AOPA Pilot,* Vol. 11 (November 1968), p. 60.

31. *Report of the Aviation Human Resources Study Board,* pp. 65–67.

32. See "A Study to Determine the Feasibility of Establishing a National Program for Training Skilled Aviation Personnel," prepared by Arizona State University for the Economic Development Administration (U.S. Government Printing Office, 1967), p. I-129, for a discussion of these problems, including recommendations concerning ways of meeting the manpower "requirements" of the industry.

of total general aviation flying hours in 1931 to a peak of 71 percent in 1942, then began to diminish; but even in 1948 it continued to account for 58 percent of all general aviation flying hours, thereafter steadily declining to the 27 percent level depicted in Table 2-6.

Apart from the obvious effects of the war itself in increasing the demand for trained pilots, and the stimulation of interest in flying resulting from the war, the postwar bulge in instructional flying was due in part to the government-financed pilot training program included in the Servicemen's Readjustment Act of 1944—the so-called GI bill of rights. When these benefits were restricted in 1948 the decline began. (The parallel decline in the production of light aircraft is shown in Table 2-4.) Under present law, veterans holding private pilots' licenses may be entitled to benefits equal in value to 90 percent of tuition if working to obtain recognized vocational objectives in the field of aviation. These could include commercial, multiengine, instrument, and air transport ratings.[33]

### Personal Use

Personal use is defined by the FAA as any use of an aircraft for personal purposes other than those associated with a business or profession, or for hire. The importance of this element of general aviation activity is due not so much to the number of aircraft primarily used for this purpose, or to the miles or hours flown, but rather to the large number of persons involved.

Of the quarter of a million or so holders of private pilots' licenses, the vast majority fly partly or wholly for pleasure or personal transportation. In response to a 1964 TIME survey of over 800 new pilots, based on a 56 percent return, 3 percent of the respondents said they flew for business only, 51 percent for pleasure only, and 40 percent for both business and pleasure.[34] In response to another questionnaire, sent to 2,693 private pilots without instrument ratings in late 1967,[35] and based on a 44 percent return,[36] 50 percent of the pilots listed pleasure as their primary reason for flying, 34 percent listed business transportation, 12 percent

33. *Public Law 90-77*, Aug. 31, 1967, sec. 302 (81 Stat. 185).

34. TIME Marketing Information, "New Pilots: A Survey of the Individuals Obtaining Pilot's Licenses in 1963," Research Report 1301 (TIME, Inc., no date; processed), pp. 1, 7.

35. Roughly speaking, possession of an instrument rating is evidence that the pilot can operate an aircraft solely on instruments, without external visual aid.

36. J. J. Eggspuehler and others, "Study to Determine the Flight Profile and Mission of the Certificated Private Pilot" (Federal Aviation Administration, 1968; processed).

the use of aircraft for personal transportation, and "other" and "no response" accounted for the remainder. The majority of qualified pilots do not own aircraft; the survey indicated that 50 percent (of those without instrument ratings) rent, 23 percent are sole owners, 20 percent are members of a flying club, 14 percent are part owners, while 15 percent obtain aircraft from friends, relatives, or employers.

The large numbers of persons who fly for other than business or commercial purposes now form the preponderant part of a highly influential sector of the general aviation community, and are represented by the Aircraft Owners and Pilots Association (AOPA). This organization, which employs roughly 150 persons at its headquarters in the Washington area, includes about 150,000 members, who own about 70 percent of the active general aviation aircraft registered in the United States.

In addition to its function of "congressional liaison," the AOPA provides a variety of services for its members, many of which are designed to enhance air safety. Despite valuable functions of this kind the AOPA has attracted a good deal of notoriety both within the general aviation industry and without, particularly over its attitude toward recent attempts made by the FAA and others to impose restrictions on general aviation activity. So far it has been remarkably successful in its attempts to defeat legislative measures detrimental to general aviation; for this reason the arguments it employs, although sometimes unreasonable, must be dealt with seriously.

Another reason for the importance of personal flying is the fact that those pilots who engage in this form of activity are, on the whole, less well qualified than those flying for other purposes. Public attention has of late been focused particularly intently on the personal flier, because of a number of accidents and near-accidents involving private aircraft. This has led to demands that general aviation be subject to ever stricter regulation.

## Current Problems

Subsequent chapters will deal in a more detailed fashion with the division of responsibility among public authorities for functions that are relevant for general aviation. Generally, the construction and operation of the airways system, which consists of air traffic control, navigational and other flight aids and services, and a vast communications network, is primarily a federal responsibility that is carried out by the Federal Aviation Administration under the provisions of the 1958 Federal Aviation Act. As a necessary accompaniment to this general function, the FAA also has power under the act to establish regulations and air traffic rules to control all civil and military operations throughout the navigable airspace of the United States, as well as to establish and administer regulations concerning safety standards for aircraft, the qualification of airmen, and standards for flying schools. It also has the important function of carrying out and supervising research and development with respect both to aircraft and air navigation facilities, and acting as a source of information on this and related matters to the aviation industry. This is in accordance with the general duty, specified in the legislation, that the FAA administrator should "encourage and foster the development of civil aeronautics and air commerce in the United States and abroad."[37]

Virtually the whole of the nation's airways system is under federal ownership and control, but responsibility for airports is more diffuse. Except for the federally owned Washington National and Dulles International, airports may be owned and operated by private, state, local, or joint public authorities, or owned by a public authority but operated by a private fixed base operator. Consequently, there is often a dual responsibility for the operation of terminal areas; for while airport runways, taxiways, aprons, hangars, terminal buildings, access roads, and automobile parking are primarily the responsibility of private, state, or local authorities, terminal airways facilities, physically located at the airport, are usually under the ownership and control of the FAA.

The problems now faced by public authorities with respect to these various functions are enormous. Most of these problems are in some way related to the phenomenal increase in demand for air transportation that has been witnessed in recent years and is predicted for the future. General aviation's contribution to this increase is expected to be considerable: most dramatic of all is the estimate that between 1969 and 1980 general aviation will be responsible for 90 percent of the annual increase in operations (landings and takeoffs) at airports with FAA control towers. The total number of general aviation operations in 1980 is expected to be more than three times that for 1969.[38]

The predicted rapidity in the growth of general aviation and the conse-

37. Federal Aviation Act of 1958, sec. 305 (72 stat. 749).
38. FAA, "Aviation Forecasts," p. 35.

quent pressure placed on the nation's airports and airways system make the role of incentives for their efficient utilization particularly important. Despite current legislative proposals to authorize greater federal expenditures, it is fair to say that public authorities with responsibilities for providing airports and airways facilities are in a state approaching despair as they see the rapid growth in demand for those facilities. Journalists and aviation interests continually warn of the dangers of future aviation "crises" that can be avoided only by a substantial program of expansion and modernization of airport and airways facilities. The problem is perhaps exhibited most clearly in the delays and dangers associated with congestion, both in the air and on the ground, at airports such as Kennedy and O'Hare.

As Levine points out, this is indeed an odd situation, for consider how pleased a private businessman would be if faced with an overwhelming demand for his product.[39] But a businessman has the market mechanism working for him; the FAA and the airport authorities, with certain exceptions, do not. The failure to enlist the aid of the price mechanism is the fundamental explanation of the difficulties now being encountered, and it appears that little attempt is being made to improve this situation at the federal, state, or local level.

This is illustrated very well by the FAA's method of forecasting aviation activity. Forecasts rely largely upon extrapolation of past trends, modified in the light of expected changes in variables such as population, technical advances, and so forth.[40] As Table 2-3 demonstrates, separate forecasts are made for various types of aircraft, for airport and airway facility planning is dependent to a significant degree on the mixture of aircraft. Forecasts are also made of the numbers of active aircraft by region, hours flown, and fuel consumed, and of aircraft operations and other use of the federal airways system. In total, such forecasts embody a good deal of technical expertise and knowledge of the workings of the airports and airways system as well as of the characteristics of the aircraft themselves. Unfortunately, this substantial edifice is constructed on somewhat shaky ground, and this applies particularly to forecasts of general aviation activity.

The basic criticism of the procedure is that the least-cost method of

39. Michael E. Levine, "Landing Fees and the Airport Congestion Problem," *Journal of Law and Economics*, Vol. 12 (April 1969), p. 80.

40. The methodology employed is explained in FAA, *General Aviation: A Study and Forecast of the Fleet and Its Use in 1975.*

achieving certain physical output targets is determined with scarcely any attention to the benefits (measured in terms of consumers' willingness to pay) that will accrue from the expenditure. This is unavoidable in the case of many services traditionally provided by public authorities, particularly "public goods" such as national defense, where the price mechanism cannot work properly. In other cases, among which may be numbered the provision of certain aviation facilities, efficient pricing and investment policies may be frustrated not by the technical difficulties of implementing a pricing policy but rather by institutional and political obstacles.

The terms "needs," "demands," and "requirements" for airport and airways facilities are used extensively (and synonymously) by aviation interests, the public at large, and, indeed, the FAA itself. In economic terms, proof of social need requires evidence that beneficiaries would be willing to pay a price for a commodity or service that is at least as large as the net cost to society of its provision. This, as far as the services supplied by the FAA are concerned, is by no means apparent and cannot be, given the present method of financing them.

Apart from relatively minor adjustments, the extrapolation method implies that the influence of changes in those variables affecting the use of airport and airway facilities will follow the same trend as in the past. As will be seen, the federal government does not levy charges based directly upon the use made of facilities by general aviation, although a contribution is recovered indirectly. Similar policies are normally followed by airport operators. Failure to adjust for changes in the influence of a price variable therefore implies a continuation of existing policy and, presumably, of overconsumption of those facilities in the future. Although the forecasting method employed by the FAA and other interested parties may (if the influence of other variables is correctly estimated) yield accurate predictions, the predictions themselves may be of economically undesirable levels of general aviation activity.

The FAA, despite attempts to improve this situation slightly, is understandably reluctant to incorporate such a change in its forecasts. Recent history has indicated only too clearly the political difficulties involved in increasing general aviation's liability for the costs incurred on its behalf. In order to avoid the problems of congestion, delay, and safety brought about by underpricing, the FAA has to plan ahead on the assumption that charges will not be raised to recover the total costs allocable to general aviation.

General aviation interests are motivated somewhat differently, but their published versions of projected general aviation growth rates differ little in principle from those of the FAA. For example, a 1968 report, produced for a body representing the manufacturers of general aviation aircraft and accessories, predicted by 1980 a general aviation fleet some 20 percent greater than that forecast by the FAA, but also noted:

All of the elements of the forecast assume that no new material constraints will be imposed on the operational environment of General Aviation. Any major restrictions as to use of air space, airways and airports could significantly affect the growth of General Aviation, but for the purposes of this study it is assumed that there will be no such new restrictions.[41]

Presumably a major aim of the report, by emphasizing the value of general aviation to the community, was to avoid just this contingency. It will be argued in the following pages that there are sound reasons for ensuring that general aviation activity be constrained by raising the price it has to pay for the facilities it uses, in which case current industry and FAA forecasts would require substantial revision. The general point is that, where possible, predictions should not ignore the price variable: what that price ideally ought to be is a question considered in the next chapter.

41. R. Dixon Speas Associates, "The Magnitude and Economic Impact of General Aviation" (R. Dixon Speas Associates, 1968; processed), p. 2.

# CHAPTER THREE

# Efficiency in Pricing and Investment

THE CONCEPTS to be discussed in this chapter belong to a body of theory known as "welfare economics" from which has developed a set of rules for efficient resource allocation. Some of these rules are particularly relevant for pricing and investment decisions in the public utility field, a category that includes airport and airways facilities. The description of the theoretical background is necessarily brief and confined to portions of the theory that are particularly relevant for the problems discussed in the succeeding chapters, but a number of references are available for anyone interested in examining the subject in greater detail.[1] The practical problems encountered in applying efficient pricing and investment rules in certain other fields afford particularly valuable insights, and therefore some attention is given to recent literature on the economics of electricity and water supply and highway construction and operation.

## Marginal Cost Pricing and the Investment Decision

A policy may be roughly defined as improving efficiency in the allocation of society's scarce resources if those who gain from that policy could compensate the losers to the full monetary extent of their loss and still

1. For the theoretical background, including discussions of marginal cost pricing, see I. M. D. Little, *A Critique of Welfare Economics,* Oxford University Press, 1957. Also J. de V. Graaff, *Theoretical Welfare Economics* (Cambridge University Press, 1967). Little and de V. Graaff are both skeptical of marginal cost pricing, but there has recently been a resurgence of belief in its value for efficient public utility operation. See, for example, M. J. Farrell, "In Defence of Public-Utility Price Theory," *Oxford Economic Papers,* Vol. 10 (February 1958), pp. 109–23, as well as most of the industrial analyses referred to below.

remain better off.[2] An efficient policy is therefore one that maximizes real national income, no consideration being paid to the income distributional effects that may result. A proposition stemming from this definition is that the price of any service or commodity should be equated to the cost of producing an additional unit of it or, in other words, to its marginal cost. The argument is that, if price exceeds marginal cost, consumers have shown that they place a value on the marginal unit consumed that is at least as great as the cost to the rest of society of producing that unit, and further production is therefore justified. If, on the other hand, price is set at less than marginal cost, it can be assumed that there is oversupply of the commodity. It therefore follows that differential pricing for consumers of different types should be based solely on variation in the marginal cost attributable to each if the efficiency rules are not to be violated.

Whether or not a policy is considered to contribute toward efficiency will of course depend upon whose national income benefits the analyst is interested in increasing. Absolute reliance upon marginal cost pricing rules for aviation facilities would imply that the relevant society is neither the government, nor the FAA, nor a particular state or county, nor yet aviation interests or taxpayers at large, borrowers or lenders, but the nation as a whole. As a consequence it is necessary to distinguish between bookkeeping and real (or economic) costs. The former (for example, repayment of past loans) merely represent a transfer of income between members of the same society. Consequently, efficiency in resource allocation dictates that such costs be ignored for pricing purposes, for they represent no net loss to the community as a whole. On the other hand, the land, labor, and capital employed in the construction and operation of a particular project represent, *at the time of their employment,* real costs, in terms of resources used up and opportunities forgone. The price charged for the good or service concerned should clearly incorporate recovery of these costs if they are incurred as a result of additional consumption.

A major complication to be dealt with concerns the very definition of marginal cost. Assume that there is, at a given time, excess capacity; for example, an airport runway is less than fully utilized, or an air traffic

2. A weakness of this definition is the implication that one person's loss of $X exactly offsets another's gain of $X. For a brief discussion of the problems inherent in making "interpersonal utility comparisons," see Nancy Ruggles, "Recent Developments in the Theory of Marginal Cost Pricing," *Review of Economic Studies,* Vol. 17, No. 2 (1950), pp. 107–26.

control tower could handle more operations, even at peak hours, than it does currently. In this case, the only marginal costs are operating and maintenance costs that are a function of use—referred to as short-run marginal costs. Long-run marginal costs, on the other hand, refer to the sum of short-run marginal costs and marginal capacity costs, the latter being defined as the cost of extending capacity—for example, building a new runway—to accommodate the marginal unit of consumption.

With two definitions of marginal cost, one applicable in the short run and the other in the long run, what happens to the rule that price should equal marginal cost? A strict interpretation of the rule clearly requires that price should equal short-run marginal cost when capacity is less than fully utilized. Suppose now that demand grows over time (as is expected with respect to air transport of all kinds), and existing capacity becomes fully utilized. Price should then be raised to ration existing capacity up to the point that consumers reveal their willingness to pay a price equal to short-run marginal cost plus the annual equivalent[3] of marginal capacity cost.

At this point (that is, where price equals annual-equivalent long-run marginal cost) investment in capacity is justified. Once the investment has been carried out, however, price should fall again to short-run marginal cost, for the only real costs (or *opportunity* costs, in terms of alternative benefits forgone) are then operating costs. Price therefore plays the roles of (a) directly allocating resources efficiently when operating at less than full capacity, and (b) providing a signal to invest.

Practical problems associated with strict marginal cost pricing, as just described, immediately become apparent. First, there are particular complications where investment is "lumpy," a problem that varies considerably according to the technical circumstances of the enterprise concerned. A good illustration is provided in the case of water supply. Here, the traditional source of supply is the large reservoir, which may be some considerable distance from the area it serves. Initial costs of constructing the reservoir and laying the connecting mains are relatively high, while

3. The annual equivalent $A$ of a lump sum expenditure $E$ is defined as $A = Ei[1 + i)^n]/[(1 + i)^n - 1]$, where $i$ is the annual rate of interest and $n$ is the expected useful life of the project in years. Any demand period could be chosen, but an annual one is obviously convenient. Note that if demand is expected to continue growing, willingness to pay a price equal to annual equivalent long-run marginal cost by consumers in the first year would imply willingness to do so over the rest of the designated useful life of the asset. If not, it simply means that the useful life has been estimated incorrectly.

operating and maintenance costs are usually insignificant. This is an extreme case of "lumpiness," otherwise known as capital indivisibility. Highway construction and operation constitute another obvious example. In these two areas strict marginal cost pricing would normally involve large fluctuations in price, which would be not only administratively undesirable but would also be the source of considerable uncertainty for consumers.[4]

One solution—necessarily an imperfect one—would be to define marginal cost more broadly and set price equal to the average unit cost of incremental output, as Nelson, among others, has suggested.[5] The success of this policy obviously depends upon the degree of lumpiness and the rate of increase of demand and the consequent length of time that capacity remains idle, for although investment will be correctly signaled, short-run underutilization will be involved. In practice, of course, any version of marginal cost pricing would have to be approximate; and, in the last resort, some averaging of costs over a range of output is always required. This would also apply to electricity supply, which, as far as lumpiness is concerned, stands at the further extreme from water supply and highways: here, indivisibility of capital presents much less of a problem and strict marginal cost pricing is therefore a more feasible proposition.[6]

A contributory reason is that the large outlay on a power station may be spread over large numbers of consumers by means of a grid system. This permits some avoidance of excess capacity, which is aided by a continuing rapid increase in the demand for electricity. Another relevant characteristic of electricity supply is that the definition of capacity is fairly flexible. It is often possible to increase output with existing plant until operating costs rise to such a level that it is cheaper to increase output by investment in new plant: that is, at the point that short-run marginal costs on existing plant equal long-run marginal costs (marginal ca-

4. For a defense of this policy, see Jack Hirshleifer, James C. De Haven, and Jerome W. Milliman, *Water Supply: Economics, Technology, and Policy* (University of Chicago Press, 1960). They dismiss opposition to price fluctuations as "prejudice."

5. See James R. Nelson, "Pricing Transport Services," in Gary Fromm (ed.), *Transport Investment and Economic Development* (Brookings Institution, 1965), p. 207.

6. A standard reference on this subject is James R. Nelson (ed.), *Marginal Cost Pricing in Practice* (Prentice-Hall, 1964); see in particular the essay by Marcel Boiteux, "Peak-Load Pricing," pp. 59–89. A more recent analysis of the place of marginal cost pricing in electricity supply is to be found in Ralph Turvey, *Optimal Pricing and Investment in Electricity Supply: An Essay in Applied Welfare Economics* (London: George Allen & Unwin, 1968; MIT Press, 1969).

pacity plus operating costs associated with the new plant). Consequently, provided demand is correctly forecast and efficient investment decisions are made, there is no ambiguity in the definition of marginal cost. As Boiteux puts it, "Provided there is an optimal investment policy, short-term pricing is also long-term pricing, and there is no longer any contradiction between the two."[7] Put another way, the long-run marginal cost curve is fairly smooth, and a theoretically efficient pricing policy can be pursued without necessarily involving price fluctuations. Indivisibilities, when they occur, are therefore of little account. Turvey's position is that price should be equated to the average level of marginal cost over a range of output, and that in a large and expanding electricity supply system, indivisibilities can safely be ignored.[8] Such a policy will be referred to here as *average incremental cost (AIC) pricing*.

A further problem associated with marginal cost pricing is that its use may cause the enterprise concerned to incur financial losses. This will occur when average costs are falling, for then marginal cost is less than average cost. This could be a temporary situation, arising, for example, where there is excess capacity (indicating lumpiness) and price is equated to short-run marginal cost. It could also be a situation of some permanence, even if there is perfect capital divisibility, if long-run average costs continue to decline and price is equated to long-run (equals short-run) marginal cost. If there is lumpiness, a price equal to average incremental cost would in these circumstances also result in loss-making. On the other hand, if long-run average costs are rising, profits would be made.

Any surplus that results from the application of marginal cost pricing could conceivably be used to defray other public expenditures or to reduce taxation, and few distributional or resource allocation problems would arise. Loss-making, on the other hand, may certainly be attacked on the grounds that those who benefit should pay for a service, even though the expenditure of real resources might have taken place in the past. Indeed, the possibility that efficient resource allocation could require subsidy from the remainder of society, who do not benefit from the supply of the good concerned, should lead the analyst to examine with care the fundamental objective of a pricing policy. Thus, if there is a clear conflict of interest among various groups in society, should he be concerned primarily with efficiency or primarily with the problem of income redistribution?

7. "Peak-Load Pricing," p. 70.
8. Turvey, *Optimal Pricing*, p. 45.

If consumers of a good are barely distinguishable from society at large, the grounds for pursuing a policy that might result in loss-making are stronger than cases in which consumers are a very small or select group within that society. Thus, it is easy to identify the interests of society at large with the interests of a group such as consumers of electricity, and to lay down rules that would count a dollar's worth of satisfaction of an electricity consumer as equal to a dollar's worth of satisfaction forgone by the remainder of society as a result of his consumption. But it would be less easy to do so in the case of purchasers of mink coats; indeed, one might ask why the analyst should care about efficiency in pricing for this group. It might well be argued that his main concern should be to ensure that the group is not being subsidized by the rest of society, efficient allocation being of secondary importance, to be considered only after the income distributional constraint has been satisfied.

Definition of the relevant society is therefore crucial in determining the pricing policy that should be followed, but it is necessarily a rather subjective choice. For example, how large a fraction of society should mink-coat wearers be before their interests should be identified with society as a whole? What weight should be placed upon the relative wealth of members of that group? In the case of consumers of intermediate goods, how diffuse should the ultimate benefits of their consumption be? These questions are highly relevant in determining the correct method of charging for services used by general aviation.

The problem of loss-making would be exacerbated by those who, in the interest of avoiding price fluctuations, would advocate short-run marginal cost pricing as a permanent measure. Although short-run efficiency would be achieved by this means, the investment decision would have to be determined not by consumers' revealed willingness to pay for additional capacity but by some independent estimate of the relevant demand functions. A study of the potential savings achieved by construction of a new road might, for example, be used as a signal to invest.

Short-run marginal cost pricing would normally lead to loss-making on a large scale, yet such a policy has been advocated by several leading economists.[9] This policy may be criticized not only on the grounds of equity but on efficiency grounds as well. Even if consumers are willing to

9. See, for example, A. A. Walters, *The Economics of Road User Charges*, World Bank Staff Occasional Papers, No. 5 (Johns Hopkins Press for International Bank for Reconstruction and Development, 1968). His solution may involve cross-subsidization of one group of road users by another, thus avoiding losses within the overall road budget.

pay a price that would cover the full long-run marginal cost—and average cost—their consumption entails, they have no means of revealing this directly. Governments may therefore be unwilling to appropriate money for investment that might be seen as justified on efficiency grounds if the information were available. Paradoxically, such a situation could result in a clamor from potential beneficiaries to pay charges that cover the total costs of the services they consume.

Several solutions to this dilemma have been proposed by economists, who have usually tried to obtain the best of both worlds: the advantages of marginal cost pricing and of avoiding loss-making. There are many variations on a common theme, the simplest being a two-part tariff consisting of a price equal to marginal cost plus a lump sum that covers overheads. In this way, as long as liability to the lump sum payment does not deter anyone from consuming the commodity altogether, optimal allocation can theoretically be achieved.

Similarly, efficient allocation can result, in theory, from the activities of the economist's imaginary "perfectly discriminating monopolist" who charges each consumer a price equal to the maximum that the consumer would pay, right on down to the consumer who places a value on the commodity that is equal to marginal cost.[10] Although such omniscience is rare, this general approach, popularly known as charging "what the traffic will bear," is often employed to finance airport and airways facilities—usually to the detriment of the commercial airlines and to the benefit of general aviation. A general problem with these methods is that even if they succeed in achieving efficiency in the short run, the investment decision still cannot be signaled without price fluctuations if capital indivisibility is present.

Another difficulty encountered in applying the theorems of traditional welfare economics in the real world is what economists call the "second best" problem. The problem is that what may appear at first sight to be a step in the direction of economic efficiency (for example, setting a price equal to marginal cost, or, indeed, introducing a pricing mechanism where none hitherto existed) may not be an improvement at all if nonefficient conditions prevail elsewhere in the economy. Optimality in any one sector might require a price greater to or less than marginal cost to counter inefficiencies elsewhere.

10. For an elementary discussion of these and related problems, see Alexander M. Henderson, "The Pricing of Public Utility Undertakings," *Manchester School of Economic and Social Studies,* Vol. 15 (September 1947), pp. 223–50.

In practice, in an economy with a good deal of competition, one must assume that goods and services are sold at prices that *in general* approximate long-run marginal cost. If not, the difficulties of adjusting for all imperfections would lead to the nihilistic conclusion that there are, after all, no empirical grounds for preferring any one set of pricing rules over any other.[11] But where goods or services that are in direct competition with (or are complementary to) the service in question are priced in a way that diverges blatantly from the standard set for the industry in isolation, it may be feasible to make some adjustment.[12] For example, the most efficient (and manageable) course of action, should user charges not be employed for other forms of transportation, might be to abandon the notion of introducing them in any one transport sector.

Because of the undoubted existence of imperfections in the rest of the economy, it is impossible to prove scientifically that adherence to the theoretically efficient rules for aviation-related facilities would result in an increase in global efficiency. The judgment implied in the following pages is that existing pricing and investment policies in the aviation field are so poor that, "second best" considerations notwithstanding, a shift toward the theoretical ideal is certain to be an improvement. Equally certain, however, is that it will not represent a truly optimal solution: this, in the foreseeable future, must remain an unknown quantity.

"Second best" considerations are highly relevant for the discussion of the case made by general aviation interests against the cost-recovery policy of the Federal Aviation Administration. Also of extreme importance in this controversy is the extent to which "external" effects are associated with general aviation activity. An externality can be said to exist if a firm or individual acts in a manner that benefits or harms other members of society, with no prospect of reward or liability resulting from such action. An important theoretical distinction is made by economists between technological and pecuniary externalities, but in practice the dividing line between them is often hazy, and it is easy to confuse them. Put formally, the former are those that add to (economies) or subtract from (diseconomies) society's physical production possibilities or the net satisfaction consumers can obtain from society's resources. Pecuniary externalities,

11. The informational problems emerge quite clearly in R. Rees, "Second-Best Rules for Public Enterprise Pricing," *Economica*, Vol. 35 (August 1968), pp. 260–73.

12. Turvey, *Optimal Pricing*, uses this approach in establishing optimal pricing rules for electricity supply.

on the other hand, merely represent transfers between members of the same society, no net social gain or loss being reaped as a result.

The classic case of a technological external diseconomy is river pollution, the costs of which are not borne by the parties responsible for it. In the aviation field, a good example is the cost of delay imposed by one aircraft on another when both are using a congested airport. Economic efficiency, being concerned only with activities that show a net gain or net loss to society, requires that these physical, or technological, external effects be taken into account in pricing and investment decisions. The optimal pricing rule should be redefined as price equals marginal *social* cost, which may be greater or less than marginal cost, depending upon whether technological external diseconomies or economies prevail.[13] Where strict adherence to marginal cost pricing is not feasible, the policy might therefore be to set price equal to average incremental *social* cost.

Since distributional effects are ignored, efficiency in pricing and investment is unaffected by the presence of pecuniary economies or diseconomies. For example, on purely efficiency grounds, federal subsidies to encourage location of industry in a given area would not be warranted if, as a result, equivalent economic benefits were forgone elsewhere. Efficiency criteria also ignore the fact that a net monetary gain to society may be achieved at the expense of an uncompensated monetary or nonmonetary loss to particular elements of that society, classed perhaps by income group, geographical location, or race.

This is a severe limitation in the usefulness of price as a tool for normative decision making, for, in practice, aesthetic, equity, or income distributional considerations may often override the efficiency gains that might result from a given policy. Nevertheless, use of the pricing mechanism helps to make explicit the real monetary cost to society that departure from the use of efficiency criteria may involve. The ways in which "intangible" considerations of this nature may influence policymakers will be discussed at several points in the following pages.

## Inefficiencies Where Direct Charging Is Absent

The ideal pricing and investment rules discussed at the beginning of this chapter are far removed from the methods actually used to finance

13. Marginal social cost is defined here as being net of external benefits associated with additional output or consumption.

and determine the value of general aviation airport and airways facilities. For one reason or another, the public authorities supplying these services are, almost without exception, reluctant to use price at all as a means of allocating scarce resources, let alone to follow the marginal cost pricing rules outlined above.

The inefficiencies generated by the absence of marginal cost pricing have already been alluded to. These may take an extreme form when the means of implementing a pricing mechanism do not exist (that is, when the marginal cost to the consumer is zero). In this case a consumer will continue to use a commodity up to a point that the value to him of the last unit consumed is also zero. At this point the net social "economic" loss will be the relevant marginal cost, which, when capacity is less than fully utilized, will equal short-run marginal cost.

Inefficiency is particularly evident when, at the current rate of use, existing capacity is on the verge of full utilization and for some reason rationing by price is not possible. Applying this to the case of an airport working at full capacity, the decision maker is faced with the choice among: (1) rationing by nonprice means; (2) extending capacity; or (3) allowing unrestricted congestion of airports and airspace. Since the third possibility will normally be rejected on safety grounds, the effective choice lies between investment in additional capacity and the imposition of some administrative restriction on the use of airport or airways facilities.

Generally speaking, rationing by physical or administrative means is unsatisfactory as a permanent policy for the outputs of public utilities, although nonprice rationing is currently employed by the FAA to deal with congestion at the so-called "high-density" airports. The weakness of physical rationing is that it is necessarily arbitrary and can rarely be administered in accordance with the value of the benefits derived from the services rendered. It is inefficient in allocating resources in the short run and offers absolutely no guidance for investment decisions.

The policy that is usually preferred by decision makers in this and many other public utility areas is automatically to increase capacity when existing capacity approaches full utilization. In other words, at this point more capacity is deemed to be "required." Clearly, in the absence of a signal to invest of the kind described in the previous section, it can rarely be certain that the value of the additional consumption—or usage— made possible by the investment will exceed the costs thereby incurred.

The absence of a market for a particular commodity or service does not *necessarily* preclude the achievement of efficient investment decisions. The current popularity of cost-benefit analysis is partly based on the assumption that this is so, for schemes that are the subjects of such studies are usually characterized by the absence of a market for the services they are designed to provide. Indeed, it is often *because* of this that provision of the services concerned is a public responsibility and therefore most relevant for cost-benefit analysis, in which all costs and benefits, whoever bears or receives them, should be included.

Nevertheless, the literature of cost-benefit analysis,[14] which is merely an extension of the pricing and investment rules outlined above, abounds with examples of the extreme difficulties encountered in measuring benefits when no market exists. In the absence of pricing, the demand function for project outputs has to be imputed by indirect methods, and this is often a hazardous process. For example, an extensive study by Gary Fromm[15] demonstrates that for public civil aviation expenditures, ultimate benefit estimation is not feasible unless aided by the price mechanism.[16]

Lacking any budgetary constraints, the absence of pricing and use of the "requirements" approach would almost certainly result in overinvestment. But if the guidance of the pricing mechanism is not available, budgetary constraints are more likely to prevail when, in terms of the costs and benefits of a given project, they should not. Either way, inefficiency is likely to result.

Another likely situation, which in view of the expected continued growth in aviation activity is highly relevant for airways and airports, is that investment that may be justified at some stage will be carried out too soon. For example, a present-value calculation may demonstrate that in-

14. For a summary of the literature, and a useful bibliography, see A. R. Prest and Ralph Turvey, "Cost-Benefit Analysis: A Survey," *Economic Journal,* Vol. 75 (December 1965), pp. 683–735.

15. Gary Fromm, "Economic Criteria for Federal Aviation Agency Expenditures" (United Research, Inc., 1962; processed). Summarized in Fromm, "Civil Aviation Expenditures," in Robert Dorfman (ed.), *Measuring Benefits of Government Investments* (Brookings Institution, 1965), pp. 172–216.

16. An important exception to this general rule may exist where the services provided (that is, the benefits) are *cost saving,* in which circumstances cost-benefit studies may be most useful. Within this category comes the well-known United Kingdom highway study by M. E. Beesley and D. J. Reynolds, in University of Birmingham, Road Research Laboratory, *The London-Birmingham Motorway* (London: Her Majesty's Stationery Office, 1960). On the same general theme, see Peter O. Steiner, "The Role of Alternative Cost in Project Design and Selection," *Quarterly Journal of Economics,* Vol. 79 (August 1965), pp. 417–30.

vestment in a particular facility will yield a net benefit over its lifetime, but immediate investment would not be justified if, by delaying construction a number of years, the net present value of the benefits resulting from it would be even greater.[17] This type of error, too, should be eliminated if the pricing mechanism is used correctly.

## Factors Determining the Use of Direct Charging

Despite the important role that price may play in allocating resources efficiently, there are many areas, aside from aviation, in which public authorities do not charge users a price for the services they provide. Some general influences that determine the attitude of public authorities in this respect are examined below.

One can conceive of a spectrum of activities that for one reason or another are normally carried out by public authorities or by publicly regulated private firms. The range of the spectrum depends upon a host of factors, economic, social, and political; but one can make a rough-and-ready distinction between goods and services that are normally sold by public bodies and those that are financed by some form of taxation, the payment of which may or may not be restricted to the beneficiaries.

In the former category one might place mail, electricity, and telephone services. The latter could include police, fire protection, and defense; that is, those services that are examples of the economist's traditional "collective good," which, if provided for one member of a designated community, are at once available to all. These examples do not fall neatly into the categories defined. In the United States, for instance, some telephone charges (within certain limits) are unrelated to use. Moreover, it is possible to purchase privately supplied (and normally publicly regulated) police protection. In fact, between the two extremes of services that are always, and services that are never, charged for on the basis of quantity consumed fall many publicly provided services that may or may not be supplied on that basis. For example, some roads have tolls but not others, some city centers have parking meters, some educational establishments charge fees, a price per gallon is levied on some water supplies, and so on.

17. Since we are concerned with *real* benefits and costs for society as a whole, inflationary increases in project costs do not constitute a valid reason to avoid delay in investment.

Influences determining the attitude of a public authority toward charging a price for services supplied can be categorized as follows:

1. *Presence of technological external economies.* If the consumption of a commodity results in a net real gain to society over and above that accruing directly to the purchasers, so that the marginal cost of consumption is less than its marginal *social* cost (that is, net of any external marginal benefits), the case for pricing that commodity is correspondingly weakened. Although theory states that price should equal marginal social cost, the extent of the divergence between marginal cost and marginal social cost is itself rarely known with any accuracy.[18] To the extent that this is so, price becomes less useful in aiding the investment decision or allocating resources in the short run.

It may be that the cost to a particular organization in supplying a service or commodity is less than the resulting economic benefits that accrue to the remainder of society, in which case subsidy may be justified. For instance, the presence of technological external economies may justify free or subsidized education. Also within this category are investments in projects stimulating the development of a certain activity or region within the economy, as long as development is not merely at the expense of another activity or region. Encouragement of scale economies is an example of this. Taking dynamic or growth variables of this sort into account means simply that price should be equated to the present value of the net marginal social cost of supplying a good or service.

2. *Intangible factors.* The ultimate worth of some activities or goods cannot be measured in monetary terms. Perhaps the most important example in the transportation field is connected with safety. Accidents may be measured to some degree in monetary terms (that is, costs of hospital treatment, lost productivity, and so on), but it would generally be accepted that the costs of human suffering cannot be so quantified. Another important example deals with the presence of pecuniary external economies. If free provision of the service results in, or is equivalent to, a redistribution of income that is considered favorable by policymakers, this may be used as a reason for charging a zero marginal price—or at least for subsidizing a service via a progressive tax system, particularly where consumption is likely to be of particular benefit to poorer people. The type of service is crucial here: equity arguments in favor of free medical treatment come within this category. Other intangibles could include implications

18. For a valuable popular discussion of this whole area see E. J. Mishan, *The Costs of Economic Growth* (London: Staples Press, 1967).

for governmental and democratic structures, defense, environmental quality, and so forth.

3. *Excessive cost of the price mechanism itself.* In many cases the costs of introducing a pricing mechanism are too great relative to the benefits provided. Take the case of defense: the cost of excluding people from partaking of its benefits is normally too great to be seriously considered. This is reinforced by the fact that, once provided, the service is in joint supply to all, so although the marginal cost of output may be high, the cost of supplying a marginal beneficiary is zero. Pricing would therefore be irrelevant.

A slightly different argument obtains when the marginal cost of output is very low. It has been suggested that where marginal cost is close to zero, pricing is invariably inefficient.[19] For this necessarily to be true, long-run and short-run marginal cost must both equal zero. Price, as already noted, fulfills two roles: to allocate resources in the short run and to provide a guide for the investment decision. Indeed, the benefits of obtaining an optimal investment decision may alone warrant the introduction of pricing; the fact that short-run marginal cost is zero is not a sufficient condition for its rejection. The costs of extending capacity may be substantial; consequently, so would be the benefits of deferring or obviating that investment by charging a price and thereby providing decision makers with realistic data about demand.

Ideally, the case for introducing a pricing system would itself become the subject of cost-benefit analysis. Consider the case of a commodity that is freely available to all consumers; also, desired consumption at zero price is less than capacity output of the good, and there is therefore no need for rationing by administrative device. Assume further that there is no ambiguity in the use of the term "marginal cost," implying that short-run and long-run marginal social cost are identical and that capacity can be expanded or retired in small increments: the problem of lumpiness is therefore assumed anyway.[20]

If the pricing mechanism is now introduced, there will be a reduction in consumption; the annual net saving on this account will be equal to the production cost savings less the loss in consumers' valuation of the forgone consumption. The net savings will be greater, the closer the cor-

19. See J. G. Head, "Public Goods and Public Policy," *Public Finance,* Vol. 17, No. 3 (1962), pp. 197–219.

20. A more rigorous analysis of the case for introducing pricing, given certain assumptions about the pricing policy actually followed and the nature of the long-run marginal cost function, is found in Appendix B.

respondence of the pricing policy to the efficiency criteria postulated earlier. As an offset to these savings, the pricing mechanism itself will involve certain costs. These may consist of an initial capital outlay, perhaps an investment in recording devices of some kind or the establishment of accounting and billing facilities, as well as annual operating and maintenance costs.

If consumption begins to press capacity and the policymaker is bound to make a once-for-all decision on whether to introduce a pricing system or to build new capacity, he should compare the present value of the benefits and costs of pricing with the present value of the benefits and costs of capacity expansion. Assuming that physical rationing is rejected, the decision to build additional capacity should require that the resultant consumer benefits exceed the cost of the project *less* the cost of introducing the pricing system that would otherwise be required. The difficulty of estimating consumer benefits, of course, continues to apply.

The presence of lumpiness calls for a slightly different approach. Even if capacity can be expanded incrementally, it is fairly certain that if consumption falls, excess capacity will be the immediate result, for it does not follow that capacity can be retired incrementally as well. If pricing is introduced, therefore, savings have to be calculated as two distinct elements. First, there are savings in operating costs of existing capacity; and, second, there are savings in capital and operating costs due to the deferment of a series of investments in the future. These have to be compared with the costs of the pricing mechanism to see if introduction of the latter is economically justified.

## Theory and Practice

In determining whether the pricing mechanism should be applied in the case of airport and airways facilities, the tradeoffs between monetary and nonmonetary costs and benefits of such action should be explicitly recognized. In other words, the result of a purely monetary cost-benefit analysis of the sort just described should not be the sole criterion for decision. It is possible, for example, that adverse safety or income-distributional repercussions might be considered sufficiently important to outweigh the advantages of direct charging altogether, or at least to require a form of pricing that diverges from the theoretical ideal outlined at the beginning of this chapter.

In practice, decisions regarding the allocation and supply of airport and airways facilities are rarely made in so rational a manner. The immense gulf between the theory summarized in this chapter and real-world practice will be illustrated in Chapter 4, which contains a description of the federal airways system and the way it is financed. The gulf continues to widen as the analysis is extended to encompass airport pricing and the phenomenon of congestion.

Although the marginalist approach is a requirement for efficient resource allocation, it is clear that the theoretically desirable pricing and investment rules outlined earlier can rarely be precisely followed in practice; however, the extreme shortcomings of existing policies in the aviation field indicate that even rough approximations to those rules would constitute a significant improvement. One of the main tasks in the following pages is therefore to examine the extent to which direct charging for aviation-related facilities is justified and to define a pricing policy that is at once theoretically respectable and practically feasible.

# CHAPTER FOUR

# General Aviation and the Federal Airways System

SINCE THE END of the First World War, the promotion and control of civil aviation have been the subject of almost continuous congressional inquiry, accumulating along the way a plethora of regulations and legislative enactments. It is rare that substantial pieces of legislation or regulation, even when primarily designed for or resulting from air carrier activity, do not in some way also affect general aviation. This is especially true of matters concerning the federal airways system, the construction and operation of which benefits both categories. Moreover, regulation of one segment of aircraft activity normally also has an effect on the other segment, particularly where air carriers and general aviation are joint users of federally provided and other services.

## The Statutory Basis

As a consequence, all that will be mentioned here are some of the more important developments for general aviation in the legislative history of the federal airways system. A useful landmark with which to begin is the Air Commerce Act of 1926, for prior to this date the federal government had avoided legislation pertaining to aviation—regulation, if any, being in the hands of the states. The 1926 act established an Aeronautics Branch within the Department of Commerce and, among other things, instructed the secretary of commerce to designate and establish airways; establish, operate, and maintain aids to air navigation (other than airports); and promote research and development for the improvement of these aids.

The years following the Air Commerce Act were characterized by an

45

astonishing growth in aviation activity and a furor over the allocation of airmail contracts. Severe administrative complications were unavoidable largely because three governmental agencies—the Post Office, the Interstate Commerce Commission, and the Aeronautics Branch, only the last of which was primarily concerned with aviation matters—were involved. These problems led to the passing of the Civil Aeronautics Act in 1938. The Bureau of Air Commerce (in July 1934 the name of the Aeronautics Branch had been changed to the Bureau of Air Commerce) was transferred to the newly created Civil Aeronautics Authority, as was the Bureau of Air Mail, hitherto a part of the Interstate Commerce Commission. The Civil Aeronautics Authority (slightly altered in composition and renamed Civil Aeronautics Board in 1940) was given regulatory powers over airlines' routes and fares and airmail rates, and assumed responsibilities for the airways system hitherto held by the Bureau of Air Commerce. Under the new act, however, the Civil Aeronautics Authority could acquire and operate air navigation facilities at any airport, although it was forbidden to acquire the airports themselves.

Overall, the provisions of the Civil Aeronautics Act of 1938 remain the basis for current powers and responsibilities vested in federal agencies, but an important division of responsibility for these functions was introduced in 1958. The Federal Aviation Act of that year retained the Civil Aeronautics Board but restricted its influence primarily to the establishment of routes and fares and to general economic regulation and promotional duties with respect to the air carriers. This part of the act is of little relevance here; far more important for present purposes is the portion of the act creating the Federal Aviation Agency—later to be incorporated within the Department of Transportation as the Federal Aviation Administration—and defining its fundamental duties as:

(a) The regulation of air commerce in such manner as to best promote its development and safety and fulfill the requirements of national defense;

(b) The promotion, encouragement, and development of civil aeronautics;

(c) The control of the use of the navigable airspace of the United States and the regulation of both civil and military operations in such airspace in the interest of the safety and efficiency of both;

(d) The consolidation of research and development with respect to air navigation facilities, as well as the installation and operation thereof;

(e) The development and operation of a common system of air traffic control and navigation for both military and civil aircraft.[1]

1. Federal Aviation Act of 1958, Sec. 103 (72 Stat. 740).

It should be observed, for reasons that will become clear, that there is no discrimination either in favor of or against general aviation in the foregoing. Nor is any such discrimination found elsewhere in the legislation. It is also noteworthy that the act had nothing to say about the means of financing the FAA's activities. Indeed, it was not until May 1970 that legislation specifically relating to this subject was passed. Certain aspects of this legislation—the Airport and Airway Development Act of 1970 and the Airport and Airway Revenue Act of 1970—will be discussed in some detail below.

Despite these and other significant developments that have occurred since the passing of the Federal Aviation Act, the basic responsibilities of the FAA have remained largely unchanged. Regulatory innovations, many of which have been extremely important, have been introduced within the broad range of policy laid down in the act. Normally, the procedure is that a proposed regulatory change is published in the *Federal Register,* and comments from interested parties are invited, in the light of which the proposal may be amended, withdrawn, or incorporated into a Federal Aviation Regulation. It should be noted that although reference will be made to official policy as being that of the FAA, quite often responsibility for matters of high policy is that of the secretary of transportation, to whom the administrator of the FAA is subordinate.

## The Federal Airways System

Descriptions of the federal airways system and of the services and facilities provided by the FAA for military and civil aviation can be found in the several FAA publications concerning the introduction of "user charges" legislation.[2] For descriptive purposes it is useful to divide the federal airways system into four parts—the terminal area, en route, air navigation, and flight service subsystems. The terminal area subsystem is based upon the air traffic control tower and may include airport surveillance and manual and radar approach control facilities. At the larger

2. U.S. Federal Aviation Agency, Office of Policy Development, "User Charges for the Domestic Federal Airway System" (FAA, August 1966; processed). This is reprinted in *Administration's Proposals on Airway User Charges,* Hearings before the House Committee on Ways and Means, 89 Cong. 2 sess. (1966), pp. 36–80. Subsequent references to *Airway User Charges* will quote page numbers of the latter document.

airports there may also be special radar for the detection of aircraft or ve-hicles on the airport surface, as well as approach lighting, instrument land-ing systems, visual aids, and radio navigation facilities. (It will be shown subsequently that the wide range of facilities afforded at airports of dif-ferent sizes has important implications for the achievement of an optimal pricing policy in this field.) With the exception of the federal airports, Washington National and Dulles, the provision of other terminal facili-ties and equipment (runways, taxiways, terminal buildings, and so forth) is not a federal responsibility.

Of the terminal area subsystem, the element most extensively used by general aviation is the air traffic control tower itself. It is estimated that currently some 75 percent of total operations (landings and takeoffs) recorded at the 300 or so airports with FAA-operated air traffic control towers are made by general aviation aircraft. Other terminal area facili-ties are used predominantly by aircraft operating under instrument flight rules (IFR). IFR conditions exist when weather conditions are below the minimum officially prescribed for operations under visual flight rules (VFR). Most general aviation activity takes place in VFR conditions; consequently air carriers are the main users of the rest of the terminal area subsystem.

Air carriers are also at present the main users of the en route traffic control subsystem, which is designed to facilitate safe and efficient move-ment by controlling the separation of IFR traffic along the airways. How-ever, pilots often fly IFR even when weather conditions are above the FAA-prescribed minimum. Safe separation of those aircraft thus may be achieved without visual aid under bad weather conditions, although when conditions allow VFR traffic, not subject to the same controls, reli-ance upon instruments is not sufficient. The en route subsystem consists of (a) the 27 air route traffic control centers (ARTCC), of which 21 are in the conterminous United States, (b) long-range (200 miles) radar, and (c) direct voice communications between controllers and pilots.

The air navigation subsystem provides visual, electronic, mechanical, and magnetic guidance to aircraft. The standard navigational aid is known as VORTAC. A VOR (very high frequency omnidirectional ra-dio range) is an unmanned facility that gives a pilot his bearing to or from a ground station. This enables him, by observing two or more ground stations, to plot his exact position by triangulation. VORTAC, a combination of VOR and very high frequency tactical air navigation, and

VOR DME (distance measuring equipment) provide not only direction but also distance information from a given ground installation. VOR-TAC, which is currently replacing L/MF (low- or medium-frequency aids) therefore allows location to be identified by use of a single facility. In aggregate, general aviation is a relatively unimportant user of the system.

The flight service subsystem, on the other hand, is used extensively by general aviation. Flight service stations are manned facilities, and are usually located at airports; at the end of fiscal year 1971 they numbered about 400, of which some 50 were combined station/towers. Their main function is to provide flight assistance, consisting of weather, altitude, and route information, by air-ground communication. They also initiate search and rescue operations.

Flight plans are filed at flight service stations by pilots of general aviation aircraft: when flying IFR, aircraft pass from the control of one ARTCC to another until the planned journey is complete; completion is recorded automatically. Although encouraged to do so in their training courses, general aviation pilots do not always file flight plans if flying VFR. If they do, they must report their safe arrival to the appropriate flight service station. Failure to do so may lead to the commencement of search and rescue operations, which, if not warranted by an actual emergency, may result in a fine for the offending pilot.

In addition to operating the facilities described above, the FAA carries out research and development (R&D), the costs of which are not always allocated to the four subsystems, although they may be closely related to the provision of airway facilities and services. In total the annual-equivalent cost of the domestic federal airways system for fiscal 1969 was estimated by the FAA to be almost $730 million, roughly $50 million of which consisted of expenditures on research and development projects. Maintenance and operation of the system itself were estimated at $560 million, while annual-equivalent capital costs were estimated at $120 million. Detailed estimates, broken down by type of expenditure, are given in Table 4-1.

Table 4-2 demonstrates that annual FAA expenditures on the airways system have shown a phenomenal rate of growth in the years since World War II. Despite this, the FAA has been severely criticized for its slowness in adopting new air traffic control technology. There has been especially strong pressure for increased automation of air traffic control and

**Table 4-1. Estimated Annual Cost of the Domestic Federal Airways System, by Type of Airway Facility or Service, Fiscal Year 1969**

In thousands of dollars

| Type of airway facility or service | Maintenance and operation (1) | Capital costs[a] (2) | Total (3) | Asset life (years) (4) |
|---|---|---|---|---|
| *Terminal area* | | | | |
| Traffic control towers | 69,102 | 8,508 | 77,610 | 30 |
| Manual approach control service | 5,539 | 459 | 5,998 | 15 |
| Radar approach control service | 71,813 | 10,521 | 82,334 | 15 |
| Radar approach control facilities | 27,920 | 1,926 | 29,846 | 15 |
| Precision approach radar | 1,152 | 387 | 1,539 | 13 |
| Airport surface detection equipment | 323 | 129 | 452 | 13 |
| Instrument landing systems | 18,582 | 5,518 | 24,100 | 15 |
| Approach lighting | 3,644 | 4,925 | 8,569 | 15 |
| Total, terminal area | 198,075 | 32,373 | 230,448 | — |
| *En route* | | | | |
| Traffic control centers and long-range radars | 228,443 | 58,549 | 286,992 | 20 |
| *Air navigation* | | | | |
| L/MF and VORTAC facilities[b] systems | 39,843 | 18,467 | 58,310 | 15[c] |
| *Flight service* | | | | |
| Flight service stations | 94,322 | 9,831 | 104,153 | 15 |
| *Intermediate fields* | 59 | 461 | 520 | 30 |
| Subtotal | 560,742 | 119,681 | 680,423 | — |
| Research and development | — | — | 48,941 | — |
| Total, all facilities and services | — | — | 729,364 | — |

Source: U.S. Federal Aviation Administration, unpublished data, June 6, 1969.
a. Capital charges are estimated by using an interest rate of 7 percent; the estimated average service life of each type of asset which is used is shown in column 4.
b. L/MF denotes low and medium frequencies; VORTAC denotes combination of very high frequency omnidirectional radio range and tactical air navigation systems.
c. The life of L/MF facilities is estimated at 20 years; of VORTAC facilities, 15 years.

associated facilities because of the intense physical and mental strain to which air traffic controllers are often subject.[3] This has been a major fac-

3. This is graphically described in a statement by F. Lee Bailey, General Counsel, Professional Air Traffic Controller Organization, in *Airport/Airways Development*, Hearings before the Subcommittee on Aviation of the Senate Committee on Commerce, 91 Cong. 1 sess. (1969), Pt. 1, pp. 364–74.

**Table 4-2. Estimated Expenditures on the Federal Airways System, Selected Fiscal Years, 1947–70[a]**

In millions of dollars

| Year | Operations | Facilities and equipment | Research and development | Total |
|------|-----------|--------------------------|--------------------------|-------|
| 1947 | n.a. | n.a. | n.a. | 59.5 |
| 1950 | n.a. | n.a. | n.a. | 81.6 |
| 1956 | n.a. | n.a. | n.a. | 111.9 |
| 1964 | 413.9 | 95.6 | 41.5 | 551.0 |
| 1965 | 439.6 | 77.9 | 26.9 | 544.4 |
| 1966 | 438.8 | 62.4 | 27.5 | 528.7 |
| 1967 | 458.2 | 60.6 | 30.6 | 549.4 |
| 1968 | 500.4 | 59.5 | 31.5 | 591.4 |
| 1969 | 571.9 | 74.5 | 28.2 | 674.6 |
| 1970 | 686.7 | 106.9 | 37.6 | 831.2 |

Sources: *The Budget of the United States Government—Appendix*, relevant issues.
n.a. Not available.
a. Data for 1947–56 are total obligations for the airways system, plus aircraft operation and aviation information, and all overheads. Data for 1964–70 are based on actual expenditures, constructed by applying the ratio of total actual expenditures to total obligations and applying to each account, except for facilities and equipment, which includes all expenditures. Operations includes the traffic control system and its maintenance, and installation and materiel services. Research and development includes air traffic control, navigation, and aviation weather.

tor in recent labor relations problems and consequent inconvenience for air travelers. Other sectors of the aviation industry are also exerting increasing pressure for modernization of the airways system, with primary focus on the terminal area. The Airline Pilots Association (ALPA) has been a particularly vocal group, urging, for example, the installation of instrument landing systems (ILS) at all airports served by air carriers.[4]

In 1961, a task force established by President John F. Kennedy made recommendations that, although generally accepted at the time as being desirable, have yet to be implemented. The task force (Project Beacon)[5] studied the needs of the air traffic control system in the light of the projected increase in air traffic. Its main recommendation, which, despite appearances to the contrary, is very relevant for general aviation, was that all airliners should be equipped with transponders to relay their

4. See statement by ALPA, in *Aviation Facilities Maintenance and Development*, Hearings before the House Committee on Interstate and Foreign Commerce, 91 Cong. 1 sess. (1969), Pt. 1, pp. 344–94.
5. *Report of the Task Force on Air Traffic Control, A Study of the Safe and Efficient Utilization of Airspace: Project Beacon* (Federal Aviation Agency, 1961).

identity and altitude to a computer on the ground. Along with aircraft speed, this information would appear on the air traffic controller's radar screen in alphanumerical symbols.

All air carrier aircraft are now equipped with transponders, but improvement of the complementary ground equipment has proceeded at a slower pace. At present only two terminal air traffic control centers are equipped to the standards envisaged by Project Beacon: the Common IFR Room in New York (serving Kennedy, La Guardia, and Newark) and the Atlanta airport tower. Elsewhere, controllers have to ask pilots for altitudes and manually move identification tags across the screen. So far none of the (en route) ARTCCs has the system in full operation, despite the fact that in 1961 the task force considered five years to be a "reasonable and necessary" time for most of the recommended system to be installed.

Introduction of the innovations recommended in Project Beacon would have required a doubling of the then current FAA five-year plan of capital expenditures of $250 million, but a substantial increase was delayed for some years, mainly because demands for additional expenditures were unaccompanied by politically acceptable means of financing them. However, a rapidly increasing demand for airspace and the growing danger associated with the retention of old-fashioned procedures culminated in the 1970 legislation, which was a "package deal" involving authorization for additional federal expenditures on the nation's airports and airways on the one hand and increased user charges on the other.

For a number of years prior to this date the FAA supplied data on the costs of the airways system, allocated to the three broad user categories —air carriers, general aviation, and military. Its results were continually subject to criticism from the aviation community, so the 1970 legislation provided that within two years a study should be completed to determine the appropriate method of allocating the costs of the airport and airways system among the various users. The study would also identify the proportion of costs that should be recovered from users, the remainder being assigned to the general "public benefit." Because of this clause, the FAA has abandoned its policy of publishing estimates of allocated costs, and the latest firm data from that source, for fiscal 1969, are used in the following discussion as a guide to the situation likely to be encountered in the decade beginning with fiscal 1971.

**Table 4-3. Allocation of Costs of the Domestic Federal Airways System, by User Category and by Type of Airway Facility or Service, Fiscal Year 1969[a]**

Dollar amounts in thousands

| Type of airway facility or service | Annual cost | Basis of allocation | Air carrier | | General aviation | | Military | |
|---|---|---|---|---|---|---|---|---|
| | | | Percent | Amount | Percent | Amount | Percent | Amount |
| Traffic control towers | $77,610 | Total operations | 18.7 | $14,513 | 75.3 | $58,440 | 6.0 | $4,657 |
| Manual approach control service | 5,998 | Instrument operations | 58.6 | 3,515 | 20.9 | 1,254 | 20.5 | 1,230 |
| Radar approach control service | 82,334 | Instrument operations | 76.5 | 62,986 | 17.2 | 14,161 | 6.3 | 5,187 |
| Radar approach control facilities | 29,846 | Instrument operations | 28.7 | 8,566 | 14.8 | 4,417 | 56.5 | 16,863 |
| Precision approach radar | 1,539 | Instrument approaches | 78.2 | 1,203 | 15.2 | 234 | 6.6 | 102 |
| Airport surface detection equipment | 452 | Instrument approaches | 84.1 | 380 | 13.9 | 63 | 2.0 | 9 |
| Instrument landing systems | 24,100 | Instrument approaches | 64.6 | 15,569 | 30.2 | 7,278 | 5.2 | 1,253 |
| Approach lighting | 8,569 | Instrument approaches | 65.2 | 5,587 | 29.8 | 2,554 | 5.0 | 428 |
| Traffic control centers and long-range radars | 286,992 | IFR aircraft handled[b] | 60.9 | 174,778 | 15.9 | 45,632 | 23.2 | 66,582 |
| L/MF and VORTAC facilities systems[b] | 58,310 | IFR aircraft handled | 60.9 | 35,511 | 15.9 | 9,271 | 23.2 | 13,528 |
| Flight service stations | 104,153 | Flight services | 8.4 | 8,749 | 79.5 | 82,802 | 12.1 | 12,603 |
| Intermediate fields | 520 | Flight services | 8.4 | 44 | 79.5 | 413 | 12.1 | 63 |
| Research and development projects | 48,941 | Facility average | 61.9 | 30,294 | 17.0 | 8,320 | 21.1 | 10,327 |
| Total, all facilities and services | 729,364 | | 49.6 | 361,695 | 32.2 | 234,839 | 18.2 | 132,832 |

Source: Federal Aviation Administration, unpublished data, June 13, 1969. Figures are rounded and may not add to totals.

a. Costs of Federal Aviation Administration facilities used *solely* by the military are excluded from this table, as are those attributable to international aviation, including those physically located in the United States (for example, part of the New York air route traffic control center costs are allocated to international aviation).

b. IFR denotes instrument flight rules; L/MF denotes low and medium frequencies; VORTAC denotes combination of very high frequency omnidirectional radio range and tactical air navigation systems.

# Allocated Costs and User Charges, Fiscal Year 1969

Table 4-3 portrays fiscal 1969 estimates made by the FAA of the costs of the federal airways system, allocated to air carriers, general aviation, and military users. The basis upon which allocation is made is also indicated. Roughly speaking, the method employed is to take the total annual cost of each facility (including operating, maintenance, and capital costs), and to divide this among military aircraft, air carriers, and general aviation in proportion to the use made of that facility by each of the three categories. About 80 percent of the costs attributed to general aviation are for use of the following facilities: (1) air traffic control towers; (2) traffic control centers and long-range radars; (3) flight service stations.

The fundamental problem faced by the FAA in allocating costs to broad categories of users is that most of the facilities provided are used jointly by civil and military aircraft of different types. The quantity-of-use method employed by the FAA is recognized by that body as being imperfect since, for example, certain costs of the system may not vary directly with the volume of traffic handled.[6] On the other hand, given the limited objective of the FAA, which can be summed up as an equitable method of cost recovery, this seems a relatively satisfactory method of allocation. It is, however, subject to the major reservation that even if the objective itself is the correct one, which is open to question, in assessing cost responsibility one has to be very careful in defining "use," and it appears, in one instance at least, that the FAA's method of cost allocation has underestimated the costs attributable to general aviation.

In the case of air traffic control towers, as Table 4-3 shows, the measure of use is the number of operations (landings and takeoffs) attributable to each category. This seems to be a sensible measure, but there must be some doubt as to the validity of allocating the costs of the remaining terminal facilities solely on the basis of the number of instrument approaches or operations, relatively few of which are carried out by general aviation aircraft. This applies in particular to the radar and manual approach control services and facilities located at terminal areas.

Although ostensibly provided for the benefit of IFR traffic, such facilities are often installed and used to ensure safe separation of IFR traffic from a large number of aircraft flying under VFR. A more realistic method of cost allocation might be to share the cost of radar approach control among air carriers, general aviation, and military aircraft according to the total number of operations recorded at airports where such facilities are located. Even this method would probably underestimate the true cost attributable to general aviation in one respect, that is, when the approach control installation permits the separation of general aviation aircraft that are operating from a small, towerless airport in the vi-

6. See *Airway User Charges*, p. 49, where the method is explained in detail.

cinity of the major airport. On the other hand, it may or may not overestimate the cost that should be allocated to general aviation, in that the figure for total operations does not distinguish between those made on IFR and those on VFR days. Bad (IFR) weather is a factor making for greater need (defined in terms of a given safety standard) for radar approach control services and, because of this greater need, a larger investment in them. On the other hand, when weather is good (VFR conditions), more traffic can be expected, and the need for these facilities also varies directly with the amount of traffic in the vicinity of the airport.

Should the combination of bad weather plus relatively small numbers of aircraft require greater investment in terminal area facilities than does the combination of good weather plus larger numbers of aircraft, using the number of operations as a method of cost allocation would tend to discriminate unfairly against general aviation, a relatively large proportion of whose operations are VFR. In general, however, such a method of cost allocation would certainly be preferable to the one presently employed, which absolves VFR traffic altogether from responsibility for the costs of most components of the terminal subsystem.

The costs of ARTCCs, long-range radars, L/MF, and VORTAC facilities are allocated according to the number of IFR aircraft handled. Although when estimated this way general aviation is a relatively unimportant user, the overall costs of these facilities are so large, representing almost 50 percent of total airways costs, that general aviation's allocated share still represents a considerable sum—almost 25 percent of the total costs allocated to that category. It should be noted that, although the amount of IFR traffic handled in large measure determines the staffing and workload of the ARTCCs, the point made above concerning the real load imposed on the system by VFR traffic continues to apply.

The costs of flight service stations and intermediate fields (the latter being small FAA-operated landing areas in Alaska) are allocated according to the number of flight services applicable to each category of aviation. Flight services are a measure of the workload at the stations, derived by weighting data on the number of aircraft handled, flight plans originated, pilot briefs, and flight condition messages. Intermediate fields are insignificant, but the cost of flight service stations represents roughly one-third of the total allocated to general aviation.

The methods used to allocate the costs of the airways system among broad categories of users are of crucial significance for the method of cost recovery currently employed. As has been noted, there are good reasons to doubt that the present procedure accurately or equitably reflects user cost responsibilities, and the points raised here concerning allocation of the costs of certain terminal facilities and ARTCCs on the basis of instrument operations should be closely examined in the cost-allocation study to be carried out.

Before the 1970 legislation, all FAA expenditures on the federal airways system were financed by appropriations out of general tax revenue, but specific tax liabilities, generally recognized as "user charges," were incurred by airways users. These were of two types:

1. *Ticket tax.* Passengers traveling by air carrier or scheduled air taxi paid a ticket tax of 5 percent, which went into the general fund of the federal government. (The tax had been levied at this rate since 1962; it had been 15 percent from 1944 to 1954, and 10 percent from 1954 to 1962.)

2. *Gasoline tax.* All gasoline used by civil aviation was taxed at a rate of 4 cents per gallon. Two cents of this were refundable, the remainder being credited to the Highway Trust Fund, under the provisions of the Highway Revenue Act of 1956, as amended. Data on the amount of tax actually reclaimed were never available, but an effective tax rate of 2 cents per gallon was always used by the FAA in estimating total revenue from this source. There was no tax at all on jet fuel or kerosene.

Estimates made by the FAA of the divergence between allocated costs of the airways system and the revenue collected by these methods from the various categories of aviation for fiscal year 1969 are shown in Table 4-4. At the insistence of successive administrations, similar data had been produced for several years by the FAA to reinforce the federal government's proposals that user charges—for general aviation in particular —should be increased. (Once the military share has been allocated, that category is no longer of concern here.) Indeed, Table 4-4 suggests that in 1969 general aviation was subsidized at a rate of about $220 million annually, and air carriers by about $100 million.

As already noted, use of the FAA's cost-allocation method is likely to favor general aviation, particularly with regard to the terminal subsystem and probably in the case of the en route subsystem as well. If total terminal costs were allocated on the basis of the number of operations carried out, general aviation's share for 1969 would increase to about $330 million while that of the air carriers would fall to $280 million, the relation between tax liability and allocated costs then being 4 percent and 92 per-

**Table 4-4. Allocation of Tax Liability and Costs of the Domestic Federal Airways System, by User Category, Fiscal Year 1969**

In millions of dollars

| User category and type of tax | Tax liability | Allocated costs[a] | Tax liability as percentage of cost |
|---|---|---|---|
| Military | — | 132.8 | — |
| Air carrier | | | |
| Passenger ticket tax (5 percent) | 255.5 | — | — |
| Gasoline tax (2 cents per gallon) | 2.2 | — | — |
| Total air carrier tax liability | 257.7 | 361.7 | 71 |
| General aviation | | | |
| Passenger ticket tax (5 percent) | 4.0 | — | — |
| Gasoline tax (2 cents per gallon) | 8.8 | — | — |
| Total general aviation tax liability | 12.8 | 234.8 | 5 |
| Total tax liability | 270.5 | 729.4 | 37 |

Sources: Tax liability estimated from Federal Aviation Administration, unpublished data, and *Aviation Facilities Expansion and Improvement*, H. Rept. 91-601, 91 Cong. 1 sess. (1969), p. 39; allocated costs, Table 4-3.

a. Excludes costs of Federal Aviation Administration facilities used solely by the military, and costs allocated to international aviation. In subsequent calculations none of the latter costs are attributed to general aviation.

cent, respectively. However, throughout the remainder of this book all estimates of the subsidy accruing to general aviation from its use of the airways system will be based upon the quantity-of-use method employed by the FAA, and will therefore probably be somewhat conservative.

It is clear that, even on the most generous assumptions, general aviation was heavily subsidized prior to 1970. A particularly glaring anomaly was that the operation of turboprop and turbojet aircraft owned privately by multimillionaires or used by corporations for executive transportation was completely free from user charges. These aircraft consumed untaxed kerosene, and did not carry paying passengers, so no ticket tax was applicable. Although few in number, such aircraft were becoming an increasingly important element of the general aviation fleet, and their nature was such that, compared with other general aviation aircraft, their use placed a relatively large burden on the airways system. Thus, Secretary of Transportation John A. Volpe, in discussing proposed user charges legislation, referred to the general aviation pilot who

operates an executive jet costing about three quarters of a million dollars. He pays about $420 an hour to fly this aircraft and he utilizes most of the services of our billion dollar airways system.

Should he fly IFR from New York to Boston, we estimate the total cost of the government services he receives is about $57. We estimate his IFR Chicago to Miami flight costs the government $117. But at present he pays not one penny to help defray these costs—not one penny.[7]

## The 1970 Airport and Airway Development and Revenue Acts

Subsidization of civil aviation by failure to recover from users the full cost of the federal airways system has long been the subject of debate among the various branches of the federal government. The official FAA position has been expressed as follows:

Where Agency services, activities, or expenditures provide special benefits to identifiable individuals or groups, charges should be imposed to recover the costs to the Federal Government of providing such services. . . . The Federal contribution should not act as a subsidy or an unfair influence in the competitive situation.[8]

Most people in the aviation industry pay lip service to this view, but unfortunately there is much scope for disagreement concerning the extent to which FAA services really do provide "special benefits to identifiable individuals or groups." Consequently, there is a good deal of antagonism among various elements of the aviation industry, with each group emphasizing the costs attributable to the other group.[9] In addition, the industry as a whole is keen to draw attention to the "external" benefits alleged to accrue to the public at large as a result of its activities.

Congressional appropriations committees, however, have often been concerned with the increasing burden placed on the general taxpayer as a result of the growth of aviation activity. For example, as far back as 1954 a House committee reported:

This committee has year after year called attention to the fact that the Fed-

7. Quoted from "Remarks Prepared for Delivery by Secretary of Transportation John A. Volpe before the Aero Club, Hotel Washington, Washington, D.C., June 24, 1969," in U.S. Department of Transportation, "News," 29-S-69.

8. Federal Aviation Agency, Office of Policy Development, "Policy Statement of the Federal Aviation Agency" (FAA, 1965; processed), pp. 33–34. This is in accordance with federal policy established earlier by the U.S. Bureau of the Budget in Circular A-25, "User Charges," first issued in 1959, and congressional policy in Title V of the Independent Offices Appropriation Act of 1952 (65 Stat. 290).

9. Witness, for example, the campaign waged against the airlines by the Aircraft Owners and Pilots Association. See below, p. 97.

eral Government is providing huge sums for airway facilities and operations without reimbursement from the aviation industry. The committee does not propose to continue indefinitely making recommendations for such large appropriations unless some system of airway user charges is placed in effect which will return a substantial sum to the Federal Treasury.[10]

For a number of years a similar attitude was adopted by the Bureau of the Budget, which repeatedly enforced reductions in the FAA's planned expenditures, insisting that if expenditures were to be increased they should be matched by a greater contribution from direct beneficiaries. Nevertheless, despite pressure of this kind and despite the tone of the above quotation—which, it should be noted, is far from being an isolated example—Congress has generally been reluctant to endorse repeated administration efforts to increase aviation's contribution toward the costs incurred on its behalf.[11] As a result, increasing pressure on airport and airways facilities has been virtually unchecked by taxation or pricing, while expansion of those facilities has proceeded in a somewhat haphazard fashion, with FAA budget requests being subject to considerable pruning.

It is usually agreed that the resulting problems of congestion in the air and at terminal areas are evidence of inadequate federal expenditures, but the criterion for "adequacy" is unclear. Expenditures have almost certainly been inadequate if the goal is to allow unlimited use of airways and airports at the current range of prices, but this is not a sensible constraint to accept. It is well to recall the theoretical discussion in Chapter 3 and to reiterate the point that in the absence of the guidance afforded by an efficient pricing system it is impossible to say whether expenditures are adequate or not. Indeed, the present situation illustrates the role of price only too well.

As these problems have grown in intensity, so have successive administrations' attempts to deal with them. During the late 1960s the administration and Congress were almost continually grappling with the twin issues of user charges and federal airport/airways expenditures. Details of proposals to remedy the situation sometimes varied, but in principle remained virtually unchanged through the years. In order to escape from the impasse evidenced in previous attempts, the Nixon administration en-

10. Report of the House Committee on Appropriations accompanying the Department of Commerce Appropriations Bill (H.R. 341, 83 Cong. 1 sess.) for the fiscal year 1954, as quoted in *Airway User Charges*, p. 39.

11. Every president since the Second World War has at some time proposed increased aviation user charges in his budget message to Congress. Reference to specific proposals appeared in every budget message but one between 1959 and 1970.

deavored to capitalize on the insistence of the airlines and airport operators that greatly increased expenditures on airports and airways were needed if existing standards of safety were to be maintained. The means adopted was to propose legislation authorizing increased expenditures in return for increased user charges.[12] Thus, in the summer of 1969 the administration's bill called for:

1. expenditure on the construction of airways facilities and equipment of about $250 million annually over the period 1970–79 (compared with an annual average of $93 million over the previous 10 years); and

2. an increase in federal assistance to airport authorities to an average of $250 million annually over the period 1970–79 (compared with an average appropriation of $71 million over the previous 10 years).

In return for this, the bill proposed the following changes in user charges:

1. an increase in the passenger ticket tax to 8 percent (for air taxis this was to apply to both scheduled and nonscheduled operations);

2. a new tax of $3 on passenger tickets for most international flights departing from the United States;

3. a new tax on air freight waybills of 5 percent;

4. abolition of the gasoline tax for air carriers; and

5. replacement of the existing gasoline tax for general aviation by a 9 cents per gallon (nonrefundable) tax on *all* fuel used by general aviation, unless used for purposes subject to passenger or freight taxes.

In addition, to ensure that authorizations under the bill would actually be appropriated by Congress, it proposed the establishment of a designated account (which corresponds roughly to a trust fund) into which all revenues should be paid, later to be used for further airport and airways development. The trust fund concept was one that had not been favored by the Johnson administration, and indeed still was not by budget officials, the view being that it would detract from the flexibility required by the budgetary process. Despite this, the Nixon administration felt this to be a price worth paying in order to obtain the support of the aviation industry for the user charges proposal. This was a realistic approach. The trust fund idea appealed to the industry for obvious reasons: mem-

12. See the proposed Aviation Facilities Expansion Act of 1969, H.R. 12374, 91 Cong. 1 sess. Also see the bill introduced in the Senate—S.2437, 91 Cong. 1 sess. For debates on the proposals, see in particular *Administration's Proposal on Aviation User Charges,* Hearings before the House Committee on Ways and Means, 91 Cong. 1 sess. (1969).

bers pointed to the effects of the Highway Trust Fund with some envy, and the political philosophy implied by the concept also commends itself to many.[13]

It was estimated at the time that, if implemented in their entirety for fiscal 1970, the taxes proposed in the administration's bill would have collected about $68 million from general aviation, which would correspond to roughly 30 percent of the costs allocated to that group by the FAA for 1969. (Allocated costs for 1969 are used since these are the latest estimates available.) The total that would have been collected from general aviation over the period 1971–79 was estimated at about $880 million, an average of $98 million annually.[14]

However, the administration's bill of June 1969 was to be subject to considerable modification in the following months.[15] The main debate centered on the form and rates of the user charges, but the proposed expenditures on the modernization of the airways were hardly challenged. Details of proposed airport assistance were modified, however, and are considered in a subsequent chapter.

The final version of the bill emerged from a joint conference committee and was passed by both houses and obtained presidential approval in May 1970. The act consisted of two parts. Title I was the Airport and Airway Development Act of 1970, dealing with expenditures, while Title II, the Airport and Airway Revenue Act of 1970, dealt with user

13. A leading member of one of the more influential general aviation groups told the author that a trust fund was necessary in order to prevent the receipts being used for "some socialistic purpose." On the other hand, for a convincing case *against* the trust fund approach, see testimony by James R. Nelson in *Economic Analysis and the Efficiency of Government,* Hearings before the Subcommittee on Economy in Government of the Joint Economic Committee, 91 Cong. 1 sess. (1970), p. 595.

14. In this calculation inflation was not taken into account on the cost or revenue side. Inflated costs would have had to be offset by further legislative action to change tax rates, if proportionate liability was to remain unchanged in real terms.

15. For details of the debate, see in particular *Administration's Proposal on Aviation User Charges,* Hearings; *Aviation Facilities Expansion and Improvement,* H. Rept. 91-601, 91 Cong. 1 sess. (1969); *Congressional Record,* Vol. 115, Pt. 25, 91 Cong. 1 sess. (1969), pp. 33260–33313; *Airport and Airways Development Act of 1969,* S. Rept. 91-565, 91 Cong. 1 sess. (1969); *Airport and Airway Revenue Act of 1970,* S. Rept. 91-706, 91 Cong. 2 Sess. (1970); *Congressional Record,* daily ed., February 24–26, 1970, pp. S2274–79, S2332–61, and S2484–2519, respectively; *Airport and Airway Development and Revenue Acts of 1970,* H. Rept. 91-1074, 91 Cong. 2 sess. (1970); and *Congressional Record,* daily ed., May 12–13, 1970, pp. S7043–54 and H4306–12, respectively.

**Table 4-5. Projection of General Aviation and Air Carrier Liability to User Charges, Fiscal Years 1971-80**

In millions of dollars

| User charge | 1971 | 1972 | 1973 | 1974 | 1975 | 1976 | 1977 | 1978 | 1979 | 1980 |
|---|---|---|---|---|---|---|---|---|---|---|
| *General aviation* | | | | | | | | | | |
| Fuel tax | 47.2 | 50.9 | 55.1 | 59.2 | 63.8 | 68.3 | 72.7 | 76.5 | 81.0 | 85.4 |
| Aircraft use tax | 10.4 | 11.0 | 11.8 | 12.4 | 13.2 | 14.0 | 14.7 | 15.4 | 16.2 | 17.0 |
| Waybill tax[a] | 0.5 | 0.6 | 0.6 | 0.6 | 0.6 | 0.7 | 0.8 | 0.9 | 0.9 | 1.0 |
| Passenger tax[a] | 13.8 | 15.0 | 15.8 | 16.9 | 18.2 | 19.8 | 21.4 | 23.0 | 24.7 | 26.7 |
| Taxes on tires and tubes | 1.0 | 1.0 | 1.1 | 1.2 | 1.3 | 1.4 | 1.5 | 1.6 | 1.7 | 1.8 |
| Total general aviation liability | 72.9 | 78.5 | 84.4 | 90.3 | 97.1 | 104.2 | 111.1 | 117.4 | 124.5 | 131.9 |
| *Air carrier* | | | | | | | | | | |
| Total air carrier liability | 592.9 | 647.0 | 711.3 | 781.6 | 862.6 | 958.3 | 1,054.2 | 1,158.2 | 1,269.5 | 1,405.0 |
| Total liability | 665.8 | 725.5 | 795.7 | 871.9 | 959.7 | 1,062.5 | 1,165.3 | 1,275.6 | 1,394.0 | 1,536.9 |

Sources: Fuel tax, all years, and total liability, 1971, from Federal Aviation Administration, "Accrued Liability to Civil Aviation from User Taxes—FY 1971–1980," EC-200 (May 8, 1970; processed); taxes on tires and tubes, 1971 and 1980, from *Airport and Airway Revenue Act of 1970*, S. Rept. 91-706, 91 Cong. 2 sess. (1970), p. 10; other data are estimated from EC-200 and unpublished data from FAA. Data here have been normalized and all data on revenue and cost side are in constant dollars to facilitate comparison.

a. FAA estimates incorporate 2 percent inflation factor.

charges.[16] The act created an Airport and Airway Trust Fund into which amounts equivalent to those collected from the various user charges must be transferred at least quarterly from the general fund of the Treasury. As from July 1, 1970, user charges on civil aviation are as follows:

1. A tax on commercial air carriers and air taxi operations of 8 percent of the gross amount of domestic passenger fares, which is to be fully included in the domestic tariffs. This corresponds roughly to a passenger ticket tax, the preexisting one of 5 percent being abolished.

2. A $3 per head international departure tax.

3. A 5 percent tax on domestic air freight waybills.

4. A tax of 7 cents per gallon on gasoline and kerosene used by noncommercial aviation, replacing the existing one of 2 cents per gallon on gasoline alone. Fuel used for purposes subject to passenger or freight taxes is exempt. (Commercial aviation is defined to include air taxis.)

5. As an entirely new feature, an annual registration fee (or "use tax") of $25 per aircraft, plus 2 cents per pound for piston-engined aircraft of more than 2,500 pounds "maximum certificated take-off weight" and 3½ cents per pound for turbine-powered aircraft.

Including a small tax on tires and tubes, the estimated yield from these taxes is $666 million in 1971, of which $73 million would be obtained from general aviation. Details are given in Table 4-5, which demonstrates that the fuel tax will continue to be the main source of revenue from general aviation. If liability for 1971 is related to the 1969 airways cost allocation figures, general aviation would produce revenue equivalent to just under one-third of its allocated share, quite apart from any benefits it might receive from federal aid to airports. The revenue obtained from general aviation over the ten-year period was estimated to average slightly more than $100 million annually.

On the expenditure side, the act, in common with the House and Senate versions, conformed more closely to the administration's original proposals, providing that the annual obligational authority during the period July 1, 1970, through June 30, 1980, for the acquisition, establishment, and improvement of air navigational facilities under the Federal Aviation Act of 1958 should be no less than $250 million. With legislative backing for this additional expenditure on facilities and equipment, the FAA projection of total federal expenditures on the airways is shown in Table 4-6.

16. Public Law 91-258, May 21, 1970 (84 Stat. 219).

It should be noted that the estimates of airways costs in Table 4-6 are on a different level from those given in Tables 4-1 and 4-3; there are several reasons for this. First, the capital cost element in those tables is estimated on an annualized basis, while the data here refer to estimated actual expenditures. In addition, the earlier tables relate to the *domestic* airways system and also exclude FAA expenditures on facilities used solely for military purposes. Table 4-6, on the other hand, includes expenditures on international flight service stations and other FAA facilities outside the fifty states and also includes FAA expendi-

**Table 4-6. Projection of Federal Expenditures on the Airways System, Fiscal Years 1971–80**

In millions of constant dollars

| Fiscal year | Civil | Military | Total |
|---|---|---|---|
| 1971 | 840 | 210 | 1,050 |
| 1972 | 970 | 242 | 1,212 |
| 1973 | 972 | 243 | 1,215 |
| 1974 | 965 | 241 | 1,206 |
| 1975 | 984 | 246 | 1,230 |
| 1976 | 1,042 | 260 | 1,302 |
| 1977 | 1,090 | 273 | 1,363 |
| 1978 | 1,130 | 283 | 1,413 |
| 1979 | 1,166 | 291 | 1,457 |
| 1980 | 1,200 | 300 | 1,500 |
| Total | 10,359 | 2,589 | 12,948 |

Source: *Airport and Airway Revenue Act of 1970*, S. Rept. 91-706, 91 Cong. 2 sess. (1970), p. 5.

tures for solely military use. It seems reasonable to assume that general aviation's absolute share is not increased when the airways system is defined more broadly and, *on an annualized basis,* would be retained at $235 million for 1969.

Overall expenditure estimates for the airways system are available for 1971–80, and planned investment by type of facility is also listed by the FAA,[17] but at present no estimates are available from the FAA of the annual operating costs associated with each type of facility, although in total these continue to form the bulk of FAA expenditures. Accordingly, aggregate data are used here to make a rough estimate of the extent to

17. See Federal Aviation Administration, "The National Aviation System Plan, 1970–1979" (FAA, January 1969; processed), Book 2. This does not include detailed plans for flight service stations.

which airways expenditures over the period 1971–80 should be allocated to general aviation.

For this purpose, examine the use made of airways facilities of various kinds as predicted by the FAA. Table 4-7 compares various measures of airways usage for 1969 with the corresponding annual average usage over the period 1971–80. General aviation is predicted to be responsible for about 55 percent of the increase in IFR departures, 52 percent of the increase in total IFR aircraft handled by ARTCCs, the whole of the increase in the number of contacts made by flight service stations, and 94 percent of the increase in total operations recorded at FAA-operated control towers. One reason for the expected importance of general aviation's contribution to the growth in total recorded operations is the projected increase (from 328 to 487 between 1970 and 1980) in the number of FAA control towers.[18] This will be of relatively greater benefit to general aviation, for the proportion of total air carrier operations currently recorded is much larger than the proportion of general aviation operations that take place at FAA-controlled airports.

In assessing the proportion of costs allocable to air carriers, general aviation, and the military, the number of IFR departures can be used as a rough proxy for instrument operations and approaches, and the number of contacts with flight service stations can act as a proxy for flight services. Using the FAA's quantity-of-use method of cost allocation, and bearing in mind that the fundamental reason for increasing expenditures is increasing amounts of traffic using the airways system, a rather conservative estimate would be that, at the predicted levels of activity, general aviation will be responsible for at least 50 percent of the increase in annual airways expenditures in the decade subsequent to fiscal 1970.

Total airways expenditures in 1969 were estimated at $675 million (see Table 4-2), compared with a predicted average of $1,295 million over the period 1971–80. If half of the annual increase in expenditures is allocated to general aviation and then added to its estimated liability for the 1969 base year ($235 million), the total amount annually allocable to general aviation for 1971–80 will be approximately $545 million. Since the revenue obtained from general aviation over the period is estimated at about $100 million annually, the net result will be—even with the increased user charges—an annual subsidy of about $445 million.

18. Federal Aviation Administration, *The National Aviation System Plan, 1971–1980* (1970), p. 54.

**Table 4-7. Estimates of Use of the Airways System, by Selected Measures, 1969 and 1971–80 Average**

In millions

| Period and type of estimate | Number of departures under instrument flight rules | | | | Total aircraft handled under instrument flight rules | | | | Aircraft contacted by flight service stations[a] | | | | Total operations at airports with FAA traffic control service | | | |
|---|---|---|---|---|---|---|---|---|---|---|---|---|---|---|---|---|
| | Air carrier | General aviation | Military | Total | Air carrier | General aviation | Military | Total | Air carrier | General aviation | Military | Total | Air carrier | General aviation | Military | Total |
| 1969, total | 5.2 | 1.4 | 1.6 | 8.2 | 13.1 | 3.2 | 4.6 | 20.9 | 0.8 | 8.7 | 0.6 | 10.1 | 11.0 | 44.2 | 3.3 | 58.5 |
| 1971–80 average | 7.6 | 4.4 | 1.7 | 13.7 | 19.1 | 9.7 | 4.6 | 33.4 | 0.8 | 17.5 | 0.5 | 18.8 | 15.2 | 96.6 | 2.7 | 114.5 |
| Increase, 1971–80 average over 1969 | 2.4 | 3.0 | 0.1 | 5.5 | 6.0 | 6.5 | 0 | 12.5 | 0 | 8.8 | −0.1 | 8.7 | 4.2 | 52.4 | −0.6 | 56.0 |
| Percentage of annual increase[b] | 43.6 | 54.5 | 1.8 | 100.0 | 48.0 | 52.0 | — | 100.0 | — | 101.1 | −1.1 | 100.0 | 7.5 | 93.6 | −1.1 | 100.0 |

Source: Federal Aviation Administration, Office of Policy Development, *Aviation Forecasts, Fiscal Years 1969–1980* (FAA, 1969; processed), pp. 35, 36, 38, 40.
a. One count is made for each en route, landing, or departing aircraft contacted by an FAA flight service station, regardless of the number of contacts made with an individual aircraft, but one count is made for each facility contacted by any one aircraft.
b. Percentages may not total 100 because of rounding.

Finally, it should be noted that all the official revenue estimates quoted above are based on the hypothesis that use of the airways system will not be inhibited by imposition of the increased user charges (that is, demand in the relevant price range is assumed to be inelastic). The 1970 legislation imposes a relatively small increase in general aviation aircraft operating costs,[19] so this seems a reasonable assumption to make. There are in fact no good grounds for believing otherwise. Attempts to use time series data to derive price elasticity estimates for various measures of general aviation activity have consistently come up with statistically insignificant price coefficients.

## FAA Safety Regulations

In addition to operating the airways system itself, the FAA carries out a number of "safety regulatory" functions. Over the period 1968–72 the average annual cost of these functions allocable to general aviation has been estimated at about $11 million.[20]

Of this, about $3.4 million would be spent on the assessment of technical competence and physical fitness of airmen (defined to include not only pilots but also mechanics and instructors). A roughly similar amount would be spent on the inspection and certification of aircraft engines and accessories at the design and production stages and on periodic maintenance inspections. Inspection and surveillance of air-taxi operations would account for roughly $2.5 million, with a further $1.2 million being spent on accident investigation. The remainder would be spent on support facilities and the inspection and certification of repair stations and flying schools.

Accident investigation is also the province of the National Transportation Safety Board, whose total expenditure for 1972 with respect to aviation accidents is estimated to be about $4.5 million.[21] This, of course, will apply to both air carrier and general aviation activity. Other public organizations—state aviation authorities, police, FBI, Civil Air Patrol, and the Coast Guard—are called upon as a result of aviation accidents. In total, it would not be unreasonable to assume that the cost to public

19. See Table 5-1, p. 92.
20. Federal Aviation Administration, Office of Policy Development, "FAA Services for General Aviation" (FAA, 1967; processed).
21. *The Budget of the United States Government, Fiscal Year 1972.*

authorities of general aviation accident prevention and investigation is on the order of $15 million annually.

This figure is insignificant in relation to the total costs of airway use attributable to general aviation.[22] In the next chapter, which deals with user charges policy, attention is primarily concentrated on the recovery of those costs incurred by the FAA in its operation of the federal airways system. But it must be borne in mind that the distinction between operating the airways system and carrying out the so-called safety regulatory function is largely a bookkeeping one, for the two are clearly complementary.

22. This also applies to the cost of general aviation accidents to third parties other than public authorities. See Appendix C, which also contains a general discussion of the FAA's safety regulatory role for general aviation.

# CHAPTER FIVE

# User Charges for the Federal Airways System

IN A STATEMENT made in June 1968 before a Senate committee, outlining his administration's proposed user charges legislation, the then secretary of transportation, Alan S. Boyd, affirmed "a fundamental belief in the efficiency and superiority of the market mechanism as a system for allocating scarce resources," also stating that "where there is a determination that subsidy is necessary for some overriding national objective, the subsidy should be direct, specially identified, and its purposes clearly defined."[1] This statement is unexceptionable, but the user charges that he then went on to propose, similar in form to those introduced by the administration in the following year (the passenger tax/ fuel tax package) were inconsistent with the sentiments expressed. In company with the measures that were eventually passed by Congress in 1970, they may be criticized on the grounds that (1) the form of charges does not in fact take full advantage of the benefits of the market mechanism and, indeed, may be a barrier to efficient resource allocation, and that (2) the large subsidy to general aviation has no clearly identifiable economic or social rationale.

The primary focus of attention in the present chapter is on the first of these issues, although efficiency and subsidy cannot be treated entirely separately. This is recognized in subsequent chapters, in which the interaction between the two issues of efficiency and subsidy is a constantly recurring theme.

1. *Airport Development Act of 1968,* Hearings before the Aviation Subcommittee of the Senate Committee on Commerce, 90 Cong. 2 sess. (1968), pp. 41–42.

## User Charges and Economic Efficiency

It was pointed out earlier that efficient allocation of resources can rarely be achieved in the absence of the guidance afforded by use of the market mechanism. It is therefore a very basic criticism of the 1970 user charges to say that liability to them does not adequately vary with the use made of particular facilities. This criticism arises not only because of the level of the charges but also because of their nature.

Owing to differing patterns of airway use within the general aviation sector, an equality of the real cost burden a given operator imposes on FAA facilities and the user charge he pays is largely fortuitous. This would continue to be true even if the marginal costs allocated to general aviation as a whole were matched by equivalent revenue. These user charges do not have the fundamentally important function of a price—allocating resources in an efficient or equitable manner—but are merely crude devices to recover costs from the various broad categories of aviation responsible for them.

To illustrate, suppose that aviation activity could not be continued at a level of speed and safety acceptable to the industry in the absence of the FAA facilities currently provided and that this view is accepted by aircraft operators of all types and in all parts of the country. Under these restrictive conditions, it could be said that the total sum paid by means of the fuel, passenger, and registration taxes is at least a minimum estimate of the value placed upon FAA facilities by the aviation community *as a whole*. Even here, however, the charges do not play the role of a price: even for the aviation community as a whole, the fact that users apparently place a value on FAA facilities that is at least as great as the price they pay for them is no evidence that the value placed on *marginal* installations exceeds their costs.

Moreover, a fuel or passenger tax, a rough proxy for mileage flown, does not accurately distinguish between those aircraft that make extensive use of congested air corridors and high-activity airports, and the sophisticated and expensive equipment thereby entailed, and those that make no use of them at all. Consequently, within each sector of the aviation community there will be a misallocation of resources, for there is no incentive for individual aircraft operators to make socially efficient use of

FAA facilities, no pecuniary pressure, that is, for an individual to switch from an activity entailing high resource cost to one that is less costly.

The above, of course, also implies that the suggestion that there may be a consensus on the scale and quality of FAA facilities is unrealistic. For example, some general aviation fliers claim, with justification, that they do not use the facilities and therefore place no value on them at all, while others claim that FAA facilities are inadequate for the needs of general aviation and should be expanded more rapidly. Even under a 100 percent cost recovery policy, there would no doubt be some who would continue to make the latter argument, their attitude being reinforced by the fact that the full (marginal) cost is not recovered from actual users alone but is shared among all operators.

At first sight this situation may appear to correspond to the system of paying for membership in a club; after payment of an entrance fee (the fuel, passenger, or aircraft use tax), marginal units of the facilities provided can be consumed at zero extra cost. The difference, however, is that membership in the FAA facility "club" is compulsory for all airway users, even if no use is made of those facilities. To obtain the privileges of a normal club, members pay a lump sum that can safely be presumed to be at least a minimum estimate of the value placed on membership. But for FAA facilities this does not apply; all aircraft operators are subject to the same rates of taxation, even though they may place no value at all on the facilities. Thus, although the so-called user charges may have the effect of making use of the system as a whole less than it would have been in their absence, they do not have the effect of allocating resources efficiently *within* the system because of cross-subsidization within the aviation community.

FAA policy on the choice between direct user charges (that is, those requiring the establishment of a pricing mechanism) and indirect charges, such as the fuel and passenger taxes, is worth quoting at length:

A system of direct charges, under which a specific dollar charge would be levied for each use of a component or service of the airway system, would meet the requirement of an equitable program of user charges if the direct charges were related both to the use made of and the benefits derived from individual facilities and services. However, the operational and administrative problems inherent in direct charging (e.g., charging for each flight plan filed, each radio contact made, etc.) appear to preclude its consideration for the domestic Federal Airway System in the aggregate. The large variety of facilities and services in use would require a complex schedule of fees that would have to be extensively planned before installation. A vast and expensive administrative establishment would undoubtedly be required to administer and to collect such fees throughout the United States. A further objection to direct charges is that their imposition could adversely affect the safety of flying by decreasing the readiness of some civil users to avail themselves of all appropriate facilities and services.[2]

Although written in 1966 this continues to be an accurate summary of the FAA's position, which appears to be too demanding in its approach to direct charging. It is fairly clear that the costs of introducing direct charging for the use of certain FAA facilities would exceed the benefits resulting from such action,[3] but a suitable compromise could be achieved. An improvement on existing policy could be obtained by introducing: (1) *direct charges* for the use of those facilities that are associated with landings and takeoffs; and (2) *indirect charges* for use of all other airways facilities.[4]

It is therefore recommended that federal expenditures on the terminal subsystem be recovered by means of landing charges, while remaining airways facilities (the en route traffic control, air navigation, and flight service subsystems) should be charged for—as now—on the basis of the fuel and transportation taxes, after appropriate allocation of those costs among broad categories of users. According to the FAA's method of cost allocation, therefore, almost 40 percent of general aviation's share of the costs of the domestic federal airways system would be accounted for by use of facilities subject to direct charging. Note, however, that although the terms "direct" and "indirect" will continue to be used in reference to charges, the distinction between them is not perfectly watertight. Indirect charges of the above form are not completely unrelated, and direct charges cannot be perfectly related to facility usage.

In the interests of economic efficiency, some approximation to marginal cost pricing should be employed for FAA facilities, and the task in this chapter is to see how this might be achieved in practice. The current subsidization of general aviation is not simply the by-product of applying

2. *Administration's Proposals on Airway User Charges,* Hearings before the House Committee on Ways and Means, 89 Cong. 2 sess. (1966), p. 58. Hereafter called *Airway User Charges.*
3. As described in Chapter 3 and Appendix B.
4. A similar conclusion has been reached by Gary Fromm. See his testimony in *Economic Analysis and the Efficiency of Government,* Hearings before the Subcommittee on Economy in Government of the Joint Economic Committee, 91 Cong. 1 sess. (1970), particularly pp. 568–85.

efficient pricing rules in circumstances in which marginal cost is less than average cost. Not only does the form of charging itself leave much to be desired, but in the above quotation the FAA, in distinguishing between the use made of the system and the benefits derived therefrom, stresses the equity rather than the efficiency aspect of a system of user charges, suggesting a deliberate policy of discriminating in favor of general aviation.

## Direct Charges for the Terminal Subsystem: Some Practical Issues

The emphasis on the virtue of equating price to the marginal cost that users impose on the system implies that distinctions should not be made between air carriers and general aviation or, within the general aviation category, between business and nonbusiness use, on any basis other than the costs that are involved as a result of different types of activity. Where this is unavoidable because it is not possible (or too costly) to identify individual users of particular parts of the system, the task should be to restrict the arbitrariness of such distinctions as much as possible. This however is not a problem for the terminal area subsystem, where direct charging for federally provided facilities is an eminently practicable proposition. The cost of operating a pricing system would be negligible, for it would be simple to charge a landing fee that could be collected at the same time as landing fees for *airport* use and, where applicable, a congestion tax.[5]

There are few technical difficulties attached to this solution, but one that does arise concerns the different treatment of traffic flying under instrument flight rules (IFR) and visual flight rules (VFR). Despite the FAA's method of cost allocation, which imputes a relatively large share of the burden to IFR activity, it is recommended that for charging purposes no distinction be made between IFR and VFR operations *on days when both types use a terminal facility*. This is for two reasons. First, as already pointed out, aircraft flying IFR often do so partly in order to obtain assistance in avoiding VFR traffic. Secondly, to make such a distinction would discourage general aviation operators from flying IFR.

5. Airport landing fees and congestion taxes are discussed at some length in Chapters 8 and 9.

Many are already reluctant to do so, and to encourage this tendency would be completely at odds with the FAA's function of promoting air safety.[6]

This is not, however, to agree with the FAA's rejection of direct charges *altogether* on safety grounds. Its attitude amounts to contending that some aircraft operators could not be trusted to act in a manner conducive to safety if direct charges were enforced. As applied to the terminal subsystem, the argument is that they would tend to land at airports with inadequate air traffic control or navigational facilities because it would be cheaper to do so.

A suggested solution to the problem is as follows. First, it would be fundamental to the proposed user charge policy that increases should be introduced gradually over a period of years. By this means it would be possible to estimate in advance the extent and direction of substitution of one airport for another. An airport with little in the way of FAA installations might therefore become increasingly popular as a result of the charging policy: this could be allowed to continue unchecked up to the point at which, on grounds of safety or avoidance of congestion, the FAA determines that some installation at that airport is required.[7]

Should the incremental expenditure be relatively large, price should then be raised in advance of the installation to ration existing airport capacity up to the point that potential users are willing to pay a price that will cover its costs. Prior to this stage, some operators may find it preferable to revert to use of the original airport; in which case, subject to a correct decision regarding investment, safety, and congestion costs, efficiency in the allocation of FAA resources between the two airports will have been achieved. This procedure would eventually result in a much stricter degree of federal or other public control over landing areas and therefore over general aviation operations—probably an unavoidable consequence if official standards of safety are to be maintained.

If a direct charging policy is a feasible proposition for the terminal subsystem, the next thing to deal with is the actual form of pricing that should be employed. It is suggested that price should be equated to average incremental cost, as recommended in different contexts by Nelson

6. Included as an operation is the execution of simulated instrument approaches or low passes at the airport. Training activity of this nature would require special charging arrangements.

7. In general the case for public intervention when these effects are "external" to individual users (these being defined to exclude passengers of commercial air carrier or air taxis) is clear. The case for legislation designed to protect an individual from himself is much less so.

and Turvey.[8] This, it will be recalled, is equal to the sum of marginal running costs and the cost of the marginal unit of capacity averaged over all consumption per unit of time. The technical details of the form this might take, given the peculiar characteristics of the terminal subsystem, follow in the next section. The general reader may, if he wishes, skip this without loss of continuity.

## Average Incremental Cost Pricing for the Terminal Subsystem

Practical versions of marginal cost pricing always require that some form of averaging of cost over a range of output be made, particularly when some degree of capital indivisibility is present. The solution of setting price equal to average incremental cost (AIC) for the terminal subsystem is, however, subject to certain theoretical complications quite apart from those normally encountered in departing from strictly marginal rules.

AIC pricing is here interpreted to mean that, when there is excess capacity, price should be equated to the sum of marginal operating plus average (bookkeeping) capacity costs per operation made possible by the most recent increment in capacity. As existing capacity approaches full utilization, investment in further capacity is signaled when users reveal their willingness to pay a price equal to the average cost of the next increment in capacity plus the associated marginal running costs. At this point AIC pricing conforms to strict marginal cost pricing. After investment, however, it diverges from the ideal, for the total capacity cost to be recovered via the pricing mechanism then remains unchanged until further augmentation of capacity is due. Under strict marginal cost pricing, capacity costs, once incurred, would of course cease to be relevant.

The peculiar complications involved in applying AIC pricing to terminal airways facilities arise from unavoidable ambiguity in defining an increment in capacity. This difficulty would be rather less of a problem in the case of the other utilities discussed earlier, water supply again being perhaps the best example. The important characteristic of water supply in this respect is that one can often distinguish an entirely new source of supply—an upland reservoir, for example—as being quite clearly in-

8. See above, pp. 32–33.

stalled to cater to marginal demands. Hitherto existing reservoirs then cease to be important considerations in determining average incremental cost.[9]

This certainly does not apply to the terminal airways subsystem at a single airport, even though expenditures on additional facilities and equipment may clearly cater to marginal demands. The situation here is that these facilities operate *in conjunction with existing assets* to meet marginal demands. Consequently, if all historical costs of existing assets are ignored, considerable price fluctuation can be expected to result from implementation of the rule if applied as in the water supply example.

One method of dealing with this difficulty would be to treat FAA terminal facilities as constituting an entirely new system whenever any investment takes place. The AIC pricing rule in these circumstances would then be that, if capacity is underutilized, price should be equated to the sum of (1) marginal operating costs and (2) the average bookkeeping costs of all assets *currently used*. The investment decision should then be signaled when users reveal that they are willing to pay a price that covers the average operating costs associated with the new system, plus the bookkeeping costs of all capital assets remaining in use in the system after investment has taken place.

AIC pricing is a compromise between the desire to avoid undue price fluctuations resulting from capital indivisibility and the need to stress the importance of marginal costs in the investment decision. In the latter regard it has been emphasized that only capital charges associated with assets currently employed should be used as a basis for pricing. In practice this would be a most important stipulation: the nature of the terminal airways subsystem is such that much of the investment that takes place is in equipment that *replaces* existing assets. AIC pricing would clearly require that capital charges on those assets be ignored for pricing purposes.

It should be observed that while there is excess capacity, AIC pricing (as far as the treatment of capital assets is concerned) would be equivalent to average *total* cost (ATC) pricing if decision makers defining amortization periods were equipped with perfect foresight. This is because replacement then would take place only when capital charges on those assets had been terminated. It would also correspond to ATC pricing if none of the investment replaced other assets at all. The rapidity of tech-

9. Note that even in the case of water supply, a systems approach to the calculation of marginal cost may be appropriate. This will be still more true of electricity supply and transport investments.

nical change in this area, however, suggests that these points are mainly of academic interest.

The advantage of AIC pricing is that it would eliminate loss-making resulting from capital indivisibility, but it would not do so (except where AIC turns out to be identical to ATC) if long-run average costs were falling. This is because it corresponds in the long run to marginal cost pricing, so that when long-run average costs are declining the familiar financing problems arise.

AIC pricing corresponds more closely to the theoretically ideal marginal cost pricing system, the less the degree of capital indivisibility that is present. There is some indication that increases in the volume of traffic at a given airport can, by use of the technology currently employed, be accommodated by relatively small increments of expenditure on FAA facilities, or at least by a pattern of expenditure that would not, even under strict marginal cost pricing, involve substantial fluctuations in price. Similarly, the decision to invest in an altogether new airport does not, as far as federal airways facilities are concerned, require a dramatic rise in price to signal its economic justification. In other words, indivisibility, or lumpiness, does not appear to constitute a serious problem.[10]

Evidence that this is so is provided by the differing nature of the FAA installations to be found at airports of different sizes, ranging from the general aviation landing strip with no air traffic control or navigational aids at all to an air carrier airport generously equipped with highly sophisticated equipment, such as Kennedy. In between these extremes, the size, sophistication, and type of equipment vary roughly with the size of airport. Although not invariably so, lumpiness of the marginal cost function is normally associated with high capital intensity; and it is therefore significant that in fiscal year 1969 capital costs (interest and depreciation charges) represented only 14 percent of the total annual cost of the terminal area subsystem (details in Table 4-1).

It may be argued, however, that the federal airways system is not as capital intensive as it should be; furthermore, cost data representing present and past experience may be a poor guide to the future. The charge of unduly low capital intensity of crucial elements of the airways system has recently been leveled against the FAA, special emphasis being placed on the shortcomings of the terminal area subsystem. The fo-

10. This implies that pricing and investment criteria applicable at a single airport can be generalized to apply also to the construction of an entirely new airport.

cus of the complaints, as noted in the previous chapter, is on the need for further automation, an important element of the dramatic increase in total expenditures planned for future years. This suggests that data on existing costs are an unreliable guide to the future, although how the new proposals will affect the various portions of the system remains to be seen. It is, however, conceivable that lumpiness of the terminal subsystem and the pricing problems created by excess capacity will be more evident in the future than in the past.

## Airways, Airports, and Congestion

So far no mention has been made of the pricing of airport landing and terminal areas, which offer services complementary to those of the federal airways system. From the standpoint of economic efficiency, pricing and investment decisions ideally should recognize that terminal airways facilities and the airport at which they are located form one system, even though responsibility for their operation normally lies in the hands of different authorities. Thus an airport's maximum runway acceptance rate, which defines its capacity limit, will normally be determined jointly by runway and taxiway space and the adequacy of the air traffic control system. There is a limit to the rate of operations at a given runway configuration that can be handled safely even with the most advanced air traffic control equipment.

This being the case, "second-best" theory[11] suggests that ideally the whole terminal area should be treated as a single unit for pricing purposes. One way that this could be achieved is for FAA price-fixers to compensate for any shortcomings in airport operators' pricing policies. For example, at each airport where price is less than average incremental cost, the price for FAA services should be greater than average incremental cost, and vice versa. This would cover the case in which price should be raised at capacity to signal investment, but the airport operator fails to do so. In practice, as shown below, the price general aviation aircraft operators pay for airport use is normally much less than average incremental cost—if indeed it is related to airport use at all. This would imply the need for far greater FAA charges if economic efficiency is to be the sole criterion.

11. See pp. 35, 36.

There are, however, good reasons why the dichotomized treatment of airports and airways should be maintained in this book and why pricing of FAA facilities should be dealt with in isolation from the airports at which they are located. First, to do so is to accept the proposition that as a general rule the FAA would be unable to impose a pricing system on airport operators even if it wanted to. It would be politically unrealistic to expect municipal and state airport authorities to abrogate their authority in this regard, including the right to subsidize their own airports if they see fit. Second, there is obviously a case for arguing that such intrusion in state-local affairs is unwarranted, because of the (political) desirability of local autonomy. This was the position taken by former Secretary of Transportation Boyd:

> The Federal and the State or local interests in air transportation are not identical and must be distinguished. For any number of reasons, a community might wish to build more airport capacity than it might require by objective standards. By the same token, in order to induce greater use of the facility and thereby create indirect benefits to the community, the community may choose to underprice the airport services it offers. These are all legitimate local decisions if Federal funds are not involved. And there is no reason for the Federal Government to attempt to influence airport investment decisions, where the primary objective is to create for a community or a State a competitive edge in the continuing contest to attract new business.[12]

If it is accepted that the FAA should not dictate to airport operators how they should manage their finances or allocate airport space, the implication is that it should not, through charging for its terminal facilities, correct for inefficiencies in airport pricing either. Although a subsequent chapter discusses how pricing and investment policies for airports can contribute to overall economic efficiency, it is acknowledged that this may not be the only relevant goal. Moreover, to suggest that the FAA should pursue a version of marginal cost pricing where such a policy is not employed for closely complementary services is a theoretically shaky position. On the other hand, if the ultimate objective is to achieve optimal pricing and investment throughout the aviation system, it may still be argued that it is best to begin with federal policy in the hope that a favorable "demonstration effect" results.

There are, however, certain circumstances in which FAA intervention in airport pricing not only may be desirable on efficiency grounds but, because of safety implications, be politically feasible as well. These cir-

12. *Airport Development Act of 1968,* Hearings, p. 42.

cumstances arise when an airport is operating at full capacity and there is a good deal of congestion and delay. If the local airport operator fails to raise prices or to ration capacity in some other way, the increasing risk of accidents may create an environment in which FAA intervention is made politically possible. This has already occurred in the case of the so-called "high-density airports," where the form of intervention favored by the FAA is the establishment of flight quotas, limiting the number of operations of various kinds. This policy has been challenged in the courts by general aviation interests, but the FAA's action has been upheld.[13]

The legal right and political feasibility of FAA intervention to deal with the congestion problem have therefore been established, but it is reasonable to argue that rationing by price rather than by quota is a preferable course of action.[14] Ideally, airport landing fees should incorporate not only an element related to the marginal cost imposed on airport and airways facilities but also a charge based upon the marginal delay costs imposed on other users. It would not be unreasonable to require the FAA to introduce peak hour "congestion charges," to be tacked on to the direct charges described in this section, even though it cannot determine the pricing policies to be employed by the airport authorities themselves.

However, the phenomenon of airport congestion is in practice closely bound up with the indivisibility, or lumpiness, of those assets—runways, taxiways, terminal buildings, and so forth—that are owned and operated by state and local airport authorities. An increase in airport capacity, either by expansion of an existing airport or construction of a new one, will normally require expenditures on both federal airways and state or local airport facilities; but in both relative and absolute terms the incremental cost of the former will generally be dwarfed by that of the latter.[15] Whether or not the costs of congestion are consciously weighed in decisions to expand airport capacity, it is fairly clear that mounting delays are primarily attributable to the incremental cost of those facilities that are normally provided by state and local authorities.[16]

For this reason, detailed examination of the role of congestion charges

13. See below, p. 146.

14. This is discussed more fully in Chapter 8.

15. This is demonstrated in Table 7-3 below, p. 125, which vastly understates nonfederal costs by excluding the cost of land.

16. That inadequacy of these facilities is the primary reason for congestion is demonstrated in Civil Aeronautics Board, "Problems of Airport Congestion by 1975" (CAB, 1969; processed), referred to below, p. 136.

is deferred until the latter part of the book, where pricing and investment strategies for the whole terminal area, consisting of federal, state, and local facilities, are outlined. To avoid repetition, consideration of details of the form that congestion charges should take and their relevance for the investment decision is also deferred.

## Indirect Charges for Nonterminal Subsystems

Any system of indirect charging is necessarily imperfect from the aspects both of efficiency in resource allocation and of equity. The acceptance of indirect charges for the remainder of the airways system, however, implies agreement with the FAA position that the costs of operating a pricing system for the en route, air navigation, and flight service subsystems would exceed the benefits derived therefrom.

The costs, as indicated in the FAA statement quoted earlier,[17] would be primarily of two forms. The most obvious would be the administrative expense of physically identifying and billing the individual aircraft operator each time an air-ground contact is made or a flight plan filed. While this may be fairly straightforward for scheduled air carrier traffic, it would certainly not be so for general aviation. Indeed, it would appear that installation of a device to give a unique signal for every general aviation aircraft contacted would be necessary to enable the system to work. This is technically feasible, and no doubt the automatic identification and recording of aircraft by use of transponders will become relatively less expensive as time goes on. Were it not for the second element of cost, discussed below, it is possible that as the demand for air travel grows, the relative net gain from introducing pricing would also grow.[18]

Estimation of the costs and benefits of introducing direct charging for nonterminal subsystems would receive more attention in this study if it were not for one major consideration. The official attitude is that further justification for indirect charges for use of the three nonterminal subsystems is the additional safety hazard likely to result from direct charging. Although no evidence as to the likely magnitude (monetary or nonmonetary) of such effects is available, there appear to be fairly sound reasons for acceptance of the FAA position.

17. See p. 71.
18. Optimal timing of the introduction of a pricing system, mentioned in Appendix B, then becomes a real issue.

The majority of general aviation pilots are unqualified—or, if qualified, reluctant—to take advantage of all the aids potentially made available to them by the FAA,[19] and it is likely that direct charging would be a further deterrent. This would be less clearly a matter for public concern if the only potential casualties were the pilots themselves, but the possibility that external costs might result from such behavior puts the matter in an entirely different light. Moreover, the growth in air traffic is associated with greater need for ground-air supervision; use of all the services supplied by the FAA will therefore presumably become a factor of ever-growing importance in maintaining acceptable standards of safety. There are no means of quantifying the potential effects on air safety of direct charging for nonterminal subsystems, but, as it is a fundamental duty of the FAA to assist the safe passage of aircraft, it would be unrealistic to expect the agency to establish a direct charging system the results of which could only be at variance with this objective.

In practice, therefore, the demands of equity and efficiency can probably best be satisfied by levying an indirect charge, the receipts to vary as closely as possible with use of the safety-oriented facilities, but one that does not deter an aircraft operator from using them once a decision to undertake a journey has been made. As noted earlier, the charges for general aviation that eventually materialized in the 1970 legislation included gasoline and fuel taxes, registration fees, and, where appropriate, passenger and air freight taxes.

If there is a high correlation between the liability of individual users and the burden that each places upon the system, the policymaker should follow marginal cost pricing rules as closely as practicable in establishing the indirect charge. The less accurate the proxy measure of use of the system, the less clear it is that those rules should be adhered to. But probably there is no better alternative to aiming for the best system of charging, that is, aiming for the best possible proxy measure of use and then charging in a way that conforms as closely as possible to the theoretical ideal.

For all its obvious weaknesses, the fuel tax appears to be potentially the most satisfactory method to use; and, for reasons similar to those adduced in the previous section, it should be levied at a rate that conforms as closely as possible to average incremental cost, distinguishing as far as is practicable between various categories of aircraft. For the pur-

19. See Appendix C.

poses of average incremental cost charging, the whole of the en route, air navigation, and flight service subsystems should be treated as one system.

The FAA favors the fuel tax on the grounds that the fuel consumption of any aircraft is directly related to that aircraft's weight and payload as well as to the distance flown.[20] As a general rule it is probably true that, to an individual aircraft operator, the net monetary benefit resulting from each mile flown is greater, the greater is the gross weight of his aircraft. Fuel consumption may therefore act as a measure not only of the use of the airways but also of the benefits derived from them.

A consequence of this form of cost recovery is that, within the general aviation sector, aircraft with low rates of fuel consumption receive relatively favorable treatment, a situation akin to that existing with respect to automobile gasoline taxes. This can be criticized on the grounds that, if the objective is to attain an efficient allocation of resources, price discrimination of this sort normally has perverse effects. Sometimes it *is* a legitimate device; for example, if it is necessary to cover accounting costs under conditions of increasing returns, the discriminating monopolist who charges the marginal consumer a marginal cost price, and does not exclude any others who would pay that price, is acting in accordance with the efficiency rules postulated earlier.

Normally, however, discrimination is arbitrary and is extremely difficult to apply without breaking these rules; this would seem to be particularly true in the present case. It is therefore an apparent weakness, rather than a strength, of the fuel tax if average incremental costs have to be covered by discriminating against the larger aircraft. If 100 percent (average incremental) cost recovery were effected by this means, the result would almost certainly be the encouragement of a greater than optimal amount of activity by small aircraft and less than optimal use by larger aircraft.

Paradoxically, some justification for the relatively harsh treatment of the larger aircraft may be found in the fact that mileage is not, after all, a very good proxy measure of the cost an individual operator imposes on the airways system. It need hardly be said that a journey of $X$ miles within the northeast corridor is likely to place much greater demands on the system than a journey of equal mileage undertaken, for example, within remote regions of the state of Alaska. The FAA has suggested that the larger and more sophisticated general aviation aircraft, which

20. See *Airway User Charges*, pp. 58–61, for a discussion of various possible forms of indirect charging.

are mainly used for commercial and business purposes and are to some extent competitive with the airlines, make relatively greater use of the airways in their operations.[21] For example, such aircraft might be expected to make more frequent use of air route traffic control centers, the costs of which are allocated by the FAA on the basis of the number of contacts with aircraft flying IFR. This would justify the discrimination noted, although such justification is not based upon any consideration of the relative *benefits* received by larger aircraft operators, as emphasized by the FAA, but upon relative *use*, "benefit" and "use" being quite distinct concepts.

There may, however, be occasions when the use of mileage as a measure of liability will work unjustly to the detriment of the larger aircraft. Usually they are faster, and the relatively shorter time spent in the airways is not recognized by a mileage charge and, indeed, may be discriminated against by a fuel tax. Considerable uncertainty surrounds the relationship between the incidence of the fuel tax by aircraft size and type and the costs for which each category is responsible; and at present it is not known whether fuel consumption is a more or less accurate proxy to use than mileage. There seems no reason to disagree with the FAA's position that a fuel tax is preferable to a mileage tax, mainly because the mileage tax would require the establishment of a new system of tax collection, including the installation of a device in each aircraft to record the number of hours flown, from which mileage could be calculated for different aircraft types. Since differences in the relative merits of the two methods are unknown, and both are at best very crude measures of airway use, the cost of setting up the new machinery probably would be unwarranted.

The following facts are crucial in justifying the use of the fuel tax— but only where direct charging is unavoidable. First, the machinery of tax collection already exists. Second, the method is already familiar and relatively acceptable to the aviation industry. Third, the pay-as-you-go feature is very important, particularly with respect to the smaller operator. None of these advantages would apply to a mileage tax.

Since similar considerations apply to the ticket tax payable by passengers of air taxis and to the tax on air freight waybills, little time will be devoted to them. In addition, although of growing importance, the proportion of the general aviation fleet for which these taxes are relevant remains relatively small. However, the air taxi, marking the dividing line

21. *Ibid.,* p. 59.

between the air carriers and general aviation, illustrates the difficulties inherent in distinguishing between aircraft for charging purposes on any basis other than costs imposed on the airways system. Because the air taxi is more akin to the air carrier than to most of the remainder of the general aviation fleet in its use of the airways, there is obviously a case for its inclusion in that category for purposes of cost allocation. Since over a given route the cost imposed by an air taxi is roughly similar to that imposed by an air carrier, the tax liability should be the same for each. Obviously this is not so in practice and is a further demonstration of discrimination against larger aircraft, based presumably upon some notion of equity or charging "what the traffic will bear."

If economic efficiency is the objective, the number of passengers or volume of freight should be irrelevant in determining liability for charges. Indeed, such taxes penalize those aircraft that permit the achievement of economies of scale in the use of airways facilities. A charge varying directly with mileage would be easy to administer for commercial airlines and scheduled air taxis (that is, those with specified routes). This charge should be at a common rate for both and be substituted for the passenger/freight tax now employed or proposed. The rate per mile ideally should conform closely to that payable by operators of similar aircraft liable to a fuel tax.

Finally, a word about the graduated registration fee for general aviation and air carrier aircraft. In the light of subsequent events, it is of particular interest to recall the objections raised by the FAA in 1966 to this form of taxation. The statement of the official position on the need for indirect charges, quoted earlier,[22] was followed by a discussion of the methods of indirect charging that could be employed, the conclusion being that none was superior to the fuel and transportation taxes. Although there is reason to criticize the reliance placed upon indirect charging, the objections then voiced to the registration fee were, and remain, entirely valid. A major disadvantage of the tax is its irrelevance to the use actually made of the airways system by those who pay the taxes.[23] It is clear that, for all the weaknesses of the fuel and transportation taxes, they do not match the shortcomings of the registration fee in this respect.

22. See p. 71. It is, however, fair to point out that the registration tax was not the administration's idea, but that of Congress, being first introduced in the House Ways and Means Committee. See *Aviation Facilities Expansion and Improvement,* H. Rept. 91-601, 91 Cong. 1 sess. (1969), p. 40.
23. *Airway User Charges,* p. 60.

As a general principle, lump sum taxes of this sort should be used only for the recovery of lump sum costs, such as charges for periodic aircraft inspection and initial certification. Indeed, it is somewhat surprising that there are still no special fees for original type certification or periodic airworthiness certification for general aviation or air carrier aircraft. The FAA's attempts to remedy this situation in 1967[24] were postponed in the face of objections from the industry and because this issue was overshadowed, in terms of the costs involved, by the operation of the airways system itself.

Arguments used recently in favor of registration fees do invoke the principle, although somewhat misguidedly, that they are justified by the presence of lump sum costs. The argument is that some of the costs of the airport and airways system would be incurred regardless of the volume of traffic, that is, "because many aircraft may use the system at some time, even though most of the time most of these craft are not in the air."[25]

Such a situation might call for peak-load pricing where direct charging can be applied; indeed, this argument is made below.[26] However, where indirect charging has to be used, the crucial fact to be borne in mind is the rapid rate of increase in demand for airports and airspace. This is constantly imposing pressure on existing capacity, and therefore requires a form of charging that varies as closely as possible with the use made of the system. Note also that the objective of recovering greater sums from the owners of the larger and more sophisticated aircraft can be achieved more efficiently by means of the fuel tax than by the clumsy method of varying the registration fee by weight and type of propulsion of the aircraft concerned.

There are, however, circumstances in which the graduated registration fee could usefully be employed to help finance the airways system. Where efficient pricing would result in bookkeeping losses, the very fact that the lump sum charge does *not* vary with facility usage could be put to good advantage, for it does not deter operators from using the airways when at the margin the benefits of so doing exceed the costs. The graduated registration fee seems as equitable a form of charge as any other tax that does not vary with the use of the airways. It could therefore be used

24. See Federal Aviation Administration, "FAA Information," 67-43, April 21, 1967. Fees for airman certification were also proposed. These have not materialized either.

25. *Aviation Facilities Expansion and Improvement*, H. Rept. 91-601, p. 48.

26. See Chapter 8.

to recover overhead costs either in a prolonged period of excess capacity or when in the long run average costs are falling. Although the first of these two possible circumstances is not currently relevant, the second, in view of the suggested average incremental cost pricing policy, may well be. This is, however, obviously not a valid reason for the present use of the graduated registration fee, for the other charges do not conform to efficiency criteria.

## Implementation of Airway User Charges

Estimates of the costs of the federal airways system, as used in FAA cost-allocation exercises, correspond to annual-equivalent costs of existing facilities and therefore approximate the version of incremental costs presented here. The latest official allocation is for 1969, but assume that annual-equivalent airways costs attributable to general aviation grow at the same rate as the growth in total airways expenditures between 1969 and 1971, and also that the components of these expenditures remain in the same proportion for both years.[27] If so, 100 percent cost recovery for the federal airways system would require the total amount collected from general aviation operators in fiscal 1971 to be about $289 million in landing fees and $223 million by means of the fuel/transportation tax. (The lump sum charge can be ignored, since the appropriate costs to be recovered by such a tax are relatively small.) For the purpose of this exercise, research and development costs are allocated among terminal and nonterminal subsystems in the same proportion as the size of the expenditures directly allocated to them, and terminal subsystem costs are allocated purely on the basis of the number of operations performed.

Unfortunately, it is not possible to gauge the effect that 100 percent cost recovery would have upon general aviation activity: in the economist's terminology, the elasticity of demand over the relative price range is unknown for the services of the terminal subsystem by general aviation operators and for the services of general aviation aircraft themselves. Subject to the above assumptions, it is possible to give some indication of the costs that would be borne with respect to general aviation aircraft of different sizes and types if the level of activity predicted by the FAA for 1971 were maintained *and* full-cost recovery effected. It would then be

27. Estimated total airway expenditure for fiscal year 1971 is $1,050 million. See Table 4-6.

possible to make an intelligent guess as to the effects of a 100 percent cost recovery policy on the level of general aviation activity.

### Direct Charges

For illustrative purposes the total sum payable in landing fees by general aviation is estimated according to the number of operations performed by that group. Within the general aviation category, by dividing the resulting figure of $289 million equally among the estimated 139,000 aircraft (irrespective of size or type) flying in 1971,[28] a total landing fee liability per aircraft of roughly $2,000 results. This is equivalent to about $5 per landing or takeoff and corresponds to the charge per general aviation, air carrier, or military operation at an airport where the cost per operation of FAA services is equal to the mean cost per operation for all FAA-controlled airports.

Clearly, such estimates are subject to a good deal of error. One reason is to be found in variations in the degree of sophistication of the airports at which operations are recorded. Thus, at the end of fiscal year 1969, out of the 324 airports with traffic control towers, 190 had approach control facilities, 119 had airport surveillance radar, 111 had air traffic control lighting with sequence flashing lights. Only 6 had airport surface detection equipment, and 16 had precision approach radar.[29] Since airports used primarily by general aviation are less well equipped than air carrier airports or those used jointly by the military, it is obvious that the costs here attributed to general aviation will tend to be overstated.

It would also be desirable to distinguish, within the general aviation category, between aircraft of different sizes and types in assessing their liability to landing fees. Use of average data is likely to underestimate the total liability of the larger and more sophisticated general aviation aircraft, which can be expected to make relatively greater use of FAA-controlled airports than the smaller categories. Better data are not available, but the resultant cost figures suffice as a rough guide. The procedure does at least demonstrate the amount payable in landing fees on behalf of any aircraft that carries out operations equal in number to the mean of the whole general aviation category at an "average" FAA-controlled air-

28. Federal Aviation Administration, Office of Policy Development, "Aviation Forecasts, Fiscal Years 1969–1980" (FAA, 1969; processed), p. 28.

29. See *Airport and Airways Development Act of 1969*, S. Rept. 91-565, 91 Cong. 1 sess. (1969), p. 48.

port. Moreover, in practice any such error would be irrelevant, as a landing charge established at each airport would take account of such variation. Indeed, this is illustrative of the sort of advantage to be derived from direct charging, for errors in the calculation establishing the rate of *indirect* charges not only are likely to be more frequent but also to be more serious when they do occur.

### Indirect Charges

To illustrate the liability of different categories of general aviation aircraft to indirect charges for en route services, assume that all usage is subject to a fuel tax of some sort. The liability of the relatively small air-taxi component, if such travel is to be subject to a ticket tax, should be estimated on the same basis as the fuel tax. In other words, if mileage is accepted as the best feasible measure of use of the airways system, the tax liability for an air taxi traveling $X$ miles should be roughly the same as that for a similar model (but non-air taxi) aircraft traveling an equivalent distance.

The current procedure of taxing gasoline and jet fuel consumed by general aviation aircraft at a similar rate per gallon implies the relatively harsh treatment of larger and faster aircraft. Since, for example, a typical general aviation turbojet might be expected to travel about one and one-half miles per gallon of kerosene, while a single-piston-engined one- to three-place aircraft travels about 14 miles per gallon of gasoline,[30] the liability per mile of a uniform tax is currently ten times greater for the jet than for the smaller aircraft. This is in addition to the relatively favorable treatment of smaller aircraft within each category.

To what extent is this distinction justified? There is, after all, no reason why different rates of tax should not be levied on kerosene and aviation gasoline, although the distinction between turbine- and piston-engined aircraft is about as far as one can go in allowing for variations in fuel consumption rates. But a further distinction can be made between those elements of the nonterminal airways system that may best be charged for on a simple mileage basis and those for which an alternative measure of use is preferable.

The justification given for the relatively higher tax rates for jet fuel is

30. See Federal Aviation Administration, Office of Policy Development, *General Aviation Aircraft Operating Costs* (FAA, 1969), p. 31. Some operating data for representative general aviation aircraft are also given in Table 5-1 below.

that turbine-powered aircraft make relatively greater use of the expensive en route traffic control and air navigation subsystems than piston-engined aircraft do. Unfortunately, information on the extent to which this is so is vague; but if the method used by the FAA to allocate the costs of these subsystems among the various classes of users (that is, according to the number of IFR aircraft handled) is employed, it is possible to make a crude estimate of the costs attributable to the turbine-powered segment of the general aviation fleet. (This, of course, is subject to the earlier comment that the FAA's method of cost allocation may be unduly favorable to general aviation.)

The total number of IFR aircraft handled by FAA air route traffic control centers in 1971 is predicted to be 24.5 million, of which 15.6 million are attributable to air carriers, 4.3 million to general aviation, and 4.6 million to military aircraft. The total number of miles traveled by domestic air carriers is estimated at roughly 2,170 million for 1971, corresponding to one contact per 140 miles flown.[31] The assumption here is that turbine-powered aircraft employed by general aviation place demands on the airways system that are similar to those of the air carriers, in which case contacts made by turbine-powered aircraft are also at the rate of one per 140 miles.

Total mileage for turbine-powered general aviation aircraft is estimated (as shown below) at 400 million for 1971, so the total number of contacts is 2.9 million, out of a total for all general aviation aircraft of 4.3 million. Roughly 65 percent of the costs of the en route and air navigation subsystems allocable to general aviation as a whole for 1971 is therefore allocated to turbine aircraft, the remainder to piston-engined aircraft. Recovery of these costs at the predicted rate of fuel consumption would require a tax of 27.0 cents per gallon on jet fuel and 6.2 cents per gallon on aviation gasoline.[32]

The costs of the remainder of the airways system (the flight service subsystem and intermediate fields) may now be allocated on a basis that conforms more closely to mileage covered. No official forecast is made of total general aviation mileage, but if its rate of growth between 1967 and 1971 is the same as that between 1963 and 1967, 5,780 million miles

31. Domestic mileage is about three-fourths of total mileage, which is forecast at 2,893 million for 1971. FAA, "Aviation Forecasts, Fiscal Years 1969–1980," pp. 2, 27, 38.

32. Jet fuel consumption for 1971 is estimated at 215 million gallons, and aviation gasoline, 500 million gallons. *Ibid.*, p. 31.

would be flown in 1971. If the mileage covered by turbine-powered aircraft is estimated with the aid of FAA data on average use rates and speeds of representative models,[33] the resulting figure is 400 million miles. Rather than carry out a similar calculation for piston-powered aircraft, this figure is subtracted from total mileage to obtain that attributable to the latter category. The reason is that, probably because of the greater heterogeneity of the piston-powered fleet, the definition of representative aircraft is vague; in checking this method for earlier years, poor results were obtained for piston-engined aircraft, while for turbine-powered aircraft they were quite accurate.

Although this is a somewhat unsatisfactory method, it is apparent that the proportion of total general aviation mileage flown by turbine aircraft in 1971 will be fairly small—it is here estimated to be of the order of 7 percent of the total. Accordingly, full cost recovery for the flight service subsystem and intermediate fields would require a gasoline tax of 25.3 cents per gallon and a jet fuel tax of 4.4 cents per gallon, making the total tax payable on both aviation gasoline and jet fuel about 31.5 cents per gallon. The currently proposed taxes on aviation gasoline and jet fuel therefore appear to be on the right course after all in establishing a common rate for both types of fuel. It need hardly be added that more accurate data on use, speeds, and fuel consumption are essential if indirect charging is to be a satisfactory instrument of policy. This must be a major element of the user charges and cost allocation study required by the 1970 legislation.

*Introduction of the Policy*

If activity were to be maintained at the predicted level despite increased charges, the liability faced in 1971 by operators of various types of aircraft under the provisions of the 1970 legislation would be as shown in Table 5-1. It is interesting to note that, under current legislative arrangements, the tax liability for each category of aircraft would vary between 2 and 4 percent of total aircraft operating costs. This effectively discriminates in favor of smaller aircraft in terms of the proportion of allocable airways costs that are recovered, for this would vary from 4 percent for the single-engine, piston, one- to three-place aircraft to 22 percent for turbine-powered aircraft.

33. See notes d and e, Table 5-1.

**Table 5-1. Annual Operating Costs and Liability to User Charges for Representative General Aviation Aircraft, 1971**

Costs and charges in dollars per aircraft

| Type of cost or charge | Single-engine piston, 1–3 places[a] | Single-engine piston, 4 places and over[b] | Two-engine piston[c] | Turboprop[d] | Turbojet[e] |
|---|---|---|---|---|---|
| *Operating costs* | | | | | |
| Variable | 1,208 | 2,884 | 9,490 | 69,185 | 139,210 |
| Fixed | 1,525 | 3,866 | 17,710 | 87,419 | 119,142 |
| Total | 2,733 | 6,750 | 27,200 | 156,604 | 258,352 |
| *User charges* | | | | | |
| Fuel tax[f] | 70 | 150 | 515 | 3,940 | 10,500 |
| Registration fee[g] | 25 | 25 | 125 | 360 | 500 |
| Total liability | 95 | 175 | 640 | 4,300 | 11,000 |
| Liability as percentage of allocated costs | 4 | 7 | 15 | 22 | 22 |
| Liability as percentage of total operating costs | 3 | 3 | 2 | 3 | 4 |

Sources: Operating costs and utilization data are from Federal Aviation Administration, Office of Policy Development, "General Aviation Aircraft Operating Costs" (FAA, 1969; processed), p. 31; user charges are author's estimates.

a. For example, Piper Cub 150, Cessna 150, Piper Pawnee. *Operating data used:* utilization, 150 hours per year; miles flown: 15,000; fuel consumption: 6.8 g.p.h.

b. For example, Cessna 172, Beech Bonanza V35A, Aero Commander 200. *Operating data used:* utilization, 200 hours per year; miles flown: 30,200; fuel consumption: 10.6 g.p.h.

c. For example, Beech Baron, Cessna 310, Piper Aztec. *Operating data used:* utilization, 260 hours per year; miles flown: 52,800; fuel consumption: 28.3 g.p.h.

d. For example, De Havilland Twin Otter, Turbo II Commander, Beech King Air. *Operating data used:* utilization, 450 hours per year; miles flown: 132,750; fuel consumption: 125 g.p.h.

e. For example, Learjet, Grumman Gulfstream II, Lockheed Jetstar. *Operating data used:* utilization, 500 hours per year; miles flown: 225,000; fuel consumption: 300 g.p.h.

f. 7 cents per gallon on aviation gasoline and jet fuel.

g. $25 for all aircraft, plus 2 cents a pound for piston-engined aircraft of more than 2,500 pounds maximum certificated takeoff weight, and 3½ cents per pound for turbine-powered aircraft. Representative models used for this calculation are Piper Cub 150, Cessna 172, Beech Baron, Beech King Air, and Learjet, respectively, for the five columns. Weights are from John W. R. Taylor (ed.), *Jane's All The World's Aircraft, 1969–70* (McGraw-Hill, 1969).

In absolute terms, however, larger subsidies will be obtained by operators of larger aircraft, the annual subsidy for the smallest type of aircraft listed in Table 5-1 being about $2,200 while that for a representative turbojet aircraft would be about $38,000. The proposals here eliminate all such subsidies. Table 5-2 therefore shows that relative both to operating costs and to the liability under present legislation, the proposals are much harsher for smaller than for larger aircraft, although in terms of the absolute increase in tax liability the reverse is true.

In the light of these figures it is clear that the impact of the immediate introduction of 100 percent cost recovery measures would be dramatic. Indeed, it has been suggested that "If we raised the tax as high as we

**Table 5-2. Direct and Indirect User Charges for Representative General Aviation Aircraft Assuming Full Cost Recovery, and Liability as Percentage of Operating Costs, 1971[a]**

Charges in dollars

| Type of charge or liability | Single-engine piston, 1–3 places | Single-engine piston, 4 places and over | Two-engine piston | Turboprop | Turbojet |
|---|---|---|---|---|---|
| Landing fees | 2,000 | 2,000 | 2,000 | 2,000 | 2,000 |
| Fuel tax[b] | 321 | 668 | 2,318 | 17,719 | 47,250 |
| Total liability | 2,321 | 2,668 | 4,318 | 19,719 | 49,250 |
| Liability as percentage of allocated costs | 100 | 100 | 100 | 100 | 100 |
| Liability as percentage of operating costs | 85 | 40 | 16 | 11 | 19 |

Source: Author's estimates.
a. See notes to Table 5-1.
b. 31.5 cents per gallon for aviation gasoline and jet fuel.

should to cover the deficit that is allocable to them [general aviation operators], I think it would probably eliminate all private aircraft in the United States, or come close to it."[34]

Although, as shown in the next chapter, general aviation interests have yet to demonstrate why the costs attributable to them should not be recovered in full, the immediate introduction of such a policy is not recommended; rather, the proposed landing fee/transportation tax package should be introduced gradually, say over a period of five years. This would avoid what would certainly be a sudden drop in aviation activity, resulting in hardship for such people as pilots and employees of manufacturers and fixed-base operators, and in large capital losses sustained by aircraft owners.

Another result of immediately introducing the scheme would be the creation of excess capacity in FAA facilities and airports, which would benefit nobody. These effects would be mitigated by gradual introduction of charging, which over time would allow the assumed increase in demand for general aviation services to offset, to some extent, the effect of increased costs. The best policy may therefore be to maintain the current level of general aviation activity and use of capacity, by gradually raising charges until such time as aircraft operators reveal their willingness to pay for an expansion of the system.

34. Statement by Joseph W. Barr, then under secretary of the treasury, *Airway User Charges,* p. 23.

# CHAPTER SIX

# The User Charges Controversy

GENERAL AVIATION INTERESTS oppose many of the recent proposals aimed at increasing their contribution to the financing of the federal airways system. Some of the arguments employed are clearly invalid and do not deserve serious analytical attention. Nevertheless, they are mentioned here because, whatever their merits, they have been highly successful in helping to frustrate legislation detrimental to general aviation. Other arguments deserve—and receive—more attention.

## Joint Costs and Taxation of Nonusers

The first argument is that general aviation is not subsidized, and therefore should pay no charges; because the federal airways system was designed for military aircraft and the air carriers, its existence is virtually unaffected by the presence of general aviation.[1] Federal Aviation Administration (FAA) facilities would have been built anyway, the argument runs, and general aviation bears no responsibility for their costs. To allocate costs on a proportionate use basis is therefore unjust. This raises the question of the proper allocation of joint costs—a question to which economic theory is unable to provide a completely satisfactory answer.

Use of what is known as the separable cost–remaining benefits (SCRB) method of allocation[2] would go some way toward meeting this

1. See, for example, statement by National Pilots Association in *Administration's Proposals on Airway User Charges,* Hearings before the House Committee on Ways and Means, 89 cong. 2 sess. (1966), p. 127. Hereafter referred to as *Airway User Charges.*
2. SCRB is used elsewhere by the federal government, although it is not, indeed cannot, be wholly satisfactory in its allocative effects. For a description

criticism, but given the limited objective of allocating costs equitably to various broad categories of aircraft, the straightforward quantity-of-use method employed by the FAA is essentially correct in a situation in which demand is increasing dramatically and pressure is constantly being brought to bear on the capacity of FAA facilities. The joint cost argument would have greater validity in a purely static situation in which excess capacity persisted, but FAA forecasts are that general aviation will be responsible for the largest part of the growth in aircraft activity in the foreseeable future. Since it will be the major contributor to the demand for new capacity, considerations of efficiency require that it should pay.

A related complaint is that, in the past, owners of private aircraft have been forced to invest in equipment they did not want—for example, two-way radios have been made mandatory for aircraft landing at tower-controlled airports—and the associated facilities provided by the FAA are too sophisticated for their requirements.[3] General aviation groups therefore ask whether it is proper to force persons to spend money on their aircraft so they can use the facilities and, in addition, to charge them a fee for using those facilities. Given the desirability of the regulation itself —for which the ultimate responsibility must lie with the FAA, and which in this case is not seriously queried—the answer, from the standpoint of economic efficiency, is clearly affirmative. The important thing is that, according to the cost allocation data, general aviation does use the sophisticated facilities and consequently places a burden on the system for which its members should be charged.

The previous chapter outlined the weaknesses inherent in any form of indirect charging. Similarly, general aviation interests have maintained that the user charges proposed by the FAA are not user charges at all, for they are not related to actual use of facilities in any precise way. This is put most succinctly in a statement entitled "Non-Users Should Not Be Taxed on 'User Charge' Basis,"[4] and many instances are cited of general aviation aircraft employed for such things as crop spraying, pipeline pa-

---

of the method, see United Nations, Economic Commission for Asia and the Far East, *Manual of Standards and Criteria for Planning Water Resource Projects,* Water Resources Series, No. 26 (ST/ECAFE/Ser. F/26) (U.N., 1964). SCRB is advocated by Arthur L. Webster, "Application of 'Separable Cost–Remaining Benefits' Techniques for FAA Cost Allocation and User Charges" (FAA, Office of Policy Development, 1967; processed).

3. See statement by the Aircraft Owners and Pilots Association (AOPA) in *Airway User Charges,* pp. 103, 106.

4. *Ibid.,* p. 129.

trol, and offshore drilling that never use the airways system. A further argument is that about 30,000 general aviation airplanes are not equipped with two-way radio and rarely use the airways system. Moreover, while general aviation airplanes use over 9,000 airports, only about 300 of them have federally provided control towers, yet all general aviation operators are taxed on the same basis, namely by means of the fuel or transportation tax. In view of such opposition to the concept of the user charge, it is interesting to note that the group making this argument has now seen fit to modify its attitude on the subject.[5]

A similar argument, advanced by several sectors of the general aviation community,[6] is that the passenger ticket tax for air carriers is an inefficient method of collecting revenue because aircraft with no passengers (for example, those used for pilot training or technical testing) make use of FAA facilities but are not charged. Framed in this way, the proposition is incontrovertible. But given the present method of cost allocation, general aviation should not be unduly concerned, for it merely involves a reallocation of the cost burden within the air carrier sector. And the conclusion drawn from this state of affairs differs from that drawn by certain general aviation interests: some, for example, would say that no system of user charges is workable, and the whole idea should therefore be abandoned. Thus:

There are no tools that will measure airways use reasonably accurately, either individually or in combination. Even the FAA has asserted this to be the most complex problem in user charges. Every yardstick, be it fuel consumed, aircraft operations, instrument operations, instrument approaches, flight plans, hours flown or any other, the result is the same. Each fails in some respect, separately or in any conceivable combination.[7]

The discussion in the previous chapter indicates agreement with the basic validity of such claims. Nevertheless, the proposed charging method goes some way toward meeting these objections. Moreover, even though the needs of equity and efficient resource allocation are not precisely served by the proposals, it is obvious that some proxy measure of use is more valuable than none at all. The choice lies between charging those who are probably direct users of the system—or who are certainly

5. See below, p. 109.
6. The National Aviation Trades Association (NATA), one organization supporting this position, represents fixed base operators—those who supply support facilities, airports, maintenance, and fueling operations for general aviation aircraft. See the association's arguments in *Airway User Charges*, pp. 92, 97.
7. See statement by AOPA in *Airway User Charges*, p. 105.

potential users—and those who, in general, are certainly not, that is, the general taxpayers. The alternative to an absolutely perfect method of cost allocation is *not* necessarily to abandon all attempts at cost recovery by some form of user charge.

## Air Carriers and Other Forms of Transportation

There is a noticeable amount of conflict within the aviation industry, and in particular between representatives of the airlines and of general aviation, on the subject of airport and airways use and the financing of those facilities. One clearly invalid claim made by general aviation that can readily be dismissed is that the air carriers are not charged at all for their allocated share because it is their passengers, and not they, who pay the ticket tax. If this is true, all this claim implies is that the demand for air travel by ultimate beneficiaries is inelastic in the range of prices that would exist with and without the tax.

The argument that the ticket tax is not a tax borne by the airlines because it is passed on to consumers is particularly interesting in light of the claim that the preponderant use of general aviation is for business purposes. Presumably, therefore, at least some of the aviation gasoline tax can equally be passed on to ultimate consumers. If, in fact, demand for general aviation services is not inelastic, the claim amounts to the position that it is a function of the FAA to practice price discrimination on the basis of variability in the elasticity of demand for its products.[8] But this practice should be avoided if possible, for the reasons indicated earlier.[9] In any case, it is fairly certain that general aviation groups would not wish to see such an extension of public control.[10] Finally, it is difficult to see why general aviation should be concerned over who pays for the air carrier's allotted share of FAA costs, as long as liability for covering those costs is not transferred to general aviation.

The general aviation community not only claims that it is treated unfavorably in relation to the air carriers; the complaint is also frequently made that certain nonaviation forms of transportation are subsidized.[11] It

8. See, for example, *ibid.*, p. 105. Also statement by NATA, *ibid.*, p. 92.
9. See p. 35.
10. See *ibid.*, p. 103.
11. For example, see AOPA statement in *Airport Development Act of 1968*, Hearings before the Senate Aviation Subcommittee of the Committee on Commerce, 90 Cong. 2 sess. (1968), p. 191.

seems that the major complaint is of unfairness; if there were any validity in the complaint, it could also be expressed in terms of economic efficiency, as a version of the "second-best" argument.

As has been noted, direct charging for FAA facilities should be introduced where possible, and the actual price charged should approximate marginal cost. However, it is not suggested in this particular case that marginal cost (or even average incremental cost) pricing be practiced everywhere in the transport field. In order to achieve a practicable degree of consistency with the theoretical ideal, it is argued that the case for recovering total costs from general aviation is reinforced if its direct competitors are not subsidized. That being so, the second-best argument does not seem to pose a serious obstacle to total cost recovery. The commercial airlines—the major competitors—do pay user charges of a sort already, and these cover the bulk of the airways costs allocated to them. The point implied by general aviation groups about equality of treatment is therefore accepted, but it rebounds on them: equality of treatment vis-à-vis the airlines, at least, would require a considerably higher contribution to be exacted from general aviation.

Other competitors of general aviation (and probably to a greater degree of the commercial airlines) are the railroads. Historic federal subsidization of railroads is irrelevant for current efficiency in resource allocation, and federal subsidies in this area are now negligible. In addition, the taxes paid by intercity bus operators, which are paid into the Highway Trust Fund, are estimated to cover the greater part of allocated costs.[12] Waterway users, strangely enough, are often cited by general aviation interests as candidates for the imposition of user charges.[13] This attitude gives the impression that the complaint concerns the "equity" rather than the "efficiency" benefits of extending user charges to various groups, for it is difficult to see how relevant efficiency in pricing waterways is for the treatment of general aviation.

Of more significance, it would seem, is that in the U.S. economy nearly all goods and services produced for final consumption are sold in the market, and these, in the last resort, are also competitive with aviation. The telephone call, for example, is a more important substitute for

12. See *Supplementary Report of the Highway Cost Allocation Study,* H. Doc. 124, 89 Cong. 1 sess. (1965), p. 10.

13. See, for example, the statement of the Utility Airplane Council in *Airway User Charges,* p. 130.

a long distance flight than is use of the nation's waterways.[14] Finally, as shown in Chapter 7, public airports serving general aviation are normally subsidized. If the "second-best" rule is to equate the proportion of total costs that are recovered, the complementary nature of airports and FAA facilities would suggest that the price of the latter should be raised to recover a sum in excess of total airport costs.

## Harming the "Little Guy"

The argument is also made that the FAA should be constrained in its attempts at cost recovery by the fact that the "little guy" would be harmed by such action.[15] Where official action (or inaction) of any kind results in inequity to some individual or group, there may indeed be a case for an alternative policy, even at the expense of some loss in economic efficiency. A policy that has the effect of making the poor even poorer might be an example of this. However, so might a policy that makes the rich even richer.

Prima facie, the argument that the "little guy" is harmed by user charges policy is not very sensible. Much more pertinent might be the argument that the current policy of failing to recover full costs from general aviation users is, in real terms, a subsidy to individuals in the upper and middle income groups. Beyond making the obvious point that private flying is not a poor man's occupation, however, one would be hard put to prove this statistically.

As an illustration of the dearth of statistical information, the secretary of transportation, in a 1968 statement before a Senate committee on the need for user charges,[16] could only support the administration's case in this regard by quoting a survey made by TIME five years earlier on the incomes of purchasers of new aircraft. He also stated that statistics for 1966 showed that almost 80 percent of the hours flown by general aviation were deductible for tax purposes as a business expense of the air-

14. In an oblique fashion, this is recognized by Samuel L. Brown and Wayne S. Watkins, "The Demand for Air Travel: A Regression Study of Time-Series and Cross-Sectional Data in the U.S. Domestic Market" (paper prepared for delivery at the 47th Annual Meeting of the Highway Research Board, National Research Council, Washington, D.C., January 16, 1968; processed).

15. See statement by the executive director, National Aviation Trades Association, in *Airway User Charges*, p. 92.

16. See statement by Alan S. Boyd, *Airport Development Act of 1968*, Hearings, p. 52.

craft operator. Although some claims for tax relief on aircraft use may not be entirely accurate, there is no means of checking this and no alternative to accepting the estimate that 80 percent of general aviation aircraft hours are really flown for business purposes, and that the aircraft are therefore largely intermediate, or producers', goods. If so, the benefit from their use is passed on in part to the final consumer, and there is no way of tracing the income-distributional effects—even "first-round" effects—of FAA expenditures benefiting general aviation.[17]

Data on the incomes of private aircraft owners are not only poor, but also of doubtful relevance if the aim is to show that the upper income groups are the main beneficiaries. Nevertheless, some surveys have recently been carried out by interested parties. A TIME survey of persons who bought new private planes in 1963 used a random sample of 1,088 buyers; on the basis of a 46.8 percent return, the results of answers to the question, "What was your total family income in 1963?" were as shown, by income group, in Table 6-1 (column 1). The second source of data was the Cessna Aircraft Company, which supplied the results of an unpublished survey of the total family incomes of individual owners of a wide range of Cessna aircraft manufactured in 1964, 1965, and 1966. These are shown in column 2, and are the result of the responses of 832 individual Cessna owners to 7,000 questionnaires that were sent out to owners of all kinds of aircraft in 1967. Column 3 of the table presents the results of a similar survey carried out in 1969 by the Aircraft Owners and Pilots Association.[18]

For purposes of comparison, the percentage of all families in the United States with pretax and disposable incomes falling in each income bracket is given in columns 4 and 5 of Table 6-1. Both are given because it is not clear from the way the questionnaires were formulated whether the data in columns 1, 2, and 3 refer to the one or the other.

17. One could argue that the definition of "legitimate" business use requires that the net profit resulting from expenditure on aircraft use should be greater than that resulting from any other equivalent expenditure on inputs that do not themselves yield intrinsic satisfaction to the businessman. If an aircraft is used when there is a cheaper alternative, or more profitable use of an equivalent expenditure, *and this is known*, the net profitability of the alternative is a minimum measure of the psychic satisfaction accruing from use of the aircraft. Theoretically this element is not really a business expense at all, and the intermediate-good argument does not apply. Unfortunately, we can do little more than state the proposition.

18. The documents from which these data are taken are cited in the note on sources accompanying Table 6-1, p. 101.

**Table 6-1. Percentage Distribution of Aircraft Owners by Income Class, Three Surveys, 1963, 1967, and 1968; and Total and Disposable Family Income, 1966**

| Income class (dollars per year) | Survey[a] | | | U.S. family income | |
| | TIME (1963) (1) | Cessna (1967) (2) | Aircraft Owners and Pilots Association (1968) (3) | Total money income (1966) (4) | Disposable income (1966) (5) |
|---|---|---|---|---|---|
| Less than 10,000 | 15 | 14 | 19 | 70 | 80 |
| 10,000–14,999 | 15 | 24 | 23 | 21 | 14 |
| 15,000–24,999 | 29 | 31 | 29 | 8 | ⎫ |
| 25,000–49,999 | 23 | 23 | 20 | ⎱ 2 | ⎬ 5 |
| 50,000 and over | 18 | 9 | 9 | ⎰ | ⎭ |
| All classes | 100 | 100 | 100 | 100 | 100 |

Sources: For 1963, TIME Marketing Information, "The Men Who Buy New Private Airplanes," Research Report 1302 (TIME Marketing Information, no date; processed), p. 2. For 1967, Cessna Aircraft Company, "Aircraft Owners Survey" (unpublished tabulation, 1967), and *Aviation Week and Space Technology*, Vol. 82 (March 15, 1965), p. 257; Vol. 84 (March 7, 1966), p. 269; Vol. 86 (March 6, 1967), p. 284. For 1968, Aircraft Owners and Pilots Association, *1969 Profile of Flying and Buying* (AOPA, 1969), Sec. 5, p. 27. Total money income data are from U.S. Bureau of the Census, *Current Population Reports*, Series P-60, No. 55, "Family Income Advances, Poverty Reduced in 1967" (1968), p. 4. Disposable income data are from University of Michigan, Survey Research Center, *1967 Survey of Consumer Finances* (University of Michigan, 1968), p. 8.

Figures are rounded and may not add to 100 percent.

a. Respondents who did not answer the question on family income are prorated among the income classes.

An exhaustive analysis of these data does not seem warranted. First, the TIME survey is likely to give a misleading impression of the affluence of the general aviation community, for it refers only to the buyers of new aircraft. New aircraft (that is, those purchased in the current year) have in recent years been a very small proportion of the total aircraft in use. For example, at the end of 1969, about half the general aviation aircraft being flown were over eight years old: this can be explained by the fact that frequent testing is required by the FAA, which has the effect of prolonging the active life of aircraft.

To a lesser degree—since aircraft of two or three years of age are included—the same limitation applies to the data supplied by Cessna. The AOPA data are probably more relevant for our purposes since they refer to individuals operating aircraft of all ages; moreover they include not only aircraft pilot/owners but also qualified pilots who do not currently own aircraft but who are, directly or indirectly, subsidized beneficiaries of FAA facilities as well (of those responding to the AOPA survey, 52 percent were sole owners). A more recent study by TIME on the characteristics of students and new pilots showed, predictably, that members of their group were less well-off than the owners (see Table 6-2). However, this understates the income status of pilots as a whole, for 39 percent of students and 25 percent of new pilots were under 25 years of age, while another survey suggests that probably over 80 percent of all private pilots are more than 30 years old.[19]

**Table 6-2. Distribution of Total Family Income of Student Pilots and New Pilots, by Income Class, 1967[a]**

| Income class (dollars per year) | Proportion of students (percent) | Proportion of new pilots (percent) |
|---|---|---|
| Less than 10,000 | 45 | 40 |
| 10,000–14,999 | 35 | 26 |
| 15,000–24,999 | 12 | 20 |
| More than 25,000 | 8 | 14 |

Source: TIME Marketing Information, "Survey on Flying (Students and New Pilots)" (TIME, Inc., no date; processed).

a. Total family income before taxes. Respondents who did not answer the question on family income were prorated among the income classes.

A further general difficulty in identifying the benefit to particular income groups that results from subsidized provision of airport and airways facilities is that not only is the real extent of business use by private individuals unknown, but the above data clearly exclude aircraft owned by corporations and air taxi operators. Both of these categories come within the definition of general aviation, but the relative responsibility they have, vis-à-vis individual usage, for costs incurred by the FAA is unknown. As far as the wealth of the owner is concerned, this omission clearly involves a downward bias. Finally, allocation of costs among income groups on the basis of any survey used is not possible unless the relationship between the income of private aircraft owners and the use made of FAA facilities is specified. So far this is unknown.

These problems could be overcome by further surveys and questionnaires, but their value probably would be limited. The lack of precision

19. J. J. Eggspuehler and others, "Study to Determine the Flight Profile and Mission of the Certificated Private Pilot" (U.S. Federal Aviation Administration, 1968; processed), p. 43.

of these data is not too important. They are clearly sufficient to show that a policy of charging for the services rendered by the FAA should not be rejected on the grounds that the "little guy" is being victimized. Relative to the commercial airlines, the general aviation operator *is* normally small but, since the commercial airlines earn approximately a normal rate of return on capital, a more relevant point is that airline passengers are assumed to have somewhat lower incomes than members of the general aviation community.[20] It is therefore fairly clear that by most people's standards the argument that charging for FAA facilities is unjust because it interferes with the simple pleasures of an impecunious few is, to say the least, weak. The proposals for charging this group on the basis of facility usage can therefore proceed without undue concern about the income-redistributional impact on the operators of general aviation aircraft. However, other, perhaps more deserving, members of society may be harmed by full cost recovery. The "external" effects of such a policy are the next focus of attention.

## Pecuniary and Technological Externalities

A fundamentally important issue raised by general aviation interests is that there is a "public interest" in general aviation activity that transcends the private interest of the aircraft owner/operator in making use of the nation's airports and airways. One general aviation group points to section 103 of the Federal Aviation Act of 1958, which happens to specify that the provision of the airways system is in the public interest.[21] From this it concludes that the system should be financed by taxation of the general public rather than by those who happen to use the system. In itself this is obviously not an argument to take seriously, but should external benefits be associated with general aviation activity, the cost of which cannot be recovered from beneficiaries directly, there may indeed be a sound case for subsidization. More generally, if external benefits *or costs* are attributable either to general aviation, to its competitors, or to complementary activities, these should be taken into account in the formulation of the pricing and cost recovery rules proposed earlier.

The most important element of the "public interest" argument consists of the view that the existence of general aviation helps to arrest the de-

20. See p. 150.
21. See statement by AOPA in *Airway User Charges*, p. 102.

cline of sparsely populated regions, thereby conferring benefits (which may be technological and/or pecuniary) for which society as a whole, rather than the aircraft operators themselves, should be called upon to pay. Spokesmen for this view refer to the federal-aid airport program (since 1970 known as the airport development program), which is clearly designed to be of particular assistance to less densely populated states; under the program, up to a certain limit, the federal government contributes 50 percent of the cost of airport construction.[22] These spokesmen argue, therefore, that "since the value of the airports is of equal importance as the airways that serve them, Congressional wisdom has been clearly expressed,"[23] implying that 50 percent of the cost (presumably after deduction of other external benefits) of the airways system should be borne by the taxpayer at large.

Numerous studies have been made of the benefits alleged to accrue to local communities as a result of the encouragement of general aviation.[24] It may be that the general conclusion reached, namely that such benefits may sometimes be substantial, is valid. Nevertheless, the concern here is with *federal* expenditures and the financing of services supplied by the federal government. Subsidization of general aviation on the grounds that local communities are beneficiaries requires some indication that there is a *federal* interest in so doing.

However, it will normally be the case that the attraction of industry to a given area (which is usually cited as the main benefit of this kind) will be at the expense of another area. If so, the gain is not to society as a whole but is merely of a redistributional nature.[25] On the other hand, a net national gain may be realized if industry is attracted from an area with full employment, where activity stimulated by general aviation will merely replace other activity, to one with a high unemployment rate, where an increase in real income may be generated.[26] There could be a

22. See pp. 112–19.

23. This is the position taken by the National Business Aircraft Association (NBAA), in hearings on the Airport Development Act in 1968.

24. A good example is supplied by Timberlake and Timberlake, "Aviation Survey, Twin City Metropolitan Area, 1961–1962," prepared for Minneapolis-St. Paul Metropolitan Airports Commission (Las Vegas, Nevada: Timberlake and Timberlake, 1962; processed).

25. See Federal Aviation Administration, Office of Policy Development, "FAA Services for General Aviation" (FAA, 1967; processed), p. 58. This topic is further discussed in Chapter 7.

26. See Gary Fromm, "Civil Aviation Expenditures," in Robert Dorfman (ed.), *Measuring Benefits of Government Investments* (Brookings Institution, 1965), pp. 208–15.

federal interest in stimulating this form of substitution, but subsidization of the whole general aviation community seems a most inefficient way of doing so, particularly when the bulk of general aviation activity is located at major urban areas anyway.[27]

It is conceivable that airport facilities are essential for the continued existence of some communities, and this is recognized by the FAA. Thus "an airport in Alaska having several operations a week and serving a village of 50 people represents the only transportation link to those people and must therefore be considered indispensable."[28] However, another alternative exists: there may be net savings to society if those people are encouraged to move elsewhere. The continued existence of outlying communities should not be taken as an absolute constraint on federal action, for there is presumably some limit to the extent to which people living in remote regions should be subsidized. The above quotation implies that there is no such limit.

The proposal that user charges be payable as far as possible by actual users would be fiercely resisted on the grounds that it would accelerate the depopulation of rural communities. Moreover, the pricing scheme for the terminal area subsystem may be particularly unpopular because, in the absence of economies of scale, the cost per aircraft may be greater at the small town airport than at one of the major air terminals. But the principle that the cost of federally provided facilities should be recovered from beneficiaries is unchanged by this fact. The normal policy should be for the FAA to charge users a landing fee, but if the relevant community government decides that there are external benefits likely to accrue to that community from general aviation (and air carrier) activity, it can opt to take over some of the responsibility for FAA expenditures and cover a proportion of the costs by transfers from the general tax fund. The remainder would be payable directly by users.

Similarly, when the FAA contemplates the installation of facilities at any airport, it should propose in advance a landing fee equal to the average incremental cost of the new system. This would give the local community a chance to decide whether or not it wants to assume a portion of the cost responsibility. If it does not, and as a result of the price increase it becomes apparent that users will not meet the additional cost, the facil-

27. See Jesse L. Sternberger, "Registered General Aviation Aircraft by Community Size, 1963–1968" (FAA, 1968; processed), p. 80.

28. From Federal Aviation Administration, Airports Service, *National Airport Plan: Fiscal Years 1968–72* (1967), p. 17.

ities should not be installed. (If this in turn means that use of the airport would create safety hazards, use of the airport should be forbidden or restricted by price increases.)

By this means local evaluation of private and external benefits would explicitly enter the decision to invest in FAA facilities, and this element of the "public interest" argument is thereby largely taken care of. However, for this to yield an optimal result requires that public decision making at the local level be considerably more enlightened than at the center. The suggestion does not stem from naïveté but merely accepts the fact that local political entities would feel themselves to be better judges of local public interest than the FAA, and therefore should be allowed to subsidize local activity if they think fit.

It is apparent that the federal government has in the past been sympathetic to the argument that sparsely populated regions should be subsidized, and there are many ways in which this is done. The allocation of aid under the federal-aid airport program has always discriminated in favor of such areas, and representatives of general aviation interests are swift to draw attention to the direct subsidization of feeder airlines.[29] There may be circumstances in which subsidization is warranted on economic efficiency grounds—for example, transferring activity from low to high unemployment regions. In addition, the federal government has certain responsibilities regarding regional variation in income, that is, distributional as well as efficiency considerations may influence its actions.

The general principles concerning the financing of FAA facilities can be adjusted to accommodate the situation in which there is deemed to be a federal interest over and above the local evaluation of those facilities as evidenced by the effective demand of community governments and private users. In certain cases subsidy may be justified by inability to pay at the local level; in these circumstances, however, the best method of aiding the economic growth of the community may not be by the free installation and operation of FAA facilities. This would be a matter of judgment in each individual case, but preferably not the judgment of the FAA itself, which is not particularly well qualified to make such a decision. The Economic Development Administration of the Department of Commerce might be in a better position to do so. Alternatively, a general subsidy could be provided to a community, to be spent according to local preferences.

29. See, for example, AOPA statement in *Airport Development Act of 1968,* Hearings, p. 181.

The free provision of FAA facilities is in any case an inefficient method of giving assistance, and presumably benefits both those communities (and individuals) that could and those that could not afford to pay for the benefits accruing from them. Should subsidies be made available to a declining region, they should be open and direct—as those to the feeder airlines are. Indeed, an alternative possibility would be to install FAA facilities, and to charge for their use, but to subsidize air transport (presumably air-taxi operations) directly if it was felt necessary to do so.

The method suggested to deal with this problem parallels thinking in Britain about the treatment of external effects accruing from the operation of nationalized industries.[30] For example, British Rail is supposed to operate a pricing policy that corresponds to "commercial" practices. Each line should at least break even, and hidden cross-subsidization is to be avoided. Where pressure exists for lines to be kept open in the "public interest," either on purely distributional grounds or because of the external technological benefits accruing from them, special application has to be made to the Ministry of Transport for an economic evaluation of the claim. In the present case, communities should be warned that the requirements for aid are very stringent, in order to avoid frivolous claims.

There are those who would argue that it is incorrect to equate the "public interest" in FAA facilities with the interest of local communities plus airport users. They contend that "transportation by air is not a local but an interstate and national program. Any weakness in the network anywhere is not merely a local weakness but a national weakness. The public interest demands that all areas be linked by air transportation as one great economic entity."[31] It is difficult to see how airport facilities supplied by the FAA—the ones that should be charged for on the basis of use—are of benefit to anyone other than the local community and actual users of the airport. For en route traffic, the above argument has some merit; a local community government is not in the best position to decide whether this sort of equipment should be installed within its territory, for the resulting benefits will normally be external to it. However, the proposed method of financing such facilities, which would involve

---

30. See *Nationalised Industries: A Review of Economic and Financial Objectives,* Cmnd. 3437 (London: Her Majesty's Stationery Office, 1967).

31. *Airport Development Act of 1968,* Hearings, pp. 273–74. Testimony of the Local Airline Service Action Committee ("formed . . . to oppose Federal plans to stop or curtail their air service and eliminate them from the mainstream of American life.").

little departure from current practice, would not discriminate at all against sparsely populated regions; indeed, the reverse would be true.

Another form of externality concerns possible benefits for defense and other emergencies that result from the existence of general aviation.[32] A good deal has been made of the ability of general aviation aircraft to operate under conditions in which larger aircraft would be useless, and their potential value in all sorts of "emergency" employment has been stressed. Most general aviation groups are of this opinion, an extreme form of which is represented by the following indictment of proposed user charges legislation:

It would be a major advantage to the Communist plan to eliminate the vast facilities and National Defense Capabilities of general aviation's fleet of over 110,000 planes. Nearly all of these planes are capable of flying and operating from dirt strips, sections of streets and highways to anywhere in the country. As recently proven, Communist led and controlled civil rights mobs rioting, burning and looting are capable of closing entire cities. It would be a very minor job for them to riot and burn the few major airline terminals . . . and put the airlines completely out of operation.[33]

It is also argued by all sectors of the industry that military preparedness is enhanced by the existence of general aviation in that the maintenance of a pool of trained pilots, operational manufacturers, and so on is ensured, and that this should be reflected in government subsidy. The point is dealt with by Fromm,[34] who argues that benefits to defense may be claimed by almost any industry, and that special treatment for civil aviation would therefore be unjustified.[35] It could be argued that if there were particular defense benefits resulting from general aviation activity, efficient use of resources would more likely be achieved by direct subsidy from the Department of Defense in those areas (for example, pilot training) where subsidy was felt to be justified.

32. This is distinct from the argument, already dealt with, that the system is to a large degree designed for the military, anyway.

33. Letter from Eugene Paules, chief pilot, Yoe Leaf Tobacco Company, to Secretary of Transportation Alan S. Boyd. *Airport Development Act of 1968,* Hearings, p. 288. In the same vein, but couched in slightly more moderate language, see statement by the National Business Aircraft Association, *Airway User Charges,* p. 88.

34. Gary Fromm, "Civil Aviation Expenditures," p. 181.

35. Similar arguments can be used to counter the claim that general aviation merits subsidy because of its foreign exchange earnings (see the statement of the Utility Airplane Council in *Airway User Charges,* p. 130) or because it acts as an import substitute.

It will be noted that this closely parallels the argument used in the case of subsidization of outlying communities, and in fact represents quite well the position taken here on user charges. The financing rules proposed should be used as a general guide, but in individual cases there may be reason to depart from them. The onus should be on general aviation interests to demonstrate why the costs attributable to them should not be recovered in full. Thus far they have failed to do so in a way that would satisfy the impartial observer.

This now appears to have been recognized by at least one important sector of the general aviation community. A change in attitude was stimulated by a combination of circumstances: the FAA's decision to restrict activity, and in particular general aviation activity, at high density airports, a substantial increase in landing fees for general aviation by the Port of New York Authority,[36] and a statement by Secretary of Transportation Alan S. Boyd to the effect that "the Federal Government has greater interest in promoting the efficiency of the common carrier system of air transportation than it does in promoting private air transportation and, where a choice must be made, the common carrier system will receive preference."[37] Fearful that the mounting cost of FAA facilities and public concern with airport delays might bring about still further regulations or legislation detrimental to general aviation, one lobbying group came out in favor of user charges prior to the passing of the 1970 legislation.[38] Needless to say, its version of acceptable user charges did not match the extent or nature of those proposed in this study.

The concern of this group was understandable: it felt that Congress would be unwilling to sanction the extension of facilities for the use of general aviation unless additional payment was received from general aviation. The point has been made by Fromm that although a zero or very low price may normally be expected to result in an overexpanded supply of the service concerned, Congress might be unwilling to permit such expansion *even though users would be willing to pay for it.*[39] Similarly, the above group, representing manufacturers of general aviation aircraft and associated industries, appeared to take the view that sales

36. These measures are described in Chapter 8.

37. *Airport Development Act of 1968*, Hearings, p. 42.

38. See statement of W. T. Piper, Jr., chairman and president of Piper Aircraft Corporation, and chairman of the Aviation Progress Committee in *Airport/Airways Development,* Hearings before the Senate Subcommittee on Aviation of the Committee on Commerce, 91 Cong. 1 sess. (1969), Pt. 1, pp. 136–43.

39. "Civil Aviation Expenditures," p. 186.

are more likely to be harmed by legislation restricting aviation than by making general aviation operators pay somewhat more for the facilities they use.

This is certainly a realistic approach: less realistic are claims made by the same group regarding the "economic benefits" alleged to result to the United States from general aviation activity. Fromm has demonstrated that it is virtually impossible to quantify the ultimate benefits of civil aviation activity[40] but the industry is less reticent on the subject. The 1968 research study produced for the Utility Airplane Council by a consulting firm included various predictions of general aviation activity—larger than those forecast by the FAA—emphasizing the size and consequent importance of general aviation in the nation's economy.[41] These led one general aviation spokesman to cite, at a congressional hearing, the contribution of general aviation to gross national product as being $3 billion in 1969, and $7 billion by 1980. To this he would add multiplier effects of these expenditures, which would bring the contribution to $6 billion in 1969 and $14 billion by 1980.[42]

Clearly, the resultant figure would be a tremendous overstatement of the *net* benefits of general aviation activity, for the approach would yield this result only if all the factors of production used would otherwise have been unemployed. But were there no general aviation, it is fairly safe to say that the bulk of the land, labor, and capital absorbed by the industry would be put to some other beneficial use. There is an element of validity in the approach to the extent that immediate imposition of a 100 percent cost recovery policy would create temporary unemployment for some resources, but introducing full cost recovery gradually should take care of this. Finally, it should be noted that the basic arguments concerning what is loosely known as the "economic impact" of general aviation are widely used by the industry to justify subsidization at the national level; they are used still more frequently to justify subsidization at the state/local level, a subject examined in more detail in the next chapter.

40. *Ibid.,* pp. 174–78.
41. R. Dixon Speas Associates, "The Magnitude and Economic Impact of General Aviation" (R. Dixon Speas Associates, 1968; processed).
42. Statement by W. T. Piper, Jr., *Airport/Airways Development,* Hearings, Pt. 1, p. 140.

# CHAPTER SEVEN

# Airport Subsidies, Pricing Practices, and General Aviation

THE FOCUS now switches from the federal airways system to the nation's public airports. The various methods currently used to finance airport operation are outlined and a further indication provided as to how far practice diverges from the theoretical ideal described in Chapter 3. The primary concern here, however, is with the extent to which general aviation is the beneficiary of any subsidies resulting from such policies, as well as of direct subsidies to public airport authorities from the federal government. Although efficiency considerations will not be neglected entirely in this chapter, detailed analysis of the appropriate pricing and investment rules, where terminal air traffic control and air navigation facilities, airport landing areas and terminal buildings are treated together as integral units, is left until Chapter 9.

For the purposes both of identifying subsidy and of determining pricing policies, it is useful to note the distinction between air carrier and general aviation airports. At the end of 1968, out of the 10,470 U.S. civil landing facilities on record with the Federal Aviation Administration, only 809 were listed as air carrier airports, which are defined to include *all* airports serving air carriers, even though general aviation activity may account for the greater part of total airport usage.[1] All air carrier airports are publicly owned, two (Dulles International and Washington National) by the federal government, the remainder by state or municipal governments.

All nonmilitary airports that are not used by any air carrier aircraft are known as general aviation airports. At the end of 1968, 6,484 of these

1. See Table 2-2.

were privately owned, the remaining 3,986 being the property of state, local, or joint public authorities. Airports in this total are broadly defined and range from the simple dirt landing strip designed for the private use of an individual aircraft owner to airports like Opa Locka and Van Nuys.

A further important distinction is that between "pure" general aviation airports and reliever airports. Reliever airports are officially defined as those that "can serve to divert general aviation traffic from a congested airline-served airport in substantial quantity."[2] In turn, an air carrier airport is defined as congested if it has at least 30,000 annual operations by air carriers and high performance military aircraft and if such operations represent the use of over 60 percent of the airport's capacity.

Officially designated as relievers for air carrier airports serving the 22 large "hubs" are 147 general aviation airports.[3] The number of relievers at each hub varies from 2 in New Orleans to 21 for the Los Angeles hub.[4] Although few in number, the reliever airports accommodate a relatively large proportion of general aviation traffic landing at FAA-controlled airports. For example, 15.9 million general aviation operations were recorded at the 22 large hub areas in 1965, representing some 60 percent of the recorded general aviation operations for that year.

## Federal Aid to Airports

### The 1946 Federal Airport Act

Before the 1970 Airport and Airway Development Act, federal aid for airport development was authorized under the provisions of the Federal Airport Act of 1946. This act provided for federal subsidies for the construction of publicly owned airport facilities on a matching basis: the fed-

2. U.S. Federal Aviation Administration, *1968 National Airport Plan, FY 1969–1973* (1968), p. 14.
3. Air traffic "hubs" are not airports; they refer to cities and standard metropolitan statistical areas (SMSAs). Hubs are defined in terms of the percentage of total enplaned passengers in the United States handled at airports serving these cities and SMSAs. Large hubs are those handling 1 percent or more, medium 0.25 to 0.99, small 0.05 to 0.24, and nonhubs those less than 0.05 percent of total enplaned passengers. See Federal Aviation Administration, *FAA Statistical Handbook of Aviation, 1969,* p. 59.
4. FAA, *1968 National Airport Plan,* p. 17.

eral government normally provided 50 percent of a particular project cost and the local sponsor the remaining 50 percent. The plan was known as the federal-aid airport program (FAAP). As of December 31, 1968, general aviation airports had received 22 percent of total assistance under the program, the details being as follows:

| Type of airport | Number of airports | Federal funds |
|---|---|---|
| Air carrier | 656 | $952.1 million |
| General aviation | 1,651 | $213.1 million |

Grants were available only for airport development consistent with the national airport plan (NAP), which, in accordance with the act, had to be prepared annually by the administrator of civil aeronautics (later, of the FAA). The NAP was designed to specify, in the light of the expected growth in air travel, the improvements and extensions of public airports throughout the United States that were necessary to "meet the needs of civil aeronautics." Although subsequent to the original passage of the act there were variations in the extent to which different items of expenditure were eligible for assistance, grants usually were available only for the construction of landing area and safety-related facilities such as runways, taxiways, aprons, lighting installations, and control towers;[5] terminal buildings were not usually eligible.

Over the years the federal-aid airport program became the object of increasing criticism. Not surprisingly, the argument voiced most frequently by aviation interests—airport operators, general aviation, and air carriers alike—was simply that the sums made available were not sufficient. It was pointed out that the Congress often did not permit the expenditure of the full amount authorized under the act and that even if it did so, aid under FAAP would be negligible when compared with the needs of the nation's airport system. The president of the Air Transport Association,[6] for example, noted that the $75 million authorized by the act (as amended in 1961) was in fact cut to a record low of $30 million in fiscal year 1969, despite receipt by the FAA of a record request by local airport operators in that year of over $455 million. And of course the timing of airport construction was affected by the uncertainty sur-

5. The construction and operation of control towers is not entirely restricted to the FAA but is sometimes carried out by the airport operator. In March 1971 there were 33 civil control towers in the United States that were not operated by the FAA.

6. See *Airport/Airways Development,* Hearings before the Subcommittee on Aviation of the Senate Committee on Commerce, 91 Cong. 1 sess. (1969), Pt. 2, pp. 627–28.

rounding the likelihood of success in obtaining priority treatment from the FAA.[7]

One criticism of particular interest here was that the proportion of federal aid allocated to *general aviation* airports was insufficient. The formula used to allocate aid by states under the Federal Airport Act was as follows: 25 percent of the aid to states was available from a discretionary fund, allocation being determined by exceptional "need" factors; the remainder was apportioned according to what is known as the area/population formula, that is, it was "apportioned by the Administrator among the several States, one-half in the proportion which the population of each State bears to the total population of all the States and one-half in the proportion which the area of each State bears to the total area of all the States."[8]

Despite this wording, grants were not necessarily channeled through state authorities but were payable directly to airport authorities. Nevertheless, cooperation between state governments or aeronautics commissions and the responsible federal body (after 1958, the FAA) was normally evident, and state approval for airport development was often a prerequisite for federal aid.

The criticisms voiced by general aviation interests[9] over their allegedly unfair treatment vis-à-vis the air carriers are difficult to substantiate or deny, even with careful perusal of the act itself and of transcripts of the congressional hearings preceding the enactment.[10] Whether or not the FAA or the various interests affected interpreted the intentions of the 1946 legislators correctly is debatable, but the allocation formula, quoted above, does lend some support to general aviation's case. Total subsidies

7. This point was made by an official of the National Association of State Aviation Officials in *Administration's Proposal on Aviation User Charges,* Hearings before the House Committee on Ways and Means, 91 Cong. 1 sess. (1969), p. 160.

8. Federal Airport Act of 1946, sec. 6(a) [60 stat. 173]. The similarity between this and the method of allocating grants from the Highway Trust Fund will be noted.

9. See, for example, the Aircraft Owners and Pilots Association statement in *Maintenance of an Adequate Airport System,* Hearings before the Aviation Subcommittee of the Senate Committee on Commerce, 90 Cong. 1 sess. (1968), pp. 121–54; National Aviation Trades Association statement, *ibid.,* pp. 242–55.

10. For the background to the legislation, see in particular *Federal Aid for Public Airports,* Hearings before a Subcommittee of the Senate Committee on Commerce, 79 Cong. 1 sess. (1945), and *Federal Aid for Public Airports,* Hearings before the House Committee on Interstate and Foreign Commerce, 79 Cong. 1 sess. (1945).

were related erratically to state population densities but, *on a per capita basis,* the formula implied that the subsidy that could be acquired by the airport operators in any one state in any year varied inversely with the population density of that state.

On a per capita basis, therefore, the less densely populated states received greater federal encouragement for airport expansion (as far as this element of the whole aviation program was concerned) than more densely populated states. It can be argued that some measure of aviation use per head of the population is a better indication of the relative reliance placed upon air travel by different communities than is the total use made of air transport by the inhabitants of those communities. Consequently, the airport subsidy should be calculated on a per capita basis to compare, as between states, its relative importance to the development of aviation. If this is accepted, federal policy as revealed by the Federal Airport Act favored the relatively greater subsidization of aviation for the inhabitants of some states than for the inhabitants of others, population density being the proxy measure of relative social need.

This suggests that there may indeed have been some validity in the complaints registered by general aviation interests. Although the provisions of the Federal Airport Act, quoted above, were not explicitly aimed at the encouragement of general aviation, the importance of the latter in facilitating communication within states, particularly between sparsely populated regions and major air traffic hubs, suggests that the use of the area-population formula implied the objective of giving particular assistance to this category of aviation. Evidence of the importance of general aviation in maintaining air links between outlying areas and major population centers is provided not only by the fact that the commercial airlines use such a small proportion of all the airports in active use in the United States, but also that 50 percent of their operations take place at only twenty-five airports. General aviation is therefore the sole, or most important, user of the great majority of the airports, and these are typically airports serving the smaller communities.

### The 1970 Legislation and the Airport Development Program

The 1970 "package deal" legislation, which authorized increased federal expenditures in return for increased user charges, went a long way toward mollifying the aviation industry and meeting its complaints about the federal-aid airport program. Two measures were largely responsible: a dramatic increase in the obligational authority for airport assistance from $75 million annually to an average of $250 million annually over the period covering fiscal years 1971–80; and the creation of an Airport and Airway Trust Fund, which was intended to ensure that the increased authorization actually would be appropriated. Details of how the money should be apportioned for the first five years were specified in the act and are shown in Table 7-1. The average annual amount apportioned for 1971–75 is $280 million. This leaves an average of $220 million annually for 1976–80.

**Table 7-1. Apportionment of Obligational Authority for Federal Airport Assistance under the Airport Development Program, Fiscal Years 1971–75**

| Type of airport and apportionment | Fiscal years 1971–75 (annual amount, in millions of dollars) |
|---|---|
| *Air carrier and reliever airports* | |
| By state, according to area and population | 80.83 |
| Hawaii, Puerto Rico, Virgin Islands, Guam, according to fixed percentage[a] | 2.50 |
| By airport, according to number of passengers | 83.33 |
| Discretionary fund | 83.33 |
| Subtotal | 250.00 |
| *General aviation airports* | |
| By state, according to area and population | 22.05 |
| Hawaii, Puerto Rico, Virgin Islands, Guam, according to fixed percentage[a] | 0.45 |
| Discretionary fund | 7.50 |
| Subtotal | 30.00 |
| Total | 280.00 |

Source: Based on Airport and Airway Development Act of 1970, Public Law 91-258, May 21, 1970 (84 Stat. 225). Figures are rounded and may not add to totals.
   a. The shares are 35 percent for Hawaii and Puerto Rico and 15 percent for Guam and the Virgin Islands.

Aside from the actual sums involved, the new legislative arrangements for federal assistance to airports (now known as the airport development program, or ADP) are similar to those in existence prior to 1970. An airport's inclusion in the NAP is a prerequisite for aid, but the requirements for inclusion are not very stringent. An airport qualifies if it can be designated as an integral part of a metropolitan system, or is a reliever airport, or if it has a regular air taxi service, or "serves the business interests of the community," or if there is evidence of "inadequate" access to another NAP airport by at least ten aircraft owners. (Access is considered to be inadequate if those ten owners would otherwise be at a distance requiring at least 30 minutes of ground travel time from the nearest alternative airport.) Airports providing access to public recreation areas or facilities or to communities that would otherwise be isolated due to inadequate surface transportation may also be included.[11]

General aviation airports of almost any kind can therefore be listed in the NAP but, although a necessary condition for federal assistance, inclusion in the plan is far from being a sufficient condition for aid. Indeed, in recent years there have been enormous differences in the expenditures on projects defined in the plan as being eligible for federal assistance and the amounts of aid actually available. Moreover, privately owned airports that are open to public use may be included in the plan, although the recommended expenditures have not been and still are not eligible for federal assistance.

In the new legislation the area/population formula is retained as a basis for allocating funds; but, whereas under the previous legislation 75 percent of the funds were apportioned by this means, in the 1970 act this proportion is reduced to 37 percent. However, 73.5 percent of the sums available for general aviation airport development are still allocated in this way. This legislative decision suggests a belated—and by now academic —vindication of general aviation's arguments on this score prior to 1970.

The 1970 act is also similar to its predecessor in that neither public parking facilities for passenger automobiles nor construction of airport buildings, other than those that are safety related, are eligible for assistance. Although air carrier interests hotly contested this restriction in hearings prior to the legislation,[12] general aviation has not been unduly concerned by it.

In purely accounting terms, the amount of federal aid that was obtained by general aviation airports under the provisions of the Federal Airport Act could be clearly identified, although the extent to which general aviation operators were actually subsidized by this means was much less clear. Still greater ambiguity surrounds the subsidization of general aviation that is likely to occur in the future under the airport develop-

11. FAA, *1968 National Airport Plan,* p. 14.
12. See, for example, statement by the president of the Air Transport Association, in *Airport/Airways Development,* Hearings, Pt. 2, pp. 666–68.

ment program, for the aid that will be available for general aviation airports is not specified even in accounting terms.

This is because of the distinction drawn in the 1970 legislation between general aviation airports on the one hand and air carrier and reliever airports on the other. (See Table 7-1.) Since 1961 the Federal Airport Act, as amended,[13] had authorized grants of up to $7 million annually to be withdrawn from the discretionary fund and used for the construction of reliever airports. The new approach, however, puts relievers in the same category as air carrier airports, thereby obscuring the extent to which general aviation airports will become the recipients of aid.

The precise amount of aid that will be available for general aviation airports is not known, but the expenditures on airports of different types recommended in the 1968 National Airport Plan may be used as a rough guide. The total recommended airport development cost for the period 1969–73 is $303.8 million for reliever and $1,312.4 million for air carrier airports. If this ratio were to be maintained under ADP (which is by no means certain), the amount annually allocable to general aviation airports would be $47 million, in addition to the $30 million explicitly authorized.

In obscuring the grants to relievers in accounting terms, the legislation serves to demonstrate that in *real* terms the extent to which general aviation operators have in the past been subsidized has in fact always been obscure; even if the reference is only to general aviation airports and even if the $47 million is an accurate forecast, it is not possible to say that general aviation will be subsidized by $77 million annually. The reason is, of course, that the decision to construct reliever airports is the outcome of demand for airport capacity imposed jointly by both general aviation and air carriers. Thus, although it is true that relievers would not have to be built if it were not for the existence of general aviation, it may also be true that they would not need to be built if it were not for air carrier activity.

A Senate committee that considered this point found that, although as a general principle general aviation should be called upon to cover the federal share of developing purely general aviation airports, this should not apply to relievers.[14] Because the reliever airport benefits not only

13. 75 Stat. 524.
14. *The National Airport System,* Interim Report of the Aviation Subcommittee of the Senate Committee on Commerce (1968), p. 12.

general aviation but also air carriers (by relieving congestion), the airlines should be called upon to pay at least a part of the costs of developing the new airport. In other words, for charging purposes, the major air traffic hub should be seen as one system, comprising both the air carrier airports and reliever airports located therein. The problem then to be faced is the allocation of joint costs between air carriers and general aviation.

This problem differs little in concept from the problem of allocating the costs of purely general aviation facilities (that is, the shorter, narrower, thinner runway) at an air carrier airport serving both categories of aircraft. It is tempting to say that the whole of the cost of the general aviation runway should be allocated to general aviation or that a subsidy for that purpose is a subsidy to general aviation, but the construction of that runway will almost certainly be the result of demands imposed jointly by both air carriers and general aviation. Moreover, the construction or extension of an air carrier runway could conceivably result solely from additional general aviation traffic. The only portion of ADP that can surely be termed a subsidy to general aviation is therefore the $30 million available for "pure" general aviation airports, but, prima facie, this is a highly conservative estimate of the real extent to which general aviation is subsidized under the program.

### Direct Charging and ADP

The 1970 act incorporates a clause suggesting that the current administration favors a greater degree of intervention in local airport management than did its predecessor.[15] The act required, for the first time in the history of federal airport assistance, that a condition of federal aid would be that "the airport operator or owner will maintain a fee and rental structure for the facilities and services being provided the airport users which will make the airport as self-sustaining as possible under the circumstances existing at that particular airport, taking into account such factors as the volume of traffic and economy of collection."[16]

This clause aroused a good deal of consternation among airport authorities. The American Association of Airport Executives (AAAE), for example, fearing that this would be the thin end of the wedge, stated that "We regard this provision as an open invitation for the federal govern-

15. See former Secretary Boyd's statement quoted earlier (p. 79).
16. Airport and Airway Development Act of 1970, sec. 18(8).

ment to get into the act of airport rate establishment or at least the authority to determine 'reasonableness' of charges."[17]

On the other hand, if the FAA is the appropriate authority to decide on priorities for aid to airports, it might be argued that it is also in the best position to decide on the extent to which aviation should be encouraged or discouraged locally by use of the pricing mechanism. However, the relevance of the quoted clause for federal airport subsidies is somewhat ambiguous; it is not clear whether the airport costs to be recovered include the ADP element or not. It is arguable that, although as a practical matter it would be easy to collect landing fees from users of airports benefiting under ADP, to achieve full cost recovery by this means would be at odds with the objectives of subsidy. Indeed, ADP would be unnecessary.

In view of the fact that the federal user charges established in the 1970 act are designed eventually to achieve total recovery of the costs of the airways system and ADP, it is probable that the FAA will not insist upon recovery of the cost of ADP by airport operators as well. But in total, the federal expenditures are to be financed by user charges, liability to which varies in large measure with the use of the airways system. As far as ADP is concerned, this arrangement can be criticized on several grounds.

First, although superficially meeting former Secretary Boyd's criteria of openness and specificity, the subsidization of airports in fact fails in this regard, for not only the recipient but also the source of subsidies should be clearly identified; an unfortunate aspect of the method of financing ADP is that it will involve cross-subsidization within the aviation community on a grand scale. It is also economically inefficient; where subsidy is considered to be justified, and the aviation community is to finance it, a lump sum charge would be the appropriate method of cost recovery, since this does not affect aircraft use at the margin.

However, one major criticism is even more fundamental. It appears that the policy of airport subsidization as currently implemented stems mainly from a reluctance on the part of airport operators to use the pricing mechanism. The guiding principle should be that, in the interest of allocative efficiency, users must pay for the airport facilities they use. There may be sound reasons for departure from this principle in individ-

17. American Association of Airport Executives, *Airport Report,* Vol. 16 (September 15, 1969), p. 2.

ual cases, but as argued in the previous chapter, the FAA is not the best authority to decide on priorities for aid to airports or on the merits of subsidy where the object is to prevent the decline of sparsely populated regions (as implied by the area/population formula) or to encourage economic growth in a particularly underprivileged area. These functions may be carried out much more effectively by a federal body specifically concerned with such problems. Obviously, there may be better methods of encouraging regional development than investing in additional airport capacity, but these are not going to be considered by a department concerned solely with aviation matters.[18] Of course, where airport subsidies *are* considered to be warranted in order to achieve these objectives, there is absolutely no reason why the aviation community should be called upon to finance them.

Although the FAA is not the appropriate body to decide upon the merits of subsidy where other than purely aviation-related considerations are involved, there remain certain circumstances in which it should retain responsibility for administering an airport subsidy program. As demonstrated in a subsequent chapter,[19] subsidy may be justified as a necessary accompaniment of efficiency in airport pricing, and this is where federal airport assistance administered by the FAA would be extremely useful. But the basis of allocation of aid among airports would be very different from that at present employed.

## State-Local Airport Subsidies and Pricing Policies

### Airport Pricing Policies

Available estimates suggest that total national expenditures on airports are slightly higher than federal expenditures on the airways system. Total public expenditures on publicly owned airports in fiscal year 1969 are

18. Provisions for aid for airport development from other federal sources in fact exist under the following legislation, although so far the sums involved have been relatively small:
  1. The Housing Act of 1954, Title VII, Urban Planning and Reserve of Planned Public Works, as amended (40 U.S.C. 460–462).
  2. The Public Works and Economic Development Act of 1965, Subchapter I, Grants for Public Works and Development Facilities, and related subchapters, as amended (42 U.S.C. 3121–3226).
  3. Appalachian Regional Development Act of 1965, as amended in 1967 (40 U.S.C. Appx. 102, 214).
  19. See p. 158.

estimated at about $838 million, compared with federal airways expenditures during that year of about $675 million. FAAP accounted for a relatively small part of the former total, as is shown by this summary of expenditures on civil airports by various levels of government in fiscal year 1969 (millions of dollars): [20]

| | |
|---|---|
| State | $ 89 |
| Local | 634 |
| Federal (national capital airports) | 11 |
| Federal-aid airport program | 104 |

In addition, a considerable amount is spent by private firms and individuals on airport development of one kind or another. No data are available on total expenditures on privately owned general aviation airports, but it has been predicted that over the period 1970–75 eighteen major airlines among them will spend almost two-thirds as much as all state and local authorities on public airport development.[21] But the main concern in this book is with *public* expenditures and the means by which costs incurred by public authorities may be recovered. It therefore appears that the airport costs relevant here are roughly of the same order of magnitude as the airways costs already discussed.

Unfortunately, the inconsistent accounting procedures employed by various airport authorities create numerous problems of interpreting published data. For similar reasons official airport financial surveys are unsatisfactory sources for determining the extent to which aviation is subsidized by state and local authorities. But they may provide some guidance, and in the absence of anything better must be used.

*General aviation airports.* One such survey, of the revenues and expenditures of public general aviation airports, was carried out by the FAA in 1969.[22] Questionnaires were sent to the 1,922 publicly owned general aviation airports, a 73 percent response rate being achieved. A distinction was made between airports operated directly by the local gov-

20. U.S. Bureau of the Census, *Governmental Finances in 1968–69* (1970), p. 23; *The Budget of the U.S. Government, Fiscal Year 1971—Appendix*, pp. 735, 737; Office of Federal Aviation Administration. Data include state expenditures on the airways and state/local expenditures on flying education, and so on, but these are a negligible part of the total.

21. See *Airport/Airways Development*, Hearings, Pt. 1, p. 164. These expenditures would, of course, be on terminal and maintenance buildings, hangars, and so forth.

22. Federal Aviation Administration, Airports Service, "FAA 1969 General Aviation Public Airport Financial Survey" (FAA, 1970; processed).

ernment unit itself and those operated by fixed base operators (FBOs). Data on operating costs (excluding depreciation) and revenues were collected only from publicly operated airports, of which 751 responded to the survey. Some results are summarized in Table 7-2.

**Table 7-2. Number of Airports and Annual Average Operating Revenues and Costs, Publicly Owned and Operated General Aviation Airports, 1968**
Money amounts in thousands of dollars

| Number of itinerant operations (thousands) | Number of airports | Revenues | Costs | Current account balance |
|---|---|---|---|---|
| 0– 4 | 560 | 2.9 | 4.1 | − 1.2 |
| 5–14 | 95 | 24.0 | 28.7 | − 4.7 |
| 15–24 | 22 | 46.3 | 46.8 | − 0.5 |
| 25–49 | 25 | 69.1 | 71.9 | − 2.8 |
| 50 and over | 49 | 249.7 | 212.6 | +37.1 |

Source: Federal Aviation Administration, Airports Service, "FAA 1969 General Aviation Public Airport Financial Survey" (FAA, 1970; processed), p. 8.

With the exception of those airports with 50,000 or more itinerant operations annually, it appears that no contribution is usually made from operating revenues toward capital development or repayment of principal and interest on past loans. Indeed, a loss on current account is usually incurred. In the case of the larger airports, it is difficult to determine how far the current account surplus goes toward meeting capital costs, for this is obscured by inconsistent accounting practices. Few more than one-third of all airports were able to report depreciation charges; 70 percent of those with annual itinerant operations of 50,000 or over did so, but the total they reported was unrealistically low.

What of the airports operated by fixed base operators? A variety of contractual arrangements between FBOs and airport owners exists, and the data here are even more scanty. The survey showed that the average rent paid to the local authority by the FBO was of the order of $2,000 annually, but that almost all capital investment, expansion, and improvement were paid for by the public authority concerned. At only 40 percent of the public airports operated by FBOs did the FBO maintain terminal buildings, and in fewer than one-fifth did the FBO maintain landing areas. Out of the 657 FBO-operated airports responding, 441 received police, 460 fire, and 403 maintenance services free of charge.

Moreover, it was observed that "in several instances" airport authorities actually paid the FBO to run the airport.

Overall, therefore, it would not be unrealistic to assume that the financial posture of the smaller airports operated by FBOs resembles that of the smaller publicly owned and operated airports: initial construction is financed out of general tax revenue, while operating revenue may or may not cover operating costs.[23] On this assumption, a rough estimate may be made of the extent to which the smaller general aviation airports will be subsidized as a result of future investment if present development plans are realized.

The larger airports present more of a problem, partly because the true extent of their contribution toward capital costs is unknown. But even if this could be determined, it would still be impossible to assign any subsidy uniquely to general aviation, because most of these airports are relievers and their construction and operation partly benefit and partly are caused by air carrier activity. An estimate of the additional subsidy that will accrue to general aviation from planned development (if present financial arrangements are maintained) must therefore be somewhat conservative, because it must exclude reliever airports.

The total planned development cost of all general aviation airports listed in the FAA's National Airport Plan for the period 1969–73 is $817 million, with a further $304 million expenditure on relievers.[24] The figure of $817 million, or about $160 million annually, would correspond to the annual subsidy to general aviation resulting from planned development if the present policy of roughly breaking even on current account for the relevant airports is maintained.[25] Since, subject to congressional appropriation, $30 million annually will be contributed by the federal government under ADP, the state-local subsidy would be about $130 million annually.

Operating revenues at general aviation airports flow from several major sources. The FAA survey indicates that for publicly owned airports the most common sources are tie-down fees, rental of hangars and agri-

23. This sort of information also suggests that the distinction between publicly and privately owned airports is a hazy one. One important result of the legal distinction is, of course, that publicly owned airports may qualify for *federal* aid.

24. *1968 National Airport Plan,* p. 31

25. This is subject to there being no dramatic change in state aviation fuel taxes; the present yield is relatively small, on the order of $2 million or $3 million annually.

cultural land, and fuel flowage fees. It can safely be assumed that a similar pattern holds with respect to the FBO-operated airports.

There is doubtless a good deal of cross-subsidization among various users of general aviation airports. Some corroborating evidence is that landing area revenue reported by respondents to the FAA questionnaire totaled 16.2 percent of all revenue, building and ground rent and "other sources" yielding 51.3 percent and 32.5 percent, respectively. Yet, judging from Table 7-3, landing areas, even excluding FAA terminal facilities, are responsible for virtually the whole of general aviation airport construction costs, and depending upon size, from 46 to 96 percent of annual operating costs.

**Table 7-3. Range of Typical Airport Construction, Maintenance, and Operating Costs, by Facility, 1966[a]**

In thousands of dollars

| Facility | Construction costs | | Annual maintenance and operating costs | |
|---|---|---|---|---|
| | Air carrier airports | General aviation airports | Air carrier airports | General aviation airports |
| Landing area | | | | |
| Runway (lighted) | 500–8,000 | 90–1,000 | 3–15 | 1.7–8 |
| Taxiway (lighted) | 300–1,000 | 10–700 | 2–14 | 0.5–6 |
| Aprons | 50–2,000 | 5–150 | 1.5–15 | 0.3–4 |
| Hangars | 200–5,000 | [b]–500 | 5–15 | [b]–5 |
| Administration buildings | 2,000–20,000 | [b]–500 | 10–50 | [b]–10 |
| Auto parking and ground services | 50–200 | 1–50 | 2–10 | 0.1–1 |
| Airport servicing facilities | 50–200 | [b]–50 | 5–25 | [b]–5 |
| Terminal air traffic control and navigational aids | 825–1,995 | 7–425 | 250–400 | 2–105 |

Source: *State and Local Public Facility Needs and Financing*, Study Prepared for the Subcommittee on Economic Progress of the Joint Economic Committee, 89 Cong. 2 sess. (1966), pp. 313–15.

a. Note that this table is restricted to airports with lighted runways and taxiways. This would exclude roughly two-thirds of all airports on record with FAA.

b. Lower limit of range is not available.

Landing fees were reported by 8 percent of all airports; 2 percent of the smallest ones and 55 percent of the largest ones did so. The main source of revenue attributable to users of the landing area was the fuel flowage fee. But, as with the federal fuel tax discussed earlier, liability is but tenuously related to the use made of a particular airport facility and it is therefore normally an unsatisfactory method of financing an airport should economic efficiency be the objective. There are, however, circumstances in which this might be a legitimate device even in terms of economic efficiency, for it may be the best method of recovering bookkeeping costs where an airport is used at less than capacity, that is, of charging what the traffic will bear with the least distortion possible. On the other hand, there is no evidence that at capacity such a policy is abandoned and landing fees raised, in order that new investment may be correctly signaled.

In fact, strong pressure is brought to bear against attempts to introduce landing fees for private aircraft users. Representatives of private and recreational fliers insist that at publicly owned airports landing fees should be paid only by aircraft operating for compensation or hire, or by those over 12,500 pounds gross weight. They are less vehement about landing fees at privately owned airports, but discourage their use in general as inhibiting "the development of general aviation."[26] They prefer the fuel flowage fee, one possible explanation for this attitude being that there is less chance of revenues thus obtained falling into the hands of the general public than if landing fees are employed. This would be most likely where the airport is publicly owned but privately operated.

At airports where landing fees are charged, the method of assessing the liability of different classes of user varies considerably. The *1968 AOPA Airport Directory* lists 37 methods used to charge general aviation aircraft for runway use at public and private airports. These include charging according to weight, purpose of use (for example, revenue or nonrevenue operations), whether the operation is itinerant or local, and so on. Fees are sometimes waived if fuel purchases are made at the airport or if operations take place during the off-season or on weekdays. (This is often because the airport is unmanned at such times and without the means of collection; it is, therefore, a sort of peak-pricing arrangement.) An interesting variation is the provision that fees should be charged all aircraft but "waived if pilot or passengers assist owner in cutting grass or with other upkeep of field."[27]

26. See *AOPA Pilot,* Vol. 12 (November 1969), p. 113.
27. Aircraft Owners and Pilots Association, *1968 AOPA Airport Directory* (AOPA, 1967), p. 16.

*Air carrier airports.* In common with general aviation airports, the larger the air carrier facility, the more likely it is to show a surplus on current account. Thus, a questionnaire sent by the Senate Committee on Commerce to all air carrier airports obtained, inter alia, the information for 1967 shown in Table 7-4.

**Table 7-4. Number of Air Carrier Airports and Mean Annual Operating Revenues and Costs, 1967**

Money amounts in thousands of dollars

| Airport annual passen-<br>ger enplanement level<br>(*thousands*) | Number<br>of<br>airports | Mean<br>operating<br>revenue | Mean<br>operating<br>expense | Mean<br>net surplus<br>or deficit (−) |
|---|---|---|---|---|
| 0–10 | 70 | 30 | 52 | −22 |
| 10–50 | 79 | 75 | 84 | −9 |
| 50–250 | 61 | 392 | 277 | 115 |
| 250–1,000 | 32 | 1,353 | 802 | 551 |
| 1,000 and over | 22 | 10,134 | 4,367 | 5,767 |

Source: *National Airport and Airway System*, S. Rept. 1335, 90 Cong. 2 sess. (1968), pp. 85–89.

Unfortunately, however, another feature that a large proportion of air carrier and general aviation airports have in common is the unsatisfactory nature of their financial data. The Senate survey achieved a response rate of over 50 percent (86 percent from large and medium hub airports), but over 35 percent of the smallest class of airports responding to the questionnaire could not provide data on revenues and expenditures, such data often being "hopelessly commingled with other municipal costs."[28] In contrast, nearly all of the airports with annual passenger enplanements exceeding one million were able to do so.

Subsidization, particularly of the smaller air carrier airports, does appear to be fairly extensive[29] but, for reasons already advanced with respect to relievers, it is not possible to define the extent to which general

28. *National Airport and Airway System,* S. Rept. 1335, 90 Cong. 2 sess. (1968), p. 76.

29. It has been estimated that of the total public outlay on airports (general aviation plus air carriers), about 34 percent had been financed out of general obligation bonds, 22 percent from FAAP, and 2 percent from state grants, while only 28 percent was financed out of revenue bonds and operating surplus, with 16 percent from "other sources." *Airport/Airways Development,* Hearings, Pt. 2, p. 590.

aviation is the true beneficiary of such a policy. If an airport jointly used is subsidized overall, general aviation operators may justly claim that it was built and is operated solely for the air carriers; general aviation may be responsible for little or no marginal cost and is therefore not subsidized. This argument, also used in connection with the federal airways system, is intuitively more appealing in this context, because most general aviation aircraft require landing areas which, compared with those needed by the airlines, are of minute dimensions. On the other hand, demands for airport capacity that stem partly from general aviation activity may best be satisfied by constructing additional runways and taxiways suitable for joint use, in which case there certainly is a positive marginal cost attributable to general aviation. This is particularly likely to be the case in light of the methods of cost recovery employed at most air carrier airports.

The subsidy question is further complicated by the failure of airport authorities to relate revenues derived from various parts of the airport complex to the particular costs involved. Apart from subsidy from federal, state, or local taxation, operating revenues may be obtained in a number of ways. The Senate Commerce Committee survey revealed that in 1967 operating revenue was received from the sources listed in Table 7-5.

**Table 7-5. Landing and Rental Fees as Percentage of Total Operating Revenues, Air Carrier Airports, 1967**

| *Airport annual passenger enplanement level (thousands)* | *Landing fees* | | *Rental fees* | *Other revenue*[a] |
|---|---|---|---|---|
| | *Total* | *From general aviation* | | |
| 0–   10 | 12 | 3 | 56 | 32 |
| 10–   50 | 21 | 4 | 45 | 36 |
| 50–  250 | 21 | 2 | 34 | 47 |
| 250–1,000 | 25 | 2 | 33 | 43 |
| 1,000 and over | 24 | 1 | 40 | 34 |

Source: *National Airport and Airway System*, S. Rept. 1335, 90 Cong. 2 sess. (1968), pp. 85-87. Figures do not add to 100 percent because of rounding.
a. Mainly revenue from concessions, auto parking, and fuel sales.

Of all airports responding to the survey, only 39 percent charged general aviation aircraft a landing fee. This proportion rose as airport size increased, from 25 percent of the smallest to 89 percent of the largest

airports. Thirteen percent of all airports charged general aviation a landing fee based on gross landing weight;[30] again, this rose from 6 percent of
the smallest airports to 51 percent of the largest. Only three airports
(Kennedy International, La Guardia, and Newark, all of which are operated by the Port of New York Authority) are known to implement a
policy of differential pricing for peak and off-peak periods, despite the
serious problems of congestion caused by peaking of demand.

Table 7-5 shows that the proportion of total operating revenue collected in landing fees grows in importance as airport size increases, rising
from 12 percent at the 0–10,000 passenger enplanement level to 24 percent at the largest airports in 1967. This is particularly interesting, for it
appears that the cost of landing areas forms a relatively smaller proportion of total expenditure as airports grow in size (see Table 7-3). In aggregate, therefore, the pricing policies of the larger airports would appear
to be more rational than those of the smaller ones.

Nevertheless, even at these airports, the proportion of total operating
revenues collected by means of a landing fee continues to be less than the
proportion of total expenditures devoted to the landing area. Moreover,
the cost of constructing and operating the landing area itself is a minimum amount for which a landing fee could legitimately be used. Particularly where it is desirable, because of congestion, to distinguish between
operations at various times of the day, part of the costs of terminal and
administrative buildings, ground access, and the like could also be included in determining a landing fee.

In addition to any subsidy received by the airport as a whole, therefore, the typical pattern is that users of landing areas are further subsidized by users of terminal areas and buildings (renters of hangars, mo-
torists, concessionaires' customers, and so forth). Users of landing areas
and users of the remainder of the airport complex may in an ultimate sense
be indistinguishable, but whether they are or not this remains an unsatisfactory situation. Allocation of airport facilities can be efficiently signaled only if the price charged for each element of the terminal system
corresponds to its cost of supply. It appears that airport operators are
content to achieve a given financial target (which, in the case of the largest airports, is simply to cover total accounting costs out of operating rev-

30. Weight is not an entirely satisfactory method of charging whether an airport is used at less than capacity or is highly congested. See the discussions on
pp. 156–57 and 139–41, respectively.

enues) without making any attempt to charge for particular facilities on the basis of their cost of supply.[31]

However, if the objective is economic efficiency rather than the achievement of an overall financial target, price should normally be set in such a way that profits are made out of the landing area when it is being used to capacity, extension being carried out only when users show they are willing to pay for it. Profits may be made either because long-run marginal costs of landing areas are rising or because there are costs caused by airport congestion that are not borne directly by the airport authority, which may nevertheless be the appropriate body to collect a fee from those responsible. Alternatively, some combination of these two influences may be present. On the other hand, as noted earlier, one cannot say categorically that subsidy of the landing area is inefficient *when it is being used at less than capacity*. In such circumstances there may be several methods of overall cost recovery, among which it is difficult to choose on grounds of economic efficiency. Indeed, it may be argued that subsidization will normally be the appropriate policy to follow when excess capacity is evident.

Since definition of the extent of public subsidy accruing to general aviation users of air carrier airports is so much a matter of subjective opinion, no attempt is made here to disentangle it from the total subsidy received by airport users. However, it is clear that at "pure" general aviation airports, where no such ambiguity arises, general aviation certainly is subsidized at the state-local level. Some of the arguments used to justify this policy are discussed below.

### Rationale of State-Local Airport Subsidies

Defense of the widespread subsidization of general aviation at the state-local level finds expression in a large number of surveys and studies that purport to establish the advantages accruing to a community from general aviation activity. The advantages usually cited include the attraction of industry, with a consequent broadening of the tax base and creation of employment, as well as the prestige that is alleged to attach to a community that appears to be progressive in its encouragement of civil

31. See Michael E. Levine, "Landing Fees and the Airport Congestion Problem," *Journal of Law and Economics*, Vol. 12 (April 1969), pp. 79–108, where this is demonstrated by example.

aviation. (Similar arguments are, of course, used with respect to the encouragement of air carrier activity.)

As noted earlier, the attraction of industry from one region to another need not result in net efficiency gains to the nation as a whole, but it may be unrealistic to expect local airport authorities to give up the privilege of subsidizing general aviation if they see fit. If one airport authority decides to subsidize general aviation by providing airport facilities and services at less than cost, other municipalities will be tempted to follow suit. Otherwise, if the loss of industry or the failure to attract new industry is their criterion, they may suffer accordingly.

Although the arguments regarding the benefits of general aviation airports in attracting industry to a locality are used so frequently, important questions arise. First, how important is the existence of a general aviation airport in determining industrial location decisions? Second, is it essential that airports be subsidized if industry is to be attracted to a given location and, if so, how effective is such a policy compared with, say, subsidization of water supply or of tax incentives? Third, even if industry *is* attracted to a locality by this means, is it necessarily true that the community benefits as a result?

Satisfactory answers to the first two questions would require a major research effort, beyond the scope of this book. A considerable amount of evidence has accumulated that substantiates the importance of the presence of aviation facilities as a determinant of industrial location, but the importance of *general* aviation facilities is much less clearly defined. Surveys and case studies bearing on the subject are summarized in *Guidelines for an Appalachian Airport System*.[32] There the point is made that surveys of overall locational determinants are more likely to be useful than individual airport case studies. Studies of industrial location rarely identify the presence of a general aviation airport as an important determinant but, when the subject is approached from a different angle and local (aircraft-owning) businessmen are asked how important general aviation facilities were in determining their locational decisions, they rate them very highly indeed. This is not a surprising result, given the inevitable bias of the parties conducting the surveys. This sort of exercise is invari-

32. Edward L. Perkins, Andrew J. Beverett, and Larry S. Goldfarb, *Guidelines for an Appalachian Airport System: Phase II,* Prepared for Appalachian Regional Commission (Palo Alto: Management and Economics Research, Inc., January 1967), pp. 40–48.

ably carried out by bodies with vested interests in the encouragement of general aviation, such as state aeronautics commissions, aircraft manufacturers, and the like.

A good example is supplied in a report issued by the Michigan Aeronautics Commission,[33] which provides an impressive list of companies and the use that they make of general aviation aircraft in the course of their business, the implication being that such business could not be conducted without convenient access to general aviation airports. The value of an aircraft as a business tool is usually stressed at the local level, but this particular fact may not be relevant in achieving the objectives of attracting industry, increasing employment, and broadening the tax base. It would not, of course, be politically wise to admit that these objectives might be achieved equally well by subsidizing a general aviation airport used by corporate-owned aircraft for other than strictly business purposes.[34]

This raises the question of what local benefits result from the attraction of industry. The Michigan Aeronautics Commission report is particularly clear in this respect and also demonstrates the condescending attitude sometimes displayed by the aviation community toward the nonflying public. Thus:

Spurred by the rise in business aviation, many communities around the country are feverishly building new airports to aid in both attracting new industry and keeping established firms. Although the business community understands the value of airports and what they mean to economic growth in the community, often the citizenry is hesitant about voting new tax measures to finance airport development or improvement, primarily because *they do not see* the direct benefit of an airport which will act as an economic generator for new industry, creating more jobs and a greater tax base.[35]

33. Michigan Aeronautics Commission, Department of Commerce, "Aviation and Economic Development" (The Commission, rev. 1969; processed), pp. 21–25.

34. One suspects that the major value of a corporate aircraft might sometimes be that it is a tax-free fringe benefit for senior executives. Since most writers on this subject have a vested interest in it, one rarely comes across such a heretical view in the literature.

35. Michigan Aeronautics Commission, "Aviation and Economic Development," p. 17 (italics supplied). Numerous other examples could be cited from aviation magazines, manufacturers' advertisements, and the publications of other interested groups. See in particular, Utility Airplane Council, *8 Steps to Airport Development: Airports Mean Business* (Washington, D.C.: The Council, no date).

One might sympathize with the citizenry in this regard, for the "broadening of the tax base" and "employment generation" arguments are particularly vague and often used when aviation enthusiasts are unable to justify on a strictly cost-benefit calculation the construction or subsidization of general aviation airports.

There may be sound reasons for a particular community to subsidize general aviation if by so doing industry is attracted to that community and if, as a result, unemployment is reduced. If local productive factors employed in aviation-related activities (including industry attracted by the airport) would otherwise have been unemployed, their value in alternative uses therefore being zero, the incomes they now receive can be counted as a net benefit of the airport development. If, on the other hand, construction of the airport and the establishment of new industries merely attract local labor from other local employment, there will be no net gain to the community, apart from the presumably slightly higher incomes or better working conditions required to induce employment mobility. It is therefore incorrect to include the whole of the incomes received from aviation-related activities as benefits—known in cost-benefit literature as secondary benefits—of airport construction or subsidization.

The attraction of industry to a community with low rates of unemployment will normally draw resources from outside the area. In these circumstances, industrial expansion will benefit the community only if growth in the population of that community is also desirable. This need not, of course, be the case, but those who attempt to justify the subsidization of general aviation in areas of low unemployment might be asked to defend their policy on these grounds.

A number of elaborate exercises have wrongly included secondary benefits in estimating the value to a particular community of an airport, as a consequence inflating the alleged value of aviation activity to enormous proportions.[36] In contrast, the reader is referred to an excellent cost-benefit study of general aviation airports, carried out by MATHE-

36. A respected and frequently quoted general aviation airport study makes this error on a gigantic scale. See Timberlake and Timberlake, "Economic Benefits to St. Paul from the Operation of the St. Paul Downtown Airport by the Metropolitan Airports Commission" (Las Vegas, Nevada: Timberlake and Timberlake, 1964; processed). See Gary Fromm's critique of this general approach in "Civil Aviation Expenditures," in Robert Dorfman (ed.), *Measuring Benefits of Government Investments* (Brookings Institution, 1965), pp. 209–15.

MATICA for the FAA.[37] In evaluating general aviation airport projects for two communities (Quakertown, Pennsylvania, and Hammontown, New Jersey), one conclusion the authors reached is that because of the high levels of prosperity in those communities, little net benefit would be derived from the employment-generating effects of airport construction and operation. As a consequence this item does not feature in the cost-benefit calculation. In itself, this finding is not very profound, attention being drawn to it simply because of the importance incorrectly attached to secondary benefits in so many other studies.

The three questions concerning the desirability of subsidizing general aviation at the local level have not been answered, for the answers will depend heavily upon the circumstances in different localities. It is hoped, however, that enough has been said to convince the reader that the arguments used so glibly by interested parties to justify the subsidization of general aviation by state and local governments should not be accepted without close scrutiny; it is conceivable that the only beneficiaries of subsidization are the members of the general aviation community themselves.

37. Nevins D. Baxter, E. Philip Howrey, and Rudolph G. Penner, "Public Investment in General Aviation Airports: An Application of Cost-Benefit Economics," prepared for the Federal Aviation Agency (Princeton: MATHEMATICA, 1967; processed). In comparison with the bulk of published work on this subject, the report is absolutely outstanding.

# CHAPTER EIGHT

# Airport Pricing: Congestion and Delays

IT WAS OBSERVED in Chapter 5 that overall efficiency in airport pricing requires that all incremental terminal system costs be taken into account, including not only those borne by the Federal Aviation Administration and airport authorities but also those incurred by aircraft operators and their passengers as a result of airport congestion. The application of efficient pricing and investment rules for the federal airways system would therefore require that complementary resources also be allocated efficiently, whether by federal action or by some other means.

The previous chapter showed that as a general rule airport authorities do not deliberately try to use price as a means of achieving efficient resource allocation, their reluctance to do so being especially marked with respect to those facilities used by general aviation. A similar conclusion applies to the methods used by public authorities to deal with the particular problem of airport congestion, which is the subject of this chapter.

The congestion problem is absolutely central to any discussion of pricing and investment policies for terminal areas, for congestion and delays are prevalent at all large and busy airports. It is also of some theoretical interest. Explicit consideration of the cost of congestion should be an integral part of the investment decision, and it adds a new dimension to the problem of efficient airport pricing, which would otherwise differ little in principle from the rules already recommended with respect to FAA terminal facilities.

This is not to say that, congestion aside, pricing of airports and terminal airways facilities can be approached identically. Although direct charges in the form of landing fees can be applied to both, an important difference is that initial lumpiness, particularly of those airports used jointly by general aviation and the commercial airlines, is much more marked than in the case of terminal airways subsystems. Consequently, when an airport is used to capacity, a considerable increase in landing fees would usually be required to signal investment in a new terminal system, whereas for terminal airways facilities alone this would not be necessary.

More important, however, is that in practice lumpiness is the basic fact underlying the prevalence of congestion, for a relatively large marginal cost of capacity extension clearly tends to make delays at once more tolerable and more difficult to remedy. Indeed, a study of fourteen major airports has demonstrated that congestion is due almost entirely to inadequacies of those facilities provided by airport authorities, as opposed to those supplied by the FAA. Major causes of delay were given as saturation of runways, insufficient runway turnoffs, lack of aprons, holding areas, and parking gates, and inadequate highway approaches. Inadequacy of air traffic control facilities was not listed as a major cause of congestion.[1]

## The Congestion Problem

Other than accidents, the increasing delays experienced by users of certain major air carrier airports have attracted the most public concern in recent years. The basic cause of delay is congestion, both on the ground and in the air. Its severity is normally determined to an important degree by the prevailing weather conditions. When weather is bad and instrument flight rules (IFR), calling for wider spacing of aircraft, are in operation, the problem is compounded. It has been estimated that at eight major terminal areas, 30 percent of delay time was experienced during IFR conditions, which were in force for only 10 percent of the time.[2]

Another crucial feature of the delay problem is that it is subject to extreme "peaking." Aircraft delays during peak hours (defined as the average delay during the two consecutive peak hours of the week) may

1. See U.S. Civil Aeronautics Board, "Problems of Airport Congestion by 1975" (CAB, 1969; processed), pp. 3–4.

2. Milton Meisner, Edward Van Duyne, and Walter Faison, "Alternative Approaches for Reducing Delays in Terminal Areas," Report RD-67-70 (U.S. Federal Aviation Administration, November 1967; processed), p. 5. The airports studied were Kennedy International, La Guardia, Newark, Washington National, Chicago O'Hare, Los Angeles, San Francisco, and Oakland.

vary from five to twenty times the average hourly delay experienced.[3] Furthermore, delays to passengers do not necessarily end upon disembarkation, for congestion of administrative buildings, access roads, and so on, is normally a peak-hour phenomenon.

The delay problem affects a relatively small number of the 10,000 or so airports used by general aviation. Although operations at the largest general aviation airports, such as Long Beach, Opa-Locka, and Van Nuys, are often subject to delay, the costs thereby entailed do not match those associated with delays at the larger air carrier airports.

The FAA does not systematically collect data on delays, other than through the daily reports received of the number of IFR flights delayed 30 minutes or more. The only information from which general conclusions may reasonably be drawn derives from the reports for 1968 by three airlines of delays at terminal areas, from which total delays to all air carriers are extrapolated by the FAA. The data are incomplete but are the best available and the extrapolation, which eliminates as far as possible any systematic bias, suggests that in 1968 delays to all commercial airlines totaled about 319,000 hours and cost some $118 million in aircraft operating costs alone.[4] This excludes the value of passenger time and the associated costs of diversions, inconvenience, missed connections, and the increased risk of midair collision. Of course it also excludes the costs incurred by general aviation aircraft using congested air carrier airports.

## The Case for Congestion Charges

Until fairly recently, neither the FAA nor the airport authorities themselves had, with certain exceptions to be dealt with below, any general policy for deterring operations contributing to such delays. The favored solution remains, where possible, to increase effective capacity by the cheapest possible means, whether by extension of an existing airport, the construction of a new one, improvement of instrument landing systems, automation of approach control facilities, or by changes in air traffic control procedures. This is despite the fact that a good deal of the necessary expenditure at a given time is solely for the purpose of accommodating peak-hour demands.

3. *Ibid.*
4. The three airlines are United, American, and Northwest. Augusta Galbreath and Richard M. Warfield, "Terminal Area Airline Delay Data, 1964–1968" (FAA, 1969; processed), p. 29.

Aircraft arrivals are normally accepted by air traffic controllers on a first-come, first-served basis—no distinction being made between peak and off-peak users—or according to the willingness of airport operators to pay for the delay costs they impose on other users of the terminal area. This situation has provoked a wave of criticism from economists,[5] who have been virtually unanimous in proclaiming the merits of flexible or peak-load pricing as a remedy for the airport congestion problem. Indeed, they have outlined the general principles so well that little more is necessary here than to reiterate some of their conclusions.[6]

An important characteristic of the congestion problem is that as the number of operations in any one period rises, the average delay per aircraft also tends to rise. For example, it has been estimated that, if at a given rate of runway use the average delay is four minutes, a 10 percent increase in activity may cause a 60 percent increase in delay, while a 20 percent increase in activity may cause an increase of as much as 200 percent.[7] This will, of course, depend upon a variety of factors: the mixture of aircraft, runway size and configuration, the ratio of arrivals to departures during the period, the degree of sophistication of air traffic control facilities, whether VFR or IFR conditions prevail, and so on.

The principle, however, remains clear: once congestion appears, the total delay caused to other aircraft by the marginal user can normally be expected to be greater than the delay he suffers in return. In other words, *marginal* delay costs exceed *average* delay costs. But in determining whether or not to use an airport at a particular time, an individual aircraft operator will be concerned only with average delay costs.

5. See, for example, Michael E. Levine, "Landing Fees and the Airport Congestion Problem," *Journal of Law and Economics,* Vol. 12 (April 1969), pp. 79–108; James R. Nelson, "Airport Landing Fees as Rentals for Congested Airspace" (U.S. Department of Transportation, Office of Economics, no date; processed); Joseph V. Yance, "Movement Time as a Cost in Airport Operations" (no date; processed); Joseph V. Yance, "The Possibilities of Pricing in Allocating Air Traffic in the Washington-Baltimore Area" (1968; processed); William D. Grampp, "An Economic Remedy for Airport Congestion: The Case for Flexible Pricing," *Business Horizons,* Vol. 11 (October 1968), pp. 21–30; and Jora R. Minasian and Ross D. Eckert, "The Economics of Airport Use, Congestion, and Safety," *California Management Review,* Vol. 11 (Spring 1969), pp. 11–24.

6. We shall, however, spend a little more time on some of the theoretical issues associated with peak pricing, mainly in order to achieve reconciliation with the general average incremental cost pricing principle outlined earlier. This appears in Chapter 9.

7. Meisner and others, "Alternative Approaches," p. 3.

The difference between average and marginal costs does not enter his calculation, for this element is "external" to him, being shared among a number of other users.[8] Socially efficient utilization of airport capacity, which requires the user to take *all* costs into account, would therefore require him to pay a price for using the airport equal to the sum of the relevant (that is, marginal) airport operating costs and marginal external delay costs. Since delays normally vary according to the time of day, flexible pricing should therefore be employed. Under such a policy, separate charges would be required for landings and takeoffs.

A result of raising charges during peak periods would be that variability in the demands placed upon airport capacity over the day would tend to be smoothed out. Over a period of time there would be a tendency for scheduled air taxis and air carriers to shift schedules, but nonscheduled air carrier and general aviation operations could be shifted from peak to off-peak periods right away. Since the demands for airport capacity on- and off-peak are interdependent (that is, the demand for capacity during peak hours will be partly determined by the price charged off-peak, and vice versa), ultimate peak and off-peak charges may have to be determined by an iterative procedure.

Delays need not be eliminated altogether by this means; some amount of delay may be consistent with economic efficiency. This would be the case if, for example, marginal external delay costs were less than the marginal cost of expanding capacity. At present, the officially prescribed "acceptable level" of delay is an average of four minutes during the consecutive two peak hours of the week.[9] But this is not based upon any economic criterion, such as the comparison of delay costs with the costs of rescheduling flights. Indeed, it cannot be; it is not possible to demonstrate the value of alternatives such as the extension of capacity at airports where congestion is experienced, for the price mechanism is inoperative.

Although all categories of aircraft are normally undercharged for operating during peak hours, it is fairly apparent that present pricing arrangements at air carrier airports are particularly favorable to general aviation. The policy of charging a landing fee based on weight, a reason-

8. For an excellent treatment of this phenomenon, see Ministry of Transport, *Road Pricing: The Economic and Technical Possibilities,* Report of a Panel set up by the Ministry of Transport (London: Her Majesty's Stationery Office, 1964).

9. Federal Aviation Administration, "Airport Capacity Criteria Used in Preparing the National Airport Plan," AC 150/5060—1A (FAA, 1968; processed), p. 1. In practice, of course, delays often exceed the "acceptable" level.

able but not entirely satisfactory device when capacity is underutilized, becomes utterly inadequate when terminal areas and airspace are congested. It would not be uncommon to find a typical general aviation aircraft paying a landing fee of $5, irrespective of the time of day it happened to be operating. It is also conceivable that one aircraft could cause delays to a number of air carriers, either on the airport surface or in the air, of, say, 30 minutes.[10] The 1968 airline delay survey mentioned earlier estimates the average operating cost attributable to delay at about $6 per minute. Even ignoring the cost of passenger time, the marginal external delay cost of that aircraft would be $180. Efficient allocation of resources would require that price should be at least equivalent to that sum.

Weight is therefore clearly an irrelevant measure to use in calculating congestion charges. The basis for charging should be the cost imposed on airport authorities and other aircraft operators and passengers by marginal users. The relative contribution to delays made by general aviation and air carrier aircraft will vary considerably from airport to airport, but few studies have been completed from which trade-offs between typical general aviation and air carrier aircraft operations can be ascertained for a given delay.

One airport that has been subjected to such an analysis is Washington National. Typical air carrier operations are more time-consuming than general aviation operations there, but the gap between them narrows as the proportion of general aviation aircraft increases. For example, to maintain a four-minute average departure delay, the time demand of a general aviation operation is 42 percent of that of an air carrier operation where less than 7.5 percent of all operations are by air carriers. The relative time demand of a typical general aviation aircraft rises to 80 percent when the proportion of air carrier operations is 42 percent of the total, and 85 percent when air carriers are responsible for between 59.5 and 85 percent of all operations.[11] Clearly, the relative time demands of various categories of aircraft should be used as a basis upon which to assess relative congestion charges. The unwarranted gains liable to accrue to light aircraft as a result of charging on the basis of weight are plain to see.

10. This is not an exaggerated figure. Where general aviation aircraft use the same runways as air carriers, the delay caused by one general aviation aircraft could easily be 100 minutes of air carrier time. Meisner and others, "Alternative Approaches," p. 42.

11. Yance, "Movement Time," p. 7.

Nelson points out that the discrimination in favor of light aircraft may be particularly large where such aircraft are equipped for IFR operations.[12] The imposition of IFR will have little, if any, effect on the number of air carrier operations, the consequence being that at predominantly air carrier airports IFR capacity is likely to be reached well before VFR capacity; the marginal operation during IFR conditions is therefore likely to cause far greater delay than the marginal operation on VFR days. An IFR-equipped general aviation aircraft using an air carrier airport during a period of poor visibility is, therefore, when landing fees are based upon weight, particularly heavily subsidized. This may not be true at predominantly general aviation airports though, for there the demand for capacity can normally be expected to fall sharply when IFR conditions prevail, and VFR capacity may be reached first.[13]

## Official Remedies for the Congestion Problem

So far, the opinion of economists concerning the desirability of peak load pricing has not carried much weight. However, a general failure of airport authorities to expand capacity sufficiently quickly was responsible, in the late 1960s, for a rapidly deteriorating situation;[14] congestion and delays grew more and more intolerable to airport operators, air traffic controllers, pilots, and passengers and owners of commercial and private aircraft. New York has usually been the area worst affected; delays and congestion reached a peak during the summer of 1968, prompting the introduction of two important measures.

First, on August 1, 1968, the Port of New York Authority raised its minimum landing charges at Kennedy, La Guardia, and Newark from $5 to $25, for aircraft seating fewer than twenty-five passengers. The increase was effective only during certain peak hours. The intention was to

12. "Airport Landing Fees," pp. 19–20.

13. The FAA study, "Alternative Approaches," predicted that for 1970 the number of operations carried out in IFR weather would be 0.25 of those carried out in VFR weather by aircraft of classes D and E, while for class C aircraft the proportion would be 0.6 (p. III-2). (Classes D and E include virtually all piston-engined aircraft used in general aviation. Class C includes smaller turboprop and turbojet and certain two-engined piston aircraft.)

14. Witness, for example, the political obstacles impeding the Port of New York Authority's attempts to find a site for the fourth major New York airport. An attempt to give the FAA authority to decide on its location was rejected in the Senate. *Congressional Record*, daily ed., February 26, 1970, pp. S2470–S2481.

encourage peak-hour general aviation users to shift to Teterboro airport, where charges remained unchanged. The immediate results of this measure were to some extent hidden by a subsequent air traffic controllers' slowdown, which may have discouraged a certain amount of general aviation traffic, but it is fairly apparent that the institution of peak-hour pricing was effective. Compared with the 1967 totals, general aviation itinerant operations at Kennedy, La Guardia, and Newark dropped 21.1 percent in August 1968, 27.7 percent in September, 26.9 percent in October, 31.4 percent in November, and 22.1 percent in December. The aggregate loss in general aviation traffic for 1968, compared with 1967, was offset to some degree by an increase in the number of general aviation operations at three of the four New Jersey airports serving the New York metropolitan area.[15] The effects of this measure on traffic for 1969 are, however, completely blurred by subsequent FAA innovations to be described below.

The Port Authority's action aroused intense opposition from general aviation interests. The Aircraft Owners and Pilots Association, for example, challenged the legality of the measure on the grounds that the $25 minimum landing fee discriminated unfairly against aircraft with fewer than twenty-five passenger seats. Following is an examination of this argument, using the rates prevailing at Kennedy as an example.

At Kennedy, the landing charge for aircraft (other than scheduled air carriers) with twenty-five passenger seats or more remained at 35 cents per thousand pounds of maximum gross weight, irrespective of time of day.[16] For the smaller aircraft this applied only during off-peak hours, the minimum charge in both cases being $5. The peak-hour minimum of $25 applied to the smaller aircraft means in effect that the charge per thousand pounds for any aircraft weighing less than about 71,000 pounds is greater than that for larger aircraft, and the proportionate burden varies inversely with the size of aircraft. For example, a Cessna 150 with a normal gross weight of 1,600 pounds would be subject to a peak landing charge equivalent to about $15.60 per thousand pounds, compared with 35 cents per thousand pounds for an aircraft with more than

15. Federal Aviation Administration, Office of Information Services, "FAA Information," 69-14, January 30, 1969, p. 1.

16. Of the three Port of New York Authority (PNYA) airports concerned, Kennedy is relatively the most generous to the smaller aircraft. The off-peak rates, maintained throughout the day for larger aircraft at La Guardia and Newark, are 95 cents and 46 cents per thousand pounds, respectively.

twenty-five seats.[17] This is the basis on which unfair discrimination was alleged.

The Port Authority was supported by a federal court decision, and in a summary judgment AOPA's request for trial was denied. The verdict was based upon the premise that commercial airliners normally represent the rights of a larger number of passengers than do general aviation flights, and, to treat them alike in "allocating scarce landing and takeoff time and space is to ignore and not to recognize the basic right of equal access to airways and landing areas."[18]

This judgment dealt with the problem in the same terms as those stressed by the AOPA—that is, *rights* of access, *unfairness,* and so forth, although of course the findings themselves were completely at odds with AOPA's demands. Although the PNYA position is preferable to that of the general aviation interests, it would be even better if the administrative distinctions between various types of operation were scrapped, and more reliance were placed by PNYA upon peak-load pricing. For example, the twenty-five passenger seat dividing line is totally arbitrary and leaves PNYA open to all sorts of legitimate criticisms and questions. A general aviation flight carrying more people than an airline flight could still be charged more for landing; and, AOPA asks, "will a cargo airliner carrying animals . . . have priority over the businessman flying his own plane?"[19]

Such questions reveal the weakness inherent in any discriminatory charging scheme, but they may be answered in a way that would hardly be in accordance with general aviation's views. In common with the PNYA judgment, AOPA stresses the benefits received from the airways, rather than the costs imposed by users, as the appropriate basis upon which charges should be levied. It was noted earlier that sellers or consumers of public services are on theoretically dangerous ground when they make this sort of judgment; much better that the various resources

17. Fees paid by scheduled air carriers at PNYA airports do not vary according to time of day and are at a lower rate still. At Kennedy, for example, "flight fees" in 1970 were of the order of 26 cents per thousand pounds takeoff weight. As is typical at air carrier airports, scheduled carriers operate under long-term lease arrangements, PNYA having recourse to collect from these carriers any deficits that are incurred during the year. Information on this subject obtained in a letter from Chief, Aviation Economics Division, PNYA, February 25, 1970.

18. Judge John Dooling, U.S. District Court, Brooklyn, quoted in *AOPA Pilot,* Vol. 12 (November 1969), p. 7.

19. *Ibid.*

used up by peak-hour airport demands should be rationed in accordance with willingness to pay for them. Consequently, if it is really more important for the businessman to use Kennedy during a peak hour than for the planeload of animals to do so, he can demonstrate this by offering to pay more than the animals' owner for the privilege.

This leads to the conclusion that a general aviation aircraft operator is unjustly treated by the introduction of a peak-hour landing fee only if his liability is greater than the real resource cost involved in his landing at that peak hour. It is fairly safe to say that this is not true of the PNYA ruling; since the peak-hour landing fee has not eliminated delays altogether, it is relevant to observe that a general aviation aircraft has only to cause delays of four air carrier minutes to generate additional air carrier operating costs of $25, quite apart from any passenger time that is lost.

It would, however, be legitimate to claim that general aviation is subject to unfair discrimination if the commercial airlines are called upon to cover a relatively smaller proportion of the costs assignable to them. If the type of aircraft were irrelevant in determining the cost of operating during peak hours, the peak-hour landing fee should be identical for all aircraft, from the Cessna 150 to the Boeing 747. But there are differences in the burden placed upon the airport operator and other users by different types of aircraft. Under the Kennedy charging scheme, a Boeing 727 on a nonscheduled flight might be charged about $47 for a peak-hour operation, while a Cessna 150 would be charged $25; it could be argued that this arrangement was nondiscriminatory only if the costs attributable to the Boeing 727's activity were double those of the Cessna 150.[20]

Calculation of the relative delay caused by various types of aircraft is a matter of great complexity, but it does appear that both air carriers and general aviation pay landing fees during peak periods that are considerably less than the real resource costs involved. The $25 fee represents a very small step in the direction of efficiency. Nevertheless, it *is* a step in the right direction and is the only example of peak-load or flexible pricing to be found among the large air carrier airports.

The existence of long-term contracts between air carriers and airports creates a stumbling block for the immediate introduction of peak pricing

20. But even then, unless the charge precisely equals the respective marginal social cost for each user—or there is subsidization of all users—controversy could arise over differences in the *absolute* subsidy received by each category of aircraft.

at PNYA and elsewhere, but achievement of such a system should be a long-term airport policy. Alternatively, the FAA could introduce the system in charging landing fees for its own terminal facilities. Unfortunately, the FAA has shown reluctance to offer wholehearted support for the principle of peak pricing; the 1967 study of terminal area delays recommended exploring the possibility of introducing flexible pricing but went no further.[21] Rather, the FAA has preferred to ration capacity by fiat. For some years, the number of operations per hour at Washington National had been limited in this way, but on June 1, 1969, flight quotas for IFR operations were introduced by the FAA at five "high density" airports. These quotas, which clearly established the preferential treatment of the air carriers, are shown in Table 8-1. Where weather and

**Table 8-1. Flight Quotas at Five High Density Airports, Effective June 1, 1969**

| Airport | Operations per hour under instrument flight rules | | | |
|---|---|---|---|---|
| | Air carrier | Air taxi | Other | Total |
| Washington National | 40 | 8 | 12 | 60 |
| Chicago O'Hare | 115 | 10 | 10 | 135 |
| Newark | 40 | 10 | 10 | 60 |
| La Guardia | 48 | 6 | 6 | 60 |
| Kennedy (5–8 p.m. peak) | 80 | 5 | 5 | 90 |
| Kennedy (other hours) | 70 | 5 | 5 | 80 |

Source: Federal Aviation Administration, "News," 69-137, December 30, 1969, pp. 1–2.

other conditions permit, provision is also made for additional operations, either IFR or VFR, in excess of these quotas.

These measures apparently achieved their object. For example, during the first four months the flight quota rule was in effect, total delays fell by about 25 percent while total operations fell by only 5 percent.[22] A "smoothing out" operation had been successfully performed. The action was recognized by the administrator, John H. Shaffer, as a stopgap measure, but only on the somewhat dubious grounds that it "doesn't contribute to continuing growth of our air transportation industry."[23]

21. Meisner and others, "Alternative Approaches," p. 67.
22. Federal Aviation Administration, "News," 69-125, November 15, 1969, p. 1.
23. *Ibid.*, p. 2.

The legality of the FAA ruling, in common with the PNYA measures, has been challenged by general aviation interest groups.[24] Similar questions were raised concerning the right to establish precedence of one sort of operation over another, again clearly illustrating the weakness of this sort of measure. PNYA was unable, or reluctant, to put all its faith in pricing as a means of allocating airport capacity; the FAA quota system, of course, fails completely in this regard. The recommendation of complete reliance on pricing would certainly be at odds with the view expressed by AOPA, which favors right of access to air carrier airports on a first-come, first-served basis, unhindered by the price mechanism or any other restriction.

## Delay Costs Attributable to General Aviation

This section presents a rough estimate of the delay costs incurred by air carrier aircraft and their passengers that result from general aviation activity. The data are for calendar year 1968; neither subsequent increases in traffic nor the PNYA and FAA actions to curb congestion are taken into account, but the estimate should provide some indication of the costs currently involved.[25] Some heroic assumptions have to be made, but the apparent importance of the subject, combined with the reluctance of any individual or organization in the aviation field to make any estimate at all, make this a task worth performing. It is believed that any error in estimating the costs attributable to general aviation is in the direction of conservatism. Since these are minimum estimates, it does not follow that remaining air carrier delay costs are solely attributable to the air carriers themselves.

### Assumptions

The following assumptions are made:

1. The peak hour for general aviation operations coincides with the peak hour for air carrier operations. This assumption is based upon a study of the capacity of airports in metropolitan areas, which although

24. See "'High Density' Rules Riddled with Contradictions," *AOPA Pilot,* Vol. 12 (April 1969), and "AOPA Files Suit to Block 'High Density Traffic Airports' Rule," *AOPA Pilot,* Vol. 12 (May 1969), p. 31.

25. The calculations suggested that about 18 percent of total delay costs caused by general aviation in 1968 were at the five airports concerned.

somewhat dated, continues to appear relevant.[26] Further assumptions are that at any given airport the average ratio of general aviation to total operations is the same at peak hours as it is off-peak, and that only *itinerant* general aviation operations contribute to air carrier delays.

2. Thirty percent of total delay time is experienced during IFR weather conditions, which are encountered 10 percent of the time.[27]

3. The ratio of general aviation operations on IFR days to those on VFR days is one-quarter. This again is a conservative estimate, corresponding to the "multiplication factor" used elsewhere with respect to the smallest general aviation aircraft for 1970.[28] (Larger piston-engined, turboprop, and turbojet aircraft used for general aviation purposes can be expected to be less sensitive to changes in weather conditions.)

4. The number of military and air carrier operations is independent of weather conditions.

5. During periods of congestion, the average delay imposed by an air carrier aircraft on other air carriers is double that imposed by a general aviation aircraft on air carriers. This assumption involves some highly complex issues, and the technical groundwork to substantiate or deny it is incomplete. Some evidence, however, is available that suggests the assumption is not unfair to general aviation.

It can be assumed, as a rough approximation, that the larger and faster general aviation aircraft—the turboprop, turbojet, and larger two- and four-engined piston aircraft—correspond to the air carriers in their time demands. Most general aviation aircraft, however, are capable of much lower performance and therefore create particular problems in assigning responsibility for delays. To begin with, their approach to an airport is much slower than that of the typical air carrier aircraft. If the spacing rules used for air carriers were observed for such aircraft also, it is fairly safe to say that the delay caused by the marginal general aviation aircraft would exceed that caused by the marginal air carrier. However, it may be possible to bring a light aircraft in steeply from a lower trajectory, between two air carrier movements, causing less delay. Further delay because of competing demands for runway space will then depend upon the availability of early runway turnoffs.

26. M. A. Warskow and I. S. Wisepart, "Capacity of Airport Systems in Metropolitan Areas: Methodology of Analysis," AIL Report 1400-4 (Deer Park, Long Island, New York: Airborne Instruments Laboratory, January 1964), p. 46, and Appendix B, pp. B-1 to B-10.

27. Meisner and others, "Alternative Approaches," p. 5.

28. *Ibid.*, p. III-2.

On VFR days, when there is a separate runway that may be used by general aviation aircraft without interfering with the flight pattern of arriving and departing air carriers, the contribution of general aviation aircraft to air carrier delays is probably fairly small. But where runways are jointly used, this is not so. And joint runway use is the rule; La Guardia apart, separate short takeoff and landing (STOL) runways continuously available to general aviation aircraft in VFR conditions are not to be found at the air carrier airports where delays are most prevalent.

Departures of light aircraft at air carrier airports with joint facilities are invariably more time-consuming than air carrier departures. First, it takes much longer for light aircraft to get away from the immediate vicinity of the airport. Second, because of the danger of wake turbulence from a preceding jet aircraft, a relatively long time must elapse before it is safe for the light aircraft to follow.

On IFR days, it is rarely possible to take full advantage of separate general aviation runways, and more stringent spacing requirements for incoming flights mean that the slow airspeed of smaller general aviation aircraft creates a "ripple" effect, causing relatively long delays for subsequent air carrier arrivals. In these conditions, to count a general aviation operation as half of an air carrier operation appears particularly generous to the former category.

The Washington National Airport study substantiates the contention that the proportion of delays here attributed to general aviation is not exaggerated. At that airport the average delay caused by general aviation aircraft becomes greater as the proportion of general aviation aircraft operations declines.[29] In light of this, it is relevant to note that at only three of the leading twenty-five air carrier airports, ranked in order of total delays, did general aviation account for more than 50 percent of total itinerant operations; air carrier activity accounted for 68.8 percent of all itinerant operations at those airports. Finally, the FAA study of eight major air carrier airports referred to above also suggests that one general aviation operation should be counted as equivalent to one-half of an air carrier operation.[30] However, it is clear that a good deal of research on the responsibility of different types of aircraft for delays at various airports is necessary before calculating an equitable and efficient congestion charge.

29. See p. 140.
30. Meisner and others, "Alternative Approaches," p. 42.

## Results

Once the foregoing assumptions were made, the proportion of general aviation to total operations was estimated at each of the twenty-five leading air carrier airports, ranked according to delay time at each.[31] A distinction was made between operations and delays on IFR and VFR days, and the total delay time and cost for each airport were allocated to general aviation where one general aviation operation counted as half an air carrier operation. Total delays and costs for the remaining airports were aggregated and dealt with in the same way. (The cost per minute of air carrier delay varied from airport to airport.)

On this basis, the total delay caused to air carrier operators by general aviation in 1968 was estimated at about 64,000 hours, which represented $23 million in aircraft operating costs.[32] At an average of 56 passengers per flight,[33] the corresponding loss in passenger time was about 3,600,000 hours. If, for illustrative purposes, a traveler's time is valued at $5 an hour,[34] the cost of lost passenger time becomes $18 million, making a total loss inflicted on airline operators and passengers by general aviation of $41.5 million.

Since scarcely any of this was recovered in the form of congestion taxes, it could be seen as a further subsidy to general aviation if it were not for the fact that congestion is a reciprocal phenomenon. Maintaining the same assumptions regarding activity during peak periods and the relative time demands of air carriers and general aviation, it is estimated that general aviation aircraft delay time attributable to the air carriers is greater than total air carrier aircraft delays caused by general aviation. But this ceases to be the case when calculated in terms of *passenger* time, for the average general aviation passenger load is only about three.[35]

31. Galbreath and Warfield, *Terminal Area Airline Delay Data, 1964–1968,* p. 30.

32. This corresponds to an average cost per minute of delay of $6.11. *Ibid.,* p. 1.

33. Based on average revenue load per aircraft for certified scheduled route air carriers including foreign lines, year ending May 31, 1968. Civil Aeronautics Board, Bureau of Accounts and Statistics, *Air Carrier Traffic Statistics,* Vol. XIV-5 (CAB, May 1968), p. 1.

34. See the discussion in Meisner and others, "Alternative Approaches," pp. 48–49, in which passenger time is alternatively valued at zero and $5 per hour.

35. Federal Aviation Agency, "General Aviation Occupant Load Factor" (FAA, 1966; processed), p. 6.

Typically, passengers of air taxis apart, one might expect the occupants of general aviation aircraft to be more wealthy than those of the commercial airlines. The 1967 Census of Transportation suggested that 38.3 percent of passengers of the commercial airlines had family incomes of below $10,000, 30.4 percent fell in the $10,000–$14,999 range, 20.9 percent in the $15,000–$24,999 range, with 10.4 percent with family incomes of $25,000 or more.[36] Clearly, airline passengers are a less wealthy group than general aviation aircraft owners and AOPA members, as comparison of these estimates with those in Table 6-1 bears out. Nevertheless, even if a general aviation occupant's time is valued at twice that of an airline passenger (that is, at $10 per hour), the combination of much smaller load factors and lower operating costs of general aviation aircraft means that the cost of general aviation delays attributable to the air carriers is relatively small—on the order of about $5 million annually. General aviation therefore apparently imposes delay costs on air carriers that were in 1968 roughly $35 million greater than those suffered in return.

Introduction of a peak pricing policy need not, even if it is perfectly consistent with economic efficiency, eliminate all these costs, for it may be that the marginal cost of delay is less than the marginal cost either of restriction or of extending capacity. But it is fairly certain that total delay costs would be reduced considerably if efficient pricing and investment policies were pursued. The theoretical problems of achieving efficiency, complicated by the factors of capital indivisibility and the differing technical requirements of various types of aircraft, are discussed in the next chapter.

36. U.S. Bureau of the Census, Census of Transportation, 1967, *National Travel Survey,* TC 67-N1 (1969), p. 23. (Respondents to the Census survey who did not answer the income question were prorated by income range.)

# CHAPTER NINE

# Airport Pricing and Economic Efficiency: A Summary

THIS CHAPTER summarizes the main conclusions previously implied concerning the appropriate rules for the allocation of airport capacity and terminal airspace. Optimal pricing and investment strategies are now discussed as if it were possible to influence both parties—the Federal Aviation Administration and state and local airport authorities—to carry them out. Because theoretical aspects of the subject become quite complex, the exposition begins by discussing airport pricing and investment in circumstances in which it is not possible to distinguish between users according to variations in costs imposed by, or benefits received from, their activities, and in which no "externalities" are present. This requires making the improbable assumptions that all aircraft are physically similar, and used for similar purposes, and that there is no variation in the costs attributable to operations carried out at different times (that is, peak problems do not arise). It also assumes away the complications caused by congestion or delay costs as capacity is approached. These assumptions are gradually relaxed, the final case being concerned with pricing and investment where users are heterogeneous, peaking of demand exists, and congestion costs are taken into account.

## Homogeneous Users, No Peaks, No Congestion

The larger and more sophisticated the airport, the greater the variety of aircraft that it can accommodate. Homogeneity of airport users would therefore be a plausible assumption at a small general aviation airport consisting of little more than a grass landing strip and rudimentary landing aids. The assumed absence of peaks is highly unrealistic but is useful to begin with in illustrating the principles involved. Even if demand does not vary by hour, day, week, or month of the year, it is a fundamental proposition that demand for airport capacity is increasing over time. As will be shown, there are circumstances in which the assumption of zero congestion costs is a reasonable one.[1]

The task is to define a pricing policy that conforms as closely as possible to the theoretical ideal and that is at the same time a practicable possibility. For reasons similar to those adduced with respect to the terminal airways subsystem when treated in isolation, the recommendation here is that average incremental cost (AIC) pricing be the rule when airports are less than fully utilized. This does not necessarily correspond to average total cost (ATC) pricing at less than capacity,[2] for replacement of assets before the end of their useful—or accounting—lives is possible. For example, runways may be extended to accommodate larger and faster aircraft, or new runway configurations may be required to cope with other technological developments, including the introduction of short takeoff and landing (STOL) and vertical takeoff and landing (VTOL) aircraft. (This is, of course, a much more important consideration when one drops the assumption of aircraft homogeneity.)

Assume that existing airport capacity approaches full use, and capacity can be increased only by the construction of an entirely new airport. Assume also that long-run airport costs are rising—that is, the AIC of a new airport, referred to as $A_2$, exceeds that of the existing one ($A_1$). This will typically be the case in practice, not only because of general inflationary tendencies but also because the cost of land near populated areas can be expected to rise in real terms over time.

If the two airports provide exactly the same quality of service to users, investment in $A_2$ would be signaled by raising price at $A_1$ until it equals the AIC associated with $A_2$. But of course $A_1$ and $A_2$ will *not* normally yield services identical in quality. For example, if $A_2$ is a greater distance than $A_1$ from the center of the urban area they are designed to serve, the surface transport cost (including travel time) per journey associated with the use of $A_2$ may exceed that associated with $A_1$. The reverse could, of course, be true. Where a quality difference of this sort exists, investment in capacity is signaled when the price paid at $A_1$ equals the AIC, which at

1. That is, when long-run marginal airport costs are falling. See p. 155.
2. Our earlier discussion of this aspect will be recalled. See pp. 76–77.

this point equals long-run marginal cost (LMC) of operations at $A_2$, plus additional (or minus any reduction in) surface transport costs incurred by users of the new airport.

Price signals alone therefore do not suffice as a guide for investment, for they must be augmented by an estimate of relative surface transport costs.[3] But price still performs the most difficult task of revealing the ultimate value placed on airport use at the margin, and the adjustment for surface transportation costs will normally be relatively straightforward. It is necessary in such calculations to assume that airport users are rational and would be willing to pay up to an extra dollar for using $A_1$ rather than $A_2$ if the net savings to them from so doing were of that amount.

The problem of lumpiness, referred to earlier, may be especially apparent where the signal for investment in $A_2$ requires a considerable increase in price at $A_1$. If AIC pricing is employed at $A_2$ and, because of lumpiness, AIC differs dramatically from short-run marginal cost, $A_2$ will be relatively overpriced as compared with $A_1$. Prices, subject to adjustments for differences in surface transport costs, will be similar, yet the *real* cost at $A_1$ will be larger than that at $A_2$. Operating and maintenance costs aside, the real cost of the marginal operation at $A_1$ will continue to be composed of the burden felt by would-be users who are denied use of $A_1$ because of the price employed to ration capacity. Economic efficiency would clearly require price at $A_2$ to be relatively lower, for no such burden exists there.

The shortcomings of the AIC pricing compromise are therefore highlighted in the multiple airport case when AIC diverges widely from short-run marginal cost, and this will be particularly marked during the early stages of $A_2$'s life. In some cases, for example, at purely general aviation airports that cater to relatively homogeneous users, lumpiness may not be a problem, for investment in a new airport may begin with little more than the purchase of land. Even here, however, it could be an important issue, and if there is an unavoidably larger lump sum expenditure at $A_2$'s inception, there may be a good case, on efficiency grounds, for some subsidization of $A_2$. The case for subsidy may become even more marked when account is taken of the fact that the cost of congestion at $A_1$ may be a par-

3. These can be estimated from surveys of the eventual destination of passengers and other aircraft operators. For an example, see Nevins D. Baxter, E. Philip Howrey, and Rudolph G. Penner, "Public Investment in General Aviation Airports: An Application of Cost-Benefit Economics," prepared for the Federal Aviation Agency (Princeton: MATHEMATICA, 1967; processed).

tial justification for investment at $A_2$. The subsidy question will be explored further when congestion costs are introduced into the discussion.

So far the reference has been to airport costs in the aggregate, with no distinction among the various parts of the airport complex for charging purposes. The principles outlined above remain valid, however, for each part. FAA air traffic control and navigational facilities at airports, runways, taxiways, and aprons should all be treated as one for charging purposes, and a landing fee levied. In addition, parts of publicly provided terminal buildings, the capacity and operating costs of which vary (depending on the number of passengers) with the number of operations in a given period, can also be charged for on this basis. The other large element of airport revenue consists of hangar and tie-down fees. Economic efficiency would dictate that if there is excess capacity the relevant fee should be zero. But in the absence of peaks, excess capacity would result only from bad planning, for parking space of this kind can normally be expanded in fairly small increments. It should therefore be possible to equate price to long-run marginal cost or marginal opportunity cost, which represents the highest amount that other users would be willing to pay at the margin.

Where there is an absolute limit on space, monopoly profits would be consistent with efficiency, although they should be used as a partial signal of the justification for investment in a new airport. Similar principles apply to charges for automobile parking, concessionaires' rentals, and other facilities. Investment in $A_2$ is therefore signaled when the total amount that users are willing to pay in any one period for additional landing areas, aircraft and automobile parking, and so forth, exceeds the total social cost of the investment calculated for a similar period, after allowing for differences in surface travel costs.

## Homogeneous Users, No Peaks, Positive Congestion Costs

Where airport capacity is approaching full utilization, resulting in increased congestion and delay, efficient allocation of resources normally requires this element of cost to be taken into account in establishing landing charges. Most delay costs associated with the marginal airport user will in fact be external, for although he himself may be delayed he will also delay a number of other users. The true *social* cost of his activity will therefore include not only the burden imposed upon the airport operator but also that imposed upon other aircraft operators.

Economic efficiency would therefore require the pricing policy defined in the previous section to be amended. The rule should now be to charge users a price equal to AIC as long as there is no congestion. When congestion does appear, the delay costs should be quantified as far as possible in monetary terms (that is, the value of passengers' time lost and the additional aircraft operating costs). Price in the region of full capacity (defined perhaps as the maximum number of operations consistent with given safety standards) should then equal the average incremental cost of airport operations plus marginal external delay costs, or the amount needed to restrict demand to capacity, whichever is greater. This may be termed average incremental *social* cost (AISC) pricing. Investment in a new airport is signaled when the benefits of the new airport (the amount that marginal users are willing to pay in any one period, adjusted for changes in surface transport costs, plus the total delay costs caused by marginal users) equal the costs of the new airport incurred for that period.

A problem attached to this solution is that some of the benefit of a new airport is realized by nonusers (that is, users of $A_1$ who would suffer less delay as a result of the construction of $A_2$), so the investment decision would be signaled before the new facility is financially viable. This possibility provides further justification for subsidizing the new airport. The problem should not arise whenever long-run marginal costs are falling, for if the sum of marginal airport and surface transport costs associated with $A_2$ is less than that for $A_1$, investment in the new airport is signaled before any delays arise at $A_1$. (Note that average incremental costs are usually falling—or at least not rising rapidly *at any one airport*. Hence this principle also applies to intra-airport investment, for which the price signal alone should be a satisfactory guide.) Where long-run marginal airport costs are falling, therefore, the question of delays should not arise.

However, if, because of bad planning, delays are occurring at $A_1$ even though long-run airport costs are falling, investment in $A_2$ under AISC pricing should bring about an actual *reduction* in congestion at $A_1$. In the normal situation, in which long-run airport costs are rising, if AISC pricing is enforced, and the timing of investment is appropriate to such a policy, this would not happen. The price charged at $A_2$ would roughly equal that at $A_1$, there would not be the incentive for aircraft operators to switch from $A_1$ to $A_2$, and the existing amount of congestion at $A_1$ would be retained.

Moreover, if $A_2$ is built too soon, an AISC pricing policy will create no incentive at all to switch from $A_1$; only if $A_2$ is built at a later than optimal date will AISC pricing at $A_1$ and $A_2$ encourage such action. In normal circumstances therefore, subsidization of $A_2$ in its early years will be necessary if delays at $A_1$ are to be reduced, and optimal use made of airport capacity. The mechanics of subsidization are briefly discussed in the following section.

## Heterogeneous Users, No Peaks, Positive Congestion Costs

Numerous problems of cost allocation arise when an airport is used by a wide variety of aircraft, perhaps ranging in size from the Cessna 150 to the Boeing 747. Such airports exhibit lumpiness to an extreme degree when first constructed, and the major task is to see how this fact can be reconciled with the incremental approach so important for efficient resource allocation.

The solution employed at many air carrier airports is to charge a landing fee that varies with aircraft weight. This method has intuitive appeal and appears to be fairly equitable, in that the cost of constructing the landing area and terminal buildings will be greater, the larger the aircraft that use the airport. The policy also has certain merits from an efficiency standpoint when there is excess capacity. Thus if the original airport investment decision was correct, it is theoretically possible to establish a scale of prices in such a way that bookkeeping costs are covered and no aircraft operator willing to pay for the real (operating and maintenance) cost[4] of his activity is excluded. Assuming that willingness to pay for airport use varies directly with aircraft weight, the airport operator may therefore act as the "discriminating monopolist" described in Chapter 3 and levy charges accordingly.

One way to approximate the theoretical ideal, and at the same time attempt to deal with the problems caused by heterogeneous users, would be to equate landing fees with the AIC appropriate to the category of aircraft concerned. Calculation of the appropriate AIC is unfortunately bound to be somewhat arbitrary, but those costs incurred solely to accommodate particular categories of aircraft (for example, the cost of additional runway length specifically for the Boeing 747, or specifically for

4. Including the AIC of FAA terminal facilities.

another group of aircraft, say those larger than the Boeing 727) may be distinguished from costs that are for the joint benefit of all categories of aircraft. The former—"separable"—costs may then be allocated to the particular class of aircraft concerned, leaving the "joint" costs to be allocated on a discriminatory basis.

Separable costs are determined by several factors. In particular, although weight is usually used as a basis for charging, runway wear and tear depend largely upon "footprint pressure"—the pressure an aircraft exerts on the airport surface. This may be but tenuously related to weight. Levine, in a helpful discussion of this subject, points out that a Boeing 727-200 has a higher footprint pressure than some models of the Boeing 747, which weigh three times as much.[5] This suggests that weight, even during periods of excess capacity, may be an inefficient measure to use as a basis for charging, for it will not encourage aircraft manufacturers or operators to design or use aircraft that impose less wear and tear on runways and taxiways. Some more complex formula involving weight, footprint pressure, and perhaps speed might be required to establish the separable cost element of a tariff schedule.

The advantage of charging for joint costs on the basis of weight is that this appears to be a rough proxy for ability to pay. Economically efficient discrimination is never easy, and any discriminatory arrangement must necessarily be somewhat arbitrary. Moreover, it may be desirable to introduce other than purely physical measures, particularly for general aviation operations. The distinctions often made between revenue and nonrevenue or business and nonbusiness operations are good examples. A general point to bear in mind is that although intuitively it may appear preferable to place a relatively large burden on the larger, faster aircraft, and on those used for commercial purposes, the cost of excluding one such operation will normally be relatively large also.

The discussion so far has been of pricing policy when an airport is being used at less than full potential capacity. The decision to invest in a new airport and the treatment of delay costs are in principle unchanged by relaxation of the homogeneity assumption. Note, however, that where delays occur at a joint use airport, the price charged general aviation aircraft should be increased to incorporate marginal external delay costs imposed on air carriers and other general aviation aircraft. This will mean a tendency for the landing fees payable by smaller aircraft to rise

5. Michael E. Levine, "Landing Fees and the Airport Congestion Problem," *Journal of Law and Economics*, Vol. 12 (April 1969), pp. 79–108.

more rapidly than those payable by larger ones, for at capacity aircraft weight becomes a relatively unimportant determinant of marginal social cost.

The signal to invest in a new airport will depend upon the cheapest means of increasing total airport capacity. If the least-cost method of accommodating the predicted mixture of aircraft over the following period begins with the construction of a general aviation airport, investment is signaled when the amount paid by *general aviation* operators, plus marginal external delay costs caused by general aviation in any period, exceeds the accounting costs of the new airport calculated for an equivalent period.[6] If a new air carrier or joint use airport is to be built, no such distinction has to be made between general aviation and air carriers.

The question of subsidizing $A_2$ now recurs. Subsidies, it will be recalled, may be justified on efficiency grounds by virtue of two influences: lumpiness of $A_2$, which if AIC pricing is employed and costs are rising, brings second-best problems to the fore, and external delay costs at $A_1$, which help to signal investment in $A_2$ before the willingness to pay of marginal users does so alone. This problem is likely to be particularly relevant where facilities are jointly used, because of the initial lumpiness of air carrier airports. (Although investment in a new general aviation airport could conceivably be signaled almost entirely by air carrier delays, the problem of financing it after construction might be eased by virtue of the smaller degree of lumpiness.)

Both influences justifying subsidization of $A_2$ stem from the benefits accruing to parties other than direct users, that is, those who continue to use $A_1$. Since the "external" beneficiaries are members of the aviation community, it would seem reasonable that the aviation community should also be the source of subsidies to particular airports. In this area, federal aid to airports would certainly be justified on grounds of economic efficiency. Indeed, the FAA could continue to act as an intermediary, in effect transferring funds from one sector of the aviation community to another. Since taxes would be unrelated to the use made of particular facilities, the assessment of liability would be as much a matter of equity as of resource allocation. A lump sum could be collected from all aircraft owners, perhaps based upon aircraft weight or value, to defray the

6. Note that total external delay costs at $A_1$ could be reduced by making it mandatory for *all* general aviation aircraft to use the new airport. But the result would be inefficient utilization of $A_1$ if those willing to pay for the real cost of using it are precluded by fiat from so doing.

costs incurred by operators of new airports, such subsidy being phased out over a period of say five years. This would certainly be an improvement on the airport subsidy program, which is more likely to hinder than to help efficient resource allocation.

## Heterogeneous Users, Congestion Costs, and the Peaking Problem

Adherence to strict marginalist rules would require off-peak consumption of any commodity to be priced at marginal operating cost, with peak consumers paying not only for the marginal operating cost of their own consumption but also for all marginal capacity costs. An exception to this would exist when off-peak consumption also contributes to demand for capacity.

Similar principles may be followed under the AIC pricing compromise. During off-peak periods price may be equated to marginal off-peak operating costs or, with a similar cost-recovery objective, discrimination can be practiced.[7] Peak users should be liable for the whole of the capacity cost of the airport complex, price for them being equated to average incremental capacity plus marginal operating costs, plus marginal delay costs where appropriate.

Investment in additional capacity should be signaled in much the same way as described in the previous section, the main difference being that willingness to pay for new facilities normally refers only to peak users. Note, however, that advantages to off-peak users may result from capacity extension. Even off-peak demand could use existing facilities to capacity, and it may therefore be necessary to ration capacity during certain off-peak hours. Off-peak demand would in those circumstances also contribute to demand for, and help to justify, further investment.

It is also conceivable that the quality of a new airport, $A_2$, may exceed that of the existing one, $A_1$. Surface transport costs, for example, could be lower at $A_2$ than at $A_1$. Off-peak users would want to take advantage of this saving; the benefits accruing to them in this respect should be taken into account in evaluating investment in $A_2$.

7. It may not be practicable to distinguish, for a large proportion of total operating costs, between those incurred solely for peak or off-peak use, that is, labor may be employed during the whole day, although used only during peak hours. This is the problem of joint cost allocation again.

A complicating factor is that variation in the pressure placed upon capacity at different times may be due to fluctuations not only in demand but also in supply. Even with demand constant, peak problems could arise, the most important reason being variability in weather conditions and visibility. Since the number of aircraft that can be handled in a given period is greater on clear days than on poor days, it might appear that landing fees charged during IFR conditions should exceed those charged when VFR prevail.

This would typically be true of predominantly air carrier airports, even though there may be a fall in demand for airport landing space during IFR conditions. At general aviation airports on the other hand, the fall in demand may be so large that capacity limits are reached not on IFR days at all but on VFR days. Whether or not this is so, there is clearly a case for varying price according to prevailing conditions of visibility.

Such a policy could be introduced quite easily. Even though peaks arising from adverse weather conditions cannot be predicted with as much certainty as purely demand-induced peaks,[8] most general aviation operators already need to be advised in advance as to whether instrument flight rules are going to be in force at an airport where they wish to land. Consequently, inefficiencies caused by inadequate price information should not constitute a serious problem.

If demand peaks and supply troughs are both to be incorporated into a flexible pricing system, there should be four pricing schedules:

VFR/off-peak demand
VFR/peak demand
IFR/off-peak demand
IFR/peak demand

A reasonable approximation to the theoretical ideal is to set price equal to marginal operating costs for each of the two off-peak demand periods, having distinguished where possible between any costs incurred solely on behalf of IFR or VFR off-peak users. The price charged peak users on VFR and IFR days should then equal the relevant AIC of the airport complex plus marginal delay costs, if any. "Relevant" average incremental cost for traffic on IFR and VFR days means the sum of (1) joint costs: those costs that would have been incurred had either IFR *or*

---

8. Although peaks caused by other forms of supply deficiency (runway construction, and so forth) may be.

VFR conditions persisted throughout the year; and (2) separable costs: those costs incurred purely for IFR or purely for VFR days (for example, an additional runway needed solely for heavier traffic on VFR days would be a separable cost).

Capacity costs that are truly joint would therefore be shared among all peak users, with no distinction between traffic on IFR and VFR days. Separable costs would be allocated, as appropriate, to IFR and VFR days. Marginal delay costs, which at a given level of demand can be expected to be greater during IFR conditions, would be added to marginal "airport costs" and if necessary, capacity could be rationed by raising price still further. The joint demands of IFR and VFR peak (and, if applicable, off-peak) users should then be used to signal the investment decision, the distinction between *marginal* joint and separable costs being maintained.

Note that peaks may be at different times of the day for IFR and VFR days. Moreover, the only peaks at general aviation airports catering largely to the recreational flier may be on summer weekends. Some airports recognize this and charge accordingly. In calculating the landing fee payable under various situations, the total number of users on IFR and VFR days in a subsequent period would have to be estimated from surveys of the number of users on both days and probability estimates of the number of IFR and VFR days during that period.

It might be argued that air carriers will be insensitive to differential prices for IFR and VFR days, as scheduling requirements do not permit any adjustment of activity. If so, the only value of the policy would be as a more equitable method of cost recovery. But to achieve the same object it would be necessary only to estimate the probable number of VFR and IFR days and charge a fixed price accordingly. However, this would be a valid alternative only in the short run, for long-term seasonal scheduling could be influenced by these measures. More certainly, flexible pricing, varying not only with demand peaks but also with supply troughs, could immediately affect the bulk of general aviation operations, an exception being the scheduled air taxis.

# CHAPTER TEN

# Conclusions

EVEN WITH THE PASSAGE of the 1970 Airport and Airway Development and Revenue Acts, the total subsidy to be received by general aviation in the foreseeable future will continue to be enormous and the institutional barriers impeding subsidy reductions will remain formidable.

## Subsidies and Economic Efficiency

If federal, state, and local aid and congestion costs are included, the difference between the costs imposed by general aviation on the rest of society and the benefits society receives in return is estimated to be about $640 million annually over the period 1971–80. Moreover, in arriving at this figure, an attempt has been made at every stage to be conservative. In particular, where problems of joint cost allocation arise (that is, for air carrier and reliever airports), the costs for which general aviation is responsible have, for the purposes of the calculation, been assumed to be zero.

It will be recalled that the major elements of the annual subsidy are as follows:

1. *Net federal aid: $475 million.* Subject to congressional appropriations, total federal airways expenditures allocated to general aviation over the period 1971–80 are estimated at $545 million annually. A further $30 million is earmarked for general aviation airports under the Airport Development Program (ADP). This is scheduled for only the first five years of the period, but a similar figure will probably hold for the second five years. To offset total annual federal expenditures of $575 million, general aviation is estimated to pay about $100 million annually in user charges.

2. *State/local airport subsidies: $130 million.* This assumes that present financing policies are maintained and airport development proceeds as envisaged in the National Airport Plan. It further assumes that the relatively small state expenditures on airways facilities, which supplement those provided by the FAA, are offset by equally small state fuel taxes and registration fees.

3. *Congestion costs: $35 million.* This assumes no change in annual cost from the 1968 figure. Even with subsequent anti-general aviation measures at New York City area airports, Washington National, and Chicago O'Hare, the general increase in traffic and congestion suggests that this will continue to be a conservative figure.

The average number of aircraft in the general aviation fleet over the period 1971–80 is expected to be about 176,000. The subsidy to general aviation therefore amounts to an average of more than $3,500 per year per aircraft. This may be compared with the annual cost that an owner privately incurs in operating and depreciating his aircraft, which ranges from $2,700 for a typical single-engined piston aircraft to $260,000 for a general aviation turbojet.[1] Since over 80 percent of the general aviation fleet falls into the former category, the astonishing result is that frequently the public at large contributes more toward the cost of safely operating a light aircraft through the nation's airspace and at its airports than does the owner himself!

Yet at the time of enactment of the user charges legislation, Congress was in a particularly self-congratulatory mood concerning the financing of federal airport and airways expenditures, as exemplified by the statement of Congressman William L. Springer (Illinois):

I think the impact and the thrust of this bill is that the general taxpayer has now . . . stopped paying the cost for the citizen who uses aviation. Whether you are flying from here to Chicago or to San Francisco—or whether you use your own plane to fly from here to Chicago or San Francisco, you will now pay your cost for doing so. That is the thrust of this bill. . . . It is, therefore, a pay-as-you-go measure and the people who fly are the people who pay.[2]

This statement, which applies to expenditures amounting to about three-quarters of the subsidy to general aviation (that is, the federal share), makes two points. First, the general taxpayer is relieved of the burden of subsidizing civil aviation and, second, because of the pay-as-

---

1. See Table 5-1.
2. *Congressional Record,* daily ed., May 13, 1970, p. H4307.

you-go feature, there is no cross-subsidization within the civil aviation sector.

Although civil aviation as a whole will not in fact pay its way for a number of years, the first of these two points is clearly an objective of the bill. The second part of the statement, however, is misleading. For the reasons already spelled out at some length, the form of charging is not as close to a pay-as-you-go system as it should be, a consequence of which being not only an economically inefficient use of aviation-related facilities, but also subsidization of certain forms of aviation activity by others. In particular, an examination of projected use of the airways system and of liability to user charges suggests that by the end of the ten-year period there will be a considerable subsidy from the air carriers to general aviation, although civil aviation in the aggregate may then be unsubsidized.

On the assumption that general aviation is responsible for 50 percent of the increase in airways expenditures over the period 1969–80 (an assumption already shown to be conservative), general aviation's share of federal airways costs in 1980 is estimated at $647 million.[3] To this may be added $30 million for subsidies to "pure" general aviation airports. Liability in that year is predicted to be $132 million, leaving a total subsidy of $545 million. Civil aviation's total liability to user charges in 1980 is estimated at $1,537 million, and total federal expenditures on civil airports and airways at $1,420 million.[4] In that year, therefore, passengers of the air carriers will contribute $545 million toward general aviation's share of federal aviation expenditures, plus a surplus of $100 million or so. It is worth repeating that in making this estimate all federal aid to airports jointly used by air carriers and general aviation and to reliever airports is allocated as a benefit to the commercial airlines.

It goes without saying that estimates made for ten years hence are subject to a good deal of error and, since the projections are in constant dollars, adjustment to tax rates would have to be made to retain liability in real terms. Nevertheless, the continued subsidization of general aviation on an ever-increasing scale is quite clearly implied by present legislative arrangements when seen in the light of predicted aviation activity. The problem is that overall cost recovery is often taken to be the only

3. This is estimated by a method similar to that employed to estimate the amount annually allocable to general aviation over 1971–80. (See p. 65.)

4. See Tables 4-5 and 4-6. To federal airways expenditures of $1,200 million, we add $220 million under ADP, this being the annual average amount remaining out of the $2.5 billion authorized after expenditures specified for fiscal years 1971–75 have been made.

criterion for an efficient and equitable user charges policy. This, of course, is entirely false.

Throughout most of this book, two major aspects of public policy toward general aviation have been examined: on one hand, the subsidy received by that group under present policies; on the other, the efficiency aspects of general aviation activity. Price and investment policies designed to achieve efficiency in resource allocation have been suggested. The question that may now arise is: Why should the taxpayer be concerned to ensure that the marginal benefits to general aviation are equated with the marginal cost of supplying airport and airways facilities? It may be argued that efficient allocation of resources used by general aviation is irrelevant for non-users so long as no subsidization takes place and that the graduated registration fee can do the job as well as any complex system of landing fees, fuel taxes, and so forth.

An immediate response could be that operators of general aviation aircraft are as much a part of the larger society whose welfare is to be maximized as is anyone else. So if the marginal cost of aviation support is less than its marginal benefit to general aviation, failure to expand the system will result in a net loss to society. But this reply may not be adequate: it may be argued that general aviation owners are such a small and select (that is, wealthy) group that they deserve to be singled out for special treatment; more specifically, they should be treated as a community separate from the remainder of society.

This argument, however, ignores the relationship between general aviation activity and the rest of the economy. For example, about three-fourths of general aviation flying hours are supposed to be for business purposes; the welfare of consumers of the final product made more readily available by general aviation should also be included. So, too, should the welfare of workers employed in aircraft manufacturing, distribution, and servicing, as well as at airports and airways installations. Certainly decisions concerning *their* future should be determined in large part by considerations of economic efficiency.

Presumably, given the choice between the elimination of subsidy by means of an efficient pricing policy or by one that is inefficient, one would always choose the former. The real problem arises when efficient pricing and the avoidance of subsidy are inconsistent with each other. This could occur when price is equated to short-run marginal cost and lumpiness is present, and will certainly occur if price is equated to short- or long-run marginal cost when long-run average costs are falling.

The nearest practicable approximation to the theoretical ideal is to equate price with average incremental cost. As long as the length of useful life of capital assets is correctly predicted in bookkeeping terms, no loss-making should arise purely from lumpiness, for in the short run average bookkeeping cost will equal average incremental cost. Moreover, where long-run average costs are rising, surpluses should accrue as a result of this pricing policy. Where long-run average costs are falling, however, losses will result.

Identification of the financial implications of average incremental cost pricing for the federal airways system would require a major study of the kind called for in the 1970 legislation; however, it appears that loss-making resulting from declining long-run costs should not constitute a serious problem. If loss-making on the account of the federal airways system *should* result, the alternatives are either to finance the deficit from the general aviation community (the graduated registration fee might be used for this purpose) or from some other source entirely. This is quite clearly a matter to be decided on grounds of equity, but subsidization of general aviation certainly seems to be more palatable when it is a byproduct of efficient pricing than when it appears to be a matter of direct policy.

There is not, of course, the same scope for levying lump sum charges on general aviation to finance airport deficits, since any charge is likely to have significant allocative effects. It is fairly safe to assume that, primarily because of ever-growing pressure on land near urban centers, average airport costs will continue to rise over time. In addition, receipts from congestion charges will be all "profit" to the state/local airport operator.


## Some Institutional Obstacles to Reform

The heavy subsidization of general aviation to date has been an important factor in encouraging its rapid rate of growth. In turn this has been matched by the development of a formidable pressure-group structure, which has strongly opposed the introduction of measures that impose costs on or otherwise restrict general aviation. As a result, subsidization of general aviation will probably continue on a large scale for some time to come, thereby stimulating still further growth. This is a vicious circle that will become increasingly difficult to break.

The most vocal representatives of general aviation interests are the Aircraft Owners and Pilots Association and the National Business Aircraft Association. The membership of these organizations includes a relatively high proportion of prominent politicians and businessmen, so that mere numbers (AOPA represents about 150,000 private owners and NBAA almost 900 corporations) tend to understate their influence.

Moreover, the seeds of influence are sown on fertile ground. It is a frequent complaint that federal agencies tend to become the representatives of the parts of society they are designed to regulate. Many views expressed by aviation interests that would immediately be rejected by an impartial observer are echoed by important elements within the FAA.

One reason is that in appointing officials to an agency that is responsible for a highly technical and complex activity, a particularly fine balance has to be struck between those who are able to understand the technicalities of the system itself and those who are able to view the activity critically, in the light of its contribution to the welfare of society as a whole. Unfortunately, those who have invested so much of their time and money in acquiring technical expertise in an area are unlikely to do anything to discourage its growth.

Officials at the state and local levels are, of course, guided by motives similar to those of their federal counterparts. The prevalence of cross-subsidization within an airport complex, referred to earlier, illustrates this. There is a powerful incentive for an airport manager to discriminate in favor of landing-area users. While his own responsibility and status in the industry are unlikely to be enhanced by the restriction of aircraft activity—even at peak hours—he will be widely acclaimed by the industry for extracting large monopoly profits from concessionaires to finance operation and extension of landing areas.

Accusations of empire-building are commonly leveled at the established civil servant, but they may also be leveled—with justification—at high-level political appointees concerned with aviation matters, because they, too, normally have a strong vested interest in the industry. As a result, although wide differences of opinion often exist within the FAA and other public aviation authorities over priorities, particularly with respect to the competing demands of general aviation and the air carriers, the prevalent view is that the growth of aviation is simply an end in itself.[5]

5. Naturally, aviation interests prefer aviation experts to be appointed to senior policymaking positions. General aviation in particular was extremely critical when

An illustration of this is the remark made by FAA Administrator John H. Shaffer, concerning the flight quotas introduced at high density airports: "Obviously we will take care of the safety problem by restriction, but that approach is not a substitute for the additional capacity required to meet demand. . . . *No one wants traffic demand restricted.*"[6]

The "requirements" approach to aviation forecasting, which was discussed in Chapter 2, is the logical accompaniment of this attitude. It also has a certain amount of statutory backing, for the Federal Aviation Act of 1958 states that it is the duty of the administrator to "encourage and foster the development of civil aeronautics and air commerce in the United States and abroad."[7] This task is obviously not going to be aided by increasing user charges, as long as the necessary facilities can be financed by other means.

Obstacles to reform of current policies toward general aviation are therefore considerable, for powerful incentives to protect the industry exist at all levels of government. Moreover, while the industry is anxious to publicize the benefits to society that result from its activity, the layman is unlikely to be equally interested in examining its arguments. Should the general taxpayer be concerned about the way in which the government spends his money, many more expensive programs will occupy his attention.

Moreover, because of the technical nature of the subject, the industry is able to present a united front against investigation by outsiders—the "rank and file of the public," to quote the Aerospace Industries Association.[8] It maintains that the only people qualified to make decisions in or about the industry are the manufacturers, pilots, and aircraft operators themselves. But if there is one major conclusion that emerges from this study, it is that aviation, in common with many other fields of endeavor, is much too important a subject to be left to such "experts."

But it is possible to end on an optimistic note. Although on the particular questions of user charges and subsidization general aviation has con-

---

in 1966 the Federal Aviation Agency was incorporated within the Department of Transportation. It continues to insist that the FAA should revert to its former status as an independent agency.

6. *Airport/Airways Development,* Hearings before the Subcommittee on Aviation of the Senate Committee on Commerce, 91 Cong. 1 sess. (1969), p. 38 (italics supplied).

7. 72 Stat. 749.

8. *The 1969 Aerospace Year Book* (Aerospace Industries Association of America, 1969), p. 255.

tinued to escape lightly, in recent years its activity has been sharply curtailed on several occasions by public authorities. The introduction of peak-hour landing fees for general aviation at the Port of New York Authority airports, FAA flight quotas at "high density" airports, and a number of changes in federal flight regulations have all been particularly restrictive to general aviation.

The significant characteristic of these measures is that, while general aviation has been harmed by them, they are certainly in the interest of general aviation's competitor for use of the nation's airports and airways, the commercial airlines. Their introduction can easily be reconciled with the general desire to see aviation expand, although here expansion of air carrier activity is encouraged at the expense of general aviation. The 1970 legislation drives a further wedge between the two elements of civil aviation. Friction between the two groups has always existed and can only be aggravated by the severe discrimination against the commercial airlines that is implied by the new user charges legislation. As to the subsidy question, it will be interesting to see if the proponents of reform of public policy toward general aviation can successfully enlist the aid of the commercial airlines and so accomplish what apparently they are unable to do alone. Once this major obstacle has been overcome, introduction of the pricing and investment policies outlined in this book would become feasible.

# APPENDIX A

# *Statistical Tables*

## Table A-1. Characteristics of Representative U.S. Manufactured General Aviation Fixed-Wing Aircraft Delivered in 1970

| Manufacturer and model[a] | Number of seats[b] | Empty weight (pounds) | Gross weight (pounds)[c] | Maximum cruise speed (miles per hour or Mach number) | Maximum range (statutory miles) | Number delivered | Price[d] (dollars) |
|---|---|---|---|---|---|---|---|
| *Single-engine piston aircraft: 1–3 places* | | | | | | | |
| Cessna 150 | 2 | 975/ 1,060 | 1,600 | 122 | 565 | 1,001 | 8,835/ 11,450 |
| Piper PA-18-150 Super Cub | 2 | 930 | 1,750 | 130 | 460 | 57 | 11,500 |
| Piper PA-28-140 Cherokee | 2 | 1,201 | 2,150 | 142 | 790 | 470 | 10,400 |
| *Single-engine piston aircraft: 4 or more places* | | | | | | | |
| Cessna 172 and 177 Cardinal | 4 | 1,250/ 1,480 | 2,300/ 2,500 | 131/142 | 640/790 | 982 | 13,425/ 17,995 |
| Cessna 180 Skywagon and 182 Skylane | 4–6 | 1,555/ 1,640 | 2,800/ 2,950 | 162/168 | 865/925 | 442 | 20,500/ 21,850 |
| Piper PA-28-180 Cherokee | 4 | 1,300 | 2,400 | 152 | 800 | 220 | 14,980 |
| Piper PA-28-180 Arrow | 4 | 1,420 | 2,500 | 170 | 995 | 30 | 18,980 |
| *Agricultural (piston) aircraft* | | | | | | | |
| Grumman G-164A AgCat | ... | ... | ... | 147 | 365/435 | 94 | 34,790/ 35,045 |
| Cessna 188 Agwagon B | ... | ... | ... | 119 | 325 | 118 | 20,995 |
| *Multi-engine piston aircraft* | | | | | | | |
| Beech Queen Air B80 | 11 | 5,060 | 8,800 | 224 | 1,200 | 7 | 192,500 |
| Beech Baron B55 | 4–6 | 3,070 | 5,100 | 225 | 1,225 | 65 | 67,950 |
| Cessna 401 and 402 | 6–10 | 3,665/ 3,779 | 6,300 | 240 | 808 | 90 | 108,500/ 111,950 |
| *Turboprop aircraft* | | | | | | | |
| Beech King Air 100 | 13 (1–2) | 6,440 | 10,600 | 248 | 1,252 | 50 | 605,000 |
| Beech Beechcraft 99A Executive | 13 (1–2) | 5,880 | 10,400 | 285 | 1,150 | 20 | 508,000 |
| *Turbojet aircraft* | | | | | | | |
| Grumman Gulfstream 2 | 19 (2) | 35,200 | 60,000 | 0.85 | 3,800 | 17 | 2,900,000 |
| Gates Learjet 24 | 6 (2) | 6,851 | 13,500 | 0.81 | 2,020 | 19 | 799,000 |
| Gates Learjet 25 | 4–8 (2) | 7,167/ 7,296 | 15,000 | 0.81 | 2,055/ 2,548 | 16 | 896,000/ 959,000 |
| Lockheed 1329 Jetstar | 10 (2) | 21,337 | 42,500 | 0.82 | 2,230 | 2 | 1,750,000 |
| North American Rockwell Sabreliner NA-265-60 | 10 (2) | 10,800 | 20,372 | 0.82 | 2,000 | 7 | 1,400,000 |

Source: *Aviation Week and Space Technology*, Vol. 94 (March 8, 1971), pp. 84, 96, 98, 154–55.

a. Models with identical power plants are grouped together.

b. For piston aircraft, figures denote the total number of seats; for turboprop and turbojet aircraft, figures not in parentheses denote the number of passenger seats and figures in parentheses denote the number of crew members.

c. For piston aircraft, figures denote the *normal* gross weight; for turboprop and turbojet aircraft, figures denote the *maximum* gross weight.

d. The prices shown are fly-away factory prices to which, for electronic equipment, the following amounts would normally be added: 1–3 place single-engine piston aircraft $600–$1,300; over 3-place single-engine piston aircraft $1,000–$2,000; multiengine piston aircraft $10,000–$35,000; turboprop aircraft $10,000–$100,000; turbojet aircraft $100,000.

**Table A-2. Active Airman Certificates Held, by Category, Selected Years, 1956–68**

| Category | 1956 | 1960 | 1964 | 1966 | 1968 |
|---|---|---|---|---|---|
| Pilot | | | | | |
|   Student | 80,494 | 99,182 | 120,743 | 165,177 | 209,406 |
|   Private | 132,525 | 138,869 | 175,574 | 222,427 | 281,728 |
|   Commercial | 72,597 | 89,904 | 108,428 | 131,539 | 164,458 |
|   Airline transport | 11,774 | 18,279 | 21,572 | 23,917 | 28,607 |
|   Other | 326 | 1,828 | 4,724 | 5,697 | 7,496 |
| Nonpilot | 148,335 | 169,598 | 195,396 | 217,132 | 250,151 |
| Flight instructor | 28,018 | 31,459 | 32,158 | 38,897 | 30,361 |

Source: *FAA Statistical Handbook of Aviation*, 1961 and 1969 editions, pp. 43 and 165, respectively.

**Table A-3. Hours and Miles of General Aviation Business Flying, Selected Years, 1948–68**

| Year | Hours flown | | Miles flown | |
|---|---|---|---|---|
| | Number (*thousands*) | Percentage of all general aviation hours | Number (*thousands*) | Percentage of all general aviation miles |
| 1948 | 2,576 | 17 | 298,945 | 20 |
| 1952 | 3,124 | 38 | 419,705 | 43 |
| 1956 | 4,600 | 45 | 672,000 | 51 |
| 1960 | 5,699 | 44 | 880,550 | 50 |
| 1964 | 5,823 | 37 | 1,046,792 | 48 |
| 1965 | 5,857 | 35 | 1,204,321 | 47 |
| 1966 | 7,057 | 33 | 1,536,158 | 46 |
| 1967 | 6,578 | 30 | 1,431,372 | 42 |
| 1968 | 6,976 | 29 | 1,406,328 | 38 |

Source: *FAA Statistical Handbook of Aviation*, 1957 and 1969 editions, pp. 44–45 and 207–08, respectively.

## Table A-4. Hours and Miles of General Aviation Commercial Flying, Selected Years, 1948–68

| Year | Hours flown Number (thousands) | Percentage of all general aviation hours | Miles flown Number (thousands) | Percentage of all general aviation miles |
|------|------|------|------|------|
| 1948 | 1,066 | 7 | 142,640 | 10 |
| 1952 | 1,727 | 21 | 217,865 | 22 |
| 1956 | 2,000 | 20 | 247,000 | 19 |
| 1960 | 2,365 | 18 | 299,387 | 17 |
| 1964 | 3,305 | 21 | 392,547 | 18 |
| 1965 | 3,348 | 20 | 461,228 | 18 |
| 1966 | 3,555 | 17 | 515,730 | 16 |
| 1967 | 3,918 | 18 | 568,502 | 16 |
| 1968 | 4,810 | 20 | 666,156 | 18 |

Source: Same as Table A-3.

## Table A-5. Hours and Miles of General Aviation Instructional Flying, Selected Years, 1948–68

| Year | Hours flown Number (thousands) | Percentage of all general aviation hours | Miles flown Number (thousands) | Percentage of all general aviation miles |
|------|------|------|------|------|
| 1948 | 8,701 | 58 | 378,660 | 34 |
| 1952 | 1,503 | 18 | 144,035 | 15 |
| 1956 | 1,500 | 15 | 158,000 | 12 |
| 1960 | 1,828 | 14 | 193,721 | 11 |
| 1964 | 2,675 | 17 | 283,506 | 13 |
| 1965 | 3,346 | 20 | 358,733 | 14 |
| 1966 | 5,674 | 27 | 646,169 | 19 |
| 1967 | 6,262 | 28 | 713,242 | 21 |
| 1968 | 6,494 | 27 | 814,190 | 22 |

Source: Same as Table A-3.

174

**Table A-6. Hours and Miles of General Aviation Personal Flying, Selected Years, 1948–68**

| Year | Hours flown | | Miles flown | |
| | Number (thousands) | Percentage of all general aviation hours | Number (thousands) | Percentage of all general aviation miles |
|---|---|---|---|---|
| 1948 | 2,606 | 17 | 225,150 | 17 |
| 1952 | 1,629 | 20 | 165,795 | 17 |
| 1956 | 2,100 | 20 | 238,000 | 18 |
| 1960 | 3,172 | 24 | 387,442 | 22 |
| 1964 | 3,777 | 24 | 436,164 | 20 |
| 1965 | 4,016 | 24 | 512,476 | 20 |
| 1966 | 4,540 | 22 | 605,912 | 18 |
| 1967 | 5,173 | 23 | 690,595 | 20 |
| 1968 | 5,532 | 23 | 777,181 | 21 |

Source: Same as Table A-3.

**Table A-7. Eligible U.S. Civil Aircraft, by Year of Manufacture, 1958–68[a]**

| Year | Number | Percentage |
|---|---|---|
| 1958 and before[b] | 52,416 | 41.2 |
| 1959 | 5,473 | 4.3 |
| 1960 | 5,080 | 4.0 |
| 1961 | 4,415 | 3.5 |
| 1962 | 4,629 | 3.6 |
| 1963 | 5,358 | 4.2 |
| 1964 | 6,985 | 5.5 |
| 1965 | 9,242 | 7.3 |
| 1966 | 12,426 | 9.8 |
| 1967 | 10,335 | 8.1 |
| 1968 | 10,805 | 8.5 |
| Total | 127,164 | 100.0 |

Source: *FAA Statistical Handbook of Aviation, 1969*, p. 191.
a. Eligible aircraft include all registered aircraft that have been inspected for airworthiness as required by FAA, and scheduled and supplemental air carriers and commercial operators operating under FAA Regulations, Parts 121 and 127.
b. Includes aircraft for which year of manufacture is unknown.

175

# The Theoretical Case for Introducing a Pricing System

WHEREVER marginal cost (*MC*) can be defined unambiguously as equal to both short-run and long-run marginal social cost and a zero price is charged for a particular commodity, consumption of any given commodity, if uninhibited by rationing, will be *OD* in Figure B-1, in which *D'D* is the demand curve. An optimal price would be associated with consumption of *OA*, and the gain from reducing consumption by *AD*

**Figure B-1. Optimal Pricing**

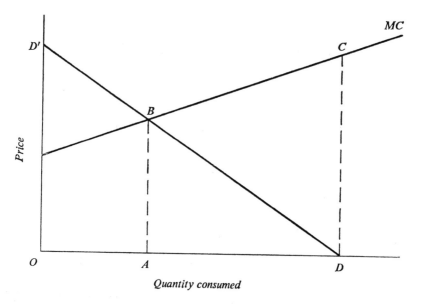

Quantity consumed

is represented by triangle *BCD*, as long as the reduction is brought about by setting a price equal to marginal cost for all consumers. If the pricing mechanism is introduced, and an optimal pricing policy (here defined as marginal cost pricing) is pursued, the benefit accruing during each demand

176

period will be defined in a similar way to $BCD$, the present value of the stream of benefits being defined by the expression

(1)
$$\int_{T}^{T+n} \left\{ \int_{x'}^{x''} [M(x) - D(x)]dx \right\} (t)e^{-rt}dt,$$

where $D$ is the demand price, $r$ is some annual social discount rate, $t$ is a one-year time period, $T$ is the time at which the pricing mechanism is introduced, $n$ the number of years the pricing mechanism is retained, $(x'' - x')$ is the reduction in the quantity of commodity $x$ consumed as a result of raising price from zero to some positive figure, and $M$ is the marginal cost of producing commodity $x$ or marginal "project" cost. To offset the benefits resulting from the use of price to ration scarce resources, the pricing mechanism itself will involve the following costs: an initial capital outlay $K$ and annual running (operating and maintenance) costs $R$. The present value of these costs can be defined as

(2)
$$\int_{T}^{T+n} R(t)e^{-rt}dt \left\{ K + \int_{T}^{T+n} R(t)e^{-rt}dt \right\}.$$

If at time $T$ the policymaker has to make a once-for-all decision on whether or not to introduce a pricing system, the theoretical answer is straightforward: he would merely compare the magnitudes of expressions (1) and (2); if the estimated benefits of the pricing mechanism exceed the costs, pricing should be introduced.[1]

The situation in which indivisible capital assets exist is illustrated in Figure B-2. Let $C_1$ be the consumption growth path when price at the margin is zero. Suppose that at time $t_0$ the current rate of consumption all but exhausts existing capacity. The policymaker then faces three possible courses of action: investing in additional capacity, investing in the means of charging a price at the margin and rationing capacity by that method, or rationing by nonprice means.

Assume further that nonprice rationing is ruled out on social grounds. The choice then lies between investing in capacity or investing in the price

1. A better solution may, however, be to defer introducing the pricing mechanism for some time and to build additional capacity in the intervening period. Optimal timing of the introduction of pricing has been covered in another context. See Jeremy J. Warford, "Water 'Requirements': The Investment Decision in the Water Supply Industry," and W. Peters, "Appendix: Notes on the Timing of the Introduction of Meters," *Manchester School of Economic and Social Studies*, Vol. 34 (January 1966), pp. 87–106, and 107–112, respectively.

mechanism. The effect of the latter will be, by raising price above zero, to reduce consumption; $C_2$ is the consumption growth path that would have existed if a pricing mechanism had always been in operation, and a given pricing policy (assuming strict marginal cost pricing with the attendant price fluctuations) followed.

**Figure B-2. Consumption, Investment, and the Introduction of Pricing**

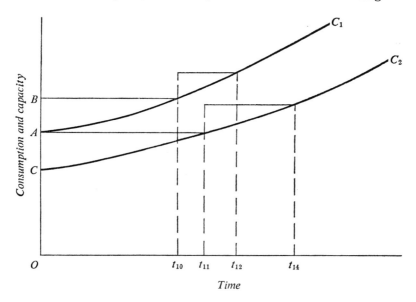

Where lumpiness is present, the benefits accruing from introducing pricing may be considered as two distinct elements. First, there will be savings due to the exclusion of demands for which consumers are unwilling to cover (in this case) marginal running costs. These savings, for any given capital stock, can be defined by expression (1). In addition, there will be gains from deferring a series of investments a number of years.

Suppose that consumption at $t_0$ is $OA$, and that this is a rate of consumption that fully utilizes existing capacity. In the absence of pricing, the best investment would increase capacity to $OB$, and this would satisfy demands up to $t_{10}$. The next investment would satisfy demands up to $t_{12}$. On the other hand, if at $t_0$ a price equal to the short-run marginal cost is charged, consumption falls to $OC$; consumption then increases along $C_2$ up to the point at which investment in capacity is required, say at $t_{11}$, and this is sufficient to satisfy demands up until $t_{14}$. Investment in the first project will then have been delayed from $t_0$ to $t_{11}$, and in the second from $t_{10}$ to $t_{14}$. (For convenience zero gestation periods are assumed for investment.)

In general, the gain from deferment of investment can be represented as:

$$(3) \qquad \sum_{i=1}^{\infty} (y_i' - y_i'') e^{-r(T_i''-T_i')}$$

where:

$y_i'$ = real cost of the $i$th investment project if undertaken at time $T'$;

$y_i''$ = real cost of the $i$th investment project if undertaken at $T''$ (the distinction between $y_i'$ and $y''$ allows for the possibility that because of technical change, the real cost of extending capacity may alter over time);

$T'$ = time of investment in the $i$th project in the absence of a pricing mechanism;

$T''$ = time of investment in the $i$th project with the pricing mechanism.

Investment in the pricing mechanism is therefore a better proposition than investment in capacity if the sum of the values of expressions (1) and (3) exceeds the value of expression (2). Expression (3) does not vary continuously with respect to time, so the timing problem would have to be solved by an iterative procedure. It was said above that investment in capacity would be "required" at $t_{11}$, meaning that at $t_{11}$ the price that consumers were willing to pay at the margin was equal to the long-run marginal cost. (Should lumpiness be important, one might expect $C_2$ in Figure B-2 to flatten out at capacity points.)

Note that, if nonprice rationing is ruled out, the value of the increment in capacity must be shown to exceed its cost *minus* the cost of introducing the pricing mechanism. Although the benefits accruing from a project may be estimated as less than its cost, investment may still be justified if the pricing costs that would otherwise be incurred are sufficient to offset the difference.

Finally, it may be argued that this description of the situation in the absence of a user price is inadequate in that rationing of a sort may still be practiced. Whether consumers of the particular product, or members of society at large, are taxed, the demand curve $D'D$ in Figure B-1 may be lower as a result of the provision of $OD$ of the commodity than it would be if the commodity were not produced at all. In other words, the costs of the output in question may exert an income effect on consumers' demand for the commodity. A priori, however, there is no way of knowing whether a shift in the demand curve will produce a greater or smaller social surplus than hitherto existed.

# The FAA's Safety-Regulatory Role and General Aviation

THE CONTRIBUTION of the Federal Aviation Administration to the safety of air travel is determined by the enforcement of safety regulations, combined with efficient operation of the airways system. The problem of enforcing safety regulations is particularly relevant in view of criticism frequently leveled at general aviation pilots. This has been dramatically illustrated from time to time by tragic midair collisions between general aviation and air carrier aircraft,[1] the most recent, in September 1969, involving a Piper Cherokee manned by a student pilot flying solo and an Allegheny Airlines DC-9 preparing to land at Indianapolis Municipal Airport.[2] Even before actual responsibility for this accident had been officially established, the death toll of 83 persons prompted a wave of public criticism, leveled both at the FAA and at the general aviation community. The FAA was criticized for permitting the use of inadequate radar equipment, but more severely for not enforcing stricter flying rules at the busier airports. These were necessary, it was alleged, because of the incompetence and irresponsibility of a minority of general aviation pilots.

Irresponsibility may take several forms, including failure of pilots to familiarize themselves with the latest technical developments that would help to maintain or improve flight proficiency and therefore standards of

---

1. Serious allegations have also been made concerning the efficiency of the FAA on the one hand and the negligence of aircraft manufacturers on the other with respect to the design of aircraft. Of the 1,200 or so fatalities resulting from general aviation accidents in 1967 one-quarter were alleged by members of the Nader Student Group of 1969 to be attributable to manufacturers' neglecting crash safety. See James Bruce and John Draper, "Crash Safety in General Aviation Aircraft" (Nader Student Group, 1970; processed).

2. In 1968 there were 37 midair collisions, all of which involved private aircraft. The Indianapolis crash was the ninth in 2½ years between private and air carrier aircraft.

safety. In 1967, the FAA stated that "a review of the accident records shows that many accidents can be ascribed to deterioration of basic airmanship and skills and to pilots' failure to keep abreast of new developments and operational procedures. In this connection, much work done by the military services shows that, in particular, procedural knowledge and activities are rapidly forgotten with time and non-use."[3]

The FAA has tried various methods of increasing pilot efficiency. For example, in 1965 it awarded a contract to the Flight Safety Foundation to persuade general aviation pilots to upgrade their proficiency in the interests of accident prevention. This was known as General Aviation Pilot Education, or Project GAPE.[4] In January 1967 it outlined a package proposal that included the introduction of a new, restrictive "basic pilot" certificate, as well as more advanced training for private and commercial certification.[5] Under pressure this was withdrawn and replaced by a proposal that periodic proficiency tests for general aviation pilots should be introduced.[6] This too has so far been unsuccessful, largely because of opposition from general aviation interests. Retesting has been opposed on the grounds that there was no statistical evidence indicating the need for it, that it would cost too much to implement, that it would damage industry and general aviation, and that, since rules cannot improve human judgment, it probably would not work anyway. It has also been argued that retesting would correct the shortcomings of a relatively small number of erring pilots and that, as reexamination of pilots was already possible under Federal Aviation Regulations, its introduction would be superfluous.[7]

These arguments simply amount to saying that the benefits of testing would be exceeded by the costs. Probably the best way to approach the problem is to conduct cost-benefit studies of introducing tests of varying degrees of severity and frequency, in order to arrive at that arrangement showing the highest net present worth. This assumes of course that, among other difficulties, the knotty problem of dealing with the valuation of

3. U.S. Federal Aviation Administration, Office of Information Services, "FAA Information," 67-88, December 29, 1967, p. 2.

4. For a description, see Robert Burkhardt, *The Federal Aviation Administration* (Praeger, 1967), p. 101.

5. FAA, "FAA Information," 67-5, January 12, 1967, p. 1.

6. FAA, "FAA Information," 67-88, December 29, 1967, p. 1.

7. See "FAA's Proficiency Proposal Attacked," *AOPA Pilot*, Vol. 11 (May 1968), p. 33.

human life can be dealt with satisfactorily.[8] If it cannot, the cost-benefit analyst can at least show the identifiable monetary costs, on the one hand, and the monetary benefits, on the other, and leave the policymaker to decide whether the number of lives saved as a result warrants the expenditure. The point that a series of different arrangements should be tried is implicit in AOPA's final argument, namely, that Federal Aviation Regulations already provide for the retesting of pilots who are suspected of being incompetent. In other words, even if the benefits of the planned scheme exceed the costs, the excess of benefits over costs of more extensive utilization of existing powers may be even greater, and to some extent the two methods would be mutually exclusive.

The AOPA in fact performs a valuable function itself, for it provides flight training clinics and other courses designed to encourage pilots to keep abreast of technical developments, often in cooperation with state aviation organizations. These have included flight instructor refresher courses and courses to prepare pilots for various FAA examinations. One series of AOPA courses that is of particular importance in view of recent controversy is that designed to prepare pilots for instrument ratings. Federal Aviation Regulations provide that no person (with certain minor exceptions) may act as pilot in command of a civil aircraft flying under instrument flight rules (IFR) or in weather conditions less than the minimum prescribed for visual flight rules (VFR) unless he has an instrument rating.[9] The instrument rating is granted by the FAA when the pilot has shown that he can handle an aircraft solely by using instruments, that is, with no external visual aid, and can operate according to the FAA's instrument flight rules.

Although airline transport pilots require instrument ratings, the rules are that private and commercial pilots need not have such ratings (in 1968 only 3 percent of nonstudent private pilots possessed the qualification). However, recent FAA actions indicate that such ability is becoming more and more necessary, for a good many rules designed to restrict VFR flying have been introduced. The impact, of course, has been felt almost entirely by general aviation operators. In particular, there was a

---

8. For a discussion of these problems, see Gary Fromm, "Aviation Safety," *Law and Contemporary Problems*, Vol. 33 (Summer 1968), pp. 590–618, and T. C. Schelling, "The Life You Save May be Your Own," in Samuel B. Chase, Jr. (ed.), *Problems in Public Expenditure Analysis* (Brookings Institution, 1968), pp. 127–76.

9. *Code of Federal Regulations*, Title 14, Part 61.3(f).

flurry of activity around the end of 1967 and the beginning of 1968, typi-
fied by the special visual flight rules (SVFR) controversy.

Normally, VFR operations can be conducted in airport control zones
if pilots have at least three miles of visibility and can remain at least
1,000 feet above, 500 feet below, and 2,000 feet laterally from clouds.
In addititon, until 1968, fixed-wing aircraft were permitted to fly under
special visual flight rules in airport control zones if the visibility was at
least one mile and pilots could remain clear of clouds. In October 1967
the FAA issued a Notice of Proposed Rule Making,[10] proposing the
elimination of SVFR operations for fixed-wing aircraft. However, this
attracted so much opposition from general aviation that the FAA modified the rule. As from April 1968, SVFR operations by fixed-wing aircraft were banned at 33 major hub airports, but permitted in the control
zones of other airports served by radar-equipped control towers; priority
was given, however, to aircraft operating under IFR.[11]

About the same time, the FAA also made more demanding the visibility and cloud clearance requirements for VFR operations between
10,000 and 14,500 feet mean sea level and lowered the floor of area positive control (APC) over the northeastern and north central United
States, within which VFR traffic is prohibited altogether.[12] Further restrictions upon VFR traffic were imposed in rules designating Kennedy,
La Guardia, Newark, O'Hare, and Washington National as "high density" airports.[13] Quotas, by category of aircraft, were imposed on the
number of IFR operations that could take place at these airports. In
comparison, VFR operations have a very low priority indeed; they can be
accepted only if they have no adverse effect on the allocated operations
for the airport concerned.

This series of measures has, understandably, aroused the wrath of general aviation interests. After drawing attention to the number of accidents precipitated by aircraft that are under full IFR control, an editorial
in the *AOPA Pilot* stated,

It's quite clear that the DOT or FAA or both (it doesn't really matter any
more) are deliberately working toward the downfall of general aviation.

10. FAA, "FAA Information," 67-45, October 10, 1967.
11. FAA, "FAA Information," 68-11, February 29, 1968.
12. FAA, "FAA Information," 68-7, February 13, 1968, and 67-68, September 20, 1967, respectively.
13. See FAA, "FAA Information," 68-76, December 3, 1968. Slight amend-
ments were made to the original rules, which were embodied in *Code of Federal
Regulations*, Title 14, Part 93.

No one knows better than they, for example, that only 20% of the country's civil pilots have instrument ratings—yet they are creating and passing rules that make it illegal to fly into major metropolitan airports without one. They are writing capricious rules and regulations that have no basis in fact, but which have what apparently is the desired effect to discourage people from buying or using general aviation aircraft.[14]

Further conflict between general aviation interests and the FAA arose out of the problems created by mixing of IFR and VFR traffic at terminal areas. These led the FAA to propose that all aircraft operating near the terminals of twenty-two major cities should be brought under ground control.[15] All aircraft, whether operating according to VFR or IFR, would be brought within the instrument flight system and would be required to be fitted with a transponder (costing about $1,000), which would permit their identification on a terminal radar screen. It was also proposed to ban student pilots from these areas. The proposals have been vigorously opposed by AOPA, which maintained that the correct solution is simply to designate separate air corridors for general aviation and air carriers.

The gulf between the FAA and the AOPA on this issue is clearly immense. The fundamental problem is to decide just what are the costs and benefits of proposed regulations, and it is fairly safe to say that usually no one really knows. Rough estimates may be made of the benefits of reducing delays by enforcement of these regulations, but what of the costs to those who are restricted? What are the costs and benefits of accident prevention; what, indeed, is the likely effect of restrictions or regulations on the accident rate?

The FAA stated that the proposals concerning flight quotas at the five airports were not intended to correct a safety problem.[16] Nevertheless, safety factors constitute an important underlying reason for the existence of the facilities provided by the FAA. It is impossible to separate the twin aims of expeditious movement of traffic and of safety. Because of the difficulty of estimating accident rates with and without rules, regulations, or certain facilities, there is ample scope for disagreement, as evidenced above. Moreover, the nature of the problem is such that experimentation is impractical.

Apart from failure to keep up with the latest developments, pilot irre-

14. *AOPA Pilot,* Vol. 11 (June 1968), p. 7.
15. FAA, "News," 69-113, September 30, 1969.
16. *Federal Register,* Vol. 33 (December 3, 1968), p. 17896.

sponsibility may take the form of dangerous or inconsiderate flying. An example that has received a good deal of attention recently is the apparent tendency of some pilots to fly while under the influence of alcohol. Suspicion has been aroused, but the case not proved, that a number of general aviation accidents in the United States were caused by alcohol.[17] Moreover, it appears that alcohol has a detrimental effect on flying performance at levels of consumption much lower than those necessary to impair automobile driving ability. But cause and effect are difficult to establish; there is for example the possibility that the type of person who drinks heavily would in any case be particularly accident-prone.[18]

What can be done about this situation? As Mohler pointed out in his 1966 report, Part 91 of the Federal Aviation Regulations covers this contingency: ". . . no person may act as a crewmember . . . of a civil aircraft while under the influence of intoxicating liquor." Nevertheless, enforcement is difficult. Mohler's conclusion was that the answer lay in "an aggressive education program for general aviation airmen."[19] In fact, some time before Mohler's report, the FAA had proposed tightening up drinking regulations, in particular stipulating minimum times between drinking and flying. This has now been done, the rule accompanying a general policy of disseminating as widely as possible information on the adverse effects of alcohol on airmen's performance. This is where FAA policy on "drunken flying" stands today.

Accident prevention is clearly a fundamental objective of FAA policy, and it does have the power to fine, suspend, or revoke the licenses of pilots breaking its rules. Firm enforcement of regulations, coupled with the recommended "aggressive education policy" mentioned above, now seems to be the FAA's general approach to the problem of pilot irresponsibility. Thus a recent move has been the employment of accident prevention officers to meet general aviation pilots and discuss safety problems with them. So far this is restricted to the central and southwest United States, but if successful the scheme will be implemented on a nationwide basis.[20]

17. See statement by Stanley R. Mohler, chief of FAA Aeromedical Applications Division, quoted in the *New York Times,* September 21, 1969.

18. See Wolfgang Schmidt, Reginald G. Smart, and Robert E. Popham, "The Role of Alcoholism in Motor Vehicle Accidents," *Traffic Safety,* Vol. 6 (December 1962), p. 21. The slight difference in context presumably does not affect the general principle.

19. Stanley R. Mohler, "Recent Findings on the Impairment of Airmanship by Alcohol" (FAA, Office of Aviation Medicine, 1966; processed), pp. 6, 7.

20. FAA, "FAA Information," 68-44, July 16, 1968, p. 1.

**Table C-1. Aircraft Accidents, Fatalities, and Accident Rates, U.S. Certificated Route Air Carriers, All Scheduled Service, 1958–69**

| | | | Accident rates | | | |
|---|---|---|---|---|---|---|
| | Number of Accidents | | Per million aircraft miles | | Per million recorded departures | |
| Year | Total | Fatal | Total | Fatal | Total | Fatal |
| 1958 | 67 | 8 | 0.068 | 0.008 | 18.44 | 2.20 |
| 1959 | 78 | 14 | 0.075 | 0.013 | 19.93 | 3.57 |
| 1960 | 72 | 12 | 0.071 | 0.009 | 18.41 | 2.33 |
| 1961 | 66 | 6 | 0.068 | 0.006 | 17.60 | 1.60 |
| 1962 | 47 | 6 | 0.046 | 0.005 | 12.57 | 1.37 |
| 1963 | 54 | 6 | 0.049 | 0.005 | 14.26 | 1.58 |
| 1964 | 59 | 11 | 0.049 | 0.008 | 14.67 | 2.53 |
| 1965 | 65 | 8 | 0.048 | 0.006 | 15.49 | 1.91 |
| 1966 | 56 | 5 | 0.038 | 0.003 | 12.81 | 1.14 |
| 1967 | 54 | 8 | 0.029 | 0.004 | 10.92 | 1.62 |
| 1968 | 56 | 13 | 0.026 | 0.005 | 10.57 | 2.08 |
| 1969p | 51 | 8 | 0.021 | 0.003 | 9.36 | 1.47 |

Sources: U.S. Department of Transportation, National Transportation Safety Board, "A Preliminary Analysis of Aircraft Accident Data: U.S. Civil Aviation, 1968" (NTSB, 1969; processed), p. 12, and "A Preliminary Analysis . . . , 1969" (NTSB, 1970; processed), p. 23.
p Preliminary.

In the final analysis, the success of aviation authorities in maintaining safety standards, and the competence of pilots, both have to be assessed in terms of accident rates. Comparative accident figures for air carriers and general aviation for 1958–69 are given in Tables C-1 and C-2.

Fromm has shown that since most accidents occur at or near terminal areas, the best simple measure of safety achievement is the accident rate per departure, rather than the traditional measure, the number of accidents per number of miles (or passenger miles) flown.[21] In 1968, while there were 10.6 accidents, 2.1 fatal accidents, and 64 fatalities per million recorded departures for U.S. domestic air carriers, the comparable figures for general aviation were 250, 35, and 70, respectively (Tables C-1 and C-2).[22] Unfortunately, while this is a satisfactory measure for air

21. Gary Fromm, "Aviation Safety." Also by the same author, "Economic Criteria for Federal Aviation Agency Expenditures" (United Research Incorporated, 1962; processed).

22. Data on fatalities are from *Airport/Airways Development*, Hearings before the Subcommittee on Aviation of the Senate Committee on Commerce, 91 Cong. 1 sess. (1969), Pt. 1, pp. 266–67.

## Table C-2. Aircraft Accidents, Fatalities, and Accident Rates, U.S. General Aviation Flying, 1958–69

| | Number of accidents | | | Accident rates | | | |
| | | | | Per million aircraft miles | | Per million recorded departures | |
| Year | Total | Fatal | Fatalities | Total | Fatal | Total | Fatal |
|---|---|---|---|---|---|---|---|
| 1958 | 4,584 | 384 | 717 | 2.8 | 0.2 | 653 | 54.7 |
| 1959 | 4,576 | 450 | 823 | 2.7 | 0.3 | 610 | 60.0 |
| 1960 | 4,793 | 429 | 787 | 2.7 | 0.2 | 647 | 57.9 |
| 1961 | 4,625 | 426 | 761 | 2.5 | 0.2 | 596 | 54.9 |
| 1962 | 4,840 | 430 | 857 | 2.5 | 0.2 | 557 | 49.5 |
| 1963 | 4,690 | 482 | 893 | 2.3 | 0.2 | 471 | 48.4 |
| 1964 | 5,069 | 526 | 1,083 | 2.3 | 0.2 | 440 | 45.7 |
| 1965 | 5,196 | 538 | 1,029 | 2.0 | 0.2 | 391 | 40.5 |
| 1966 | 5,712 | 573 | 1,149 | 1.7 | 0.2 | 342 | 34.3 |
| 1967 | 6,115 | 603 | 1,228 | 1.8 | 0.2 | 314 | 31.0 |
| 1968[a] | 4,968 | 692 | 1,399 | 1.3 | 0.2 | 250 | 34.8 |
| 1969p[a] | 4,931 | 651 | 1,388 | 1.3 | 0.2 | n.a. | n.a. |

Sources: Same as Table C-1 for first five columns (pp. 31 and 29, respectively, in the sources cited); last column, Gary Fromm, "Aviation Safety," *Law and Contemporary Problems*, Vol. 33 (Summer 1968), p. 596, and *Airport/Airways Development*, Hearings before the Subcommittee on Aviation of the Senate Committee on Commerce, 91 Cong. 1 sess. (1969), Pt. 1, pp. 266–67. Next to last column is derived from data in relevant columns.

n.a. Not available.

p Preliminary.

a. Data on total number of accidents not comparable with 1958–67 data because of change in the definition of an accident.

carriers, it is not for general aviation. The word "recorded" provides the clue to the difficulty. Departures are recorded only at those airports with FAA control towers. But whereas recorded operations account for the bulk of air carrier operations, this is certainly not true of general aviation operations, many of which take place at airports with no FAA facilities.

Accident figures per recorded departure for general aviation are therefore considerably overestimated and are of little use in facilitating comparison between the records of general aviation and the air carriers. Moreover, they are not even a good measure of progress for the general aviation sector alone. Thus a fall between 1958 and 1968 from 55 to 35 fatal general aviation accidents per million recorded departures is a precise measure of the real improvement only if the proportion of recorded to total departures remained the same over the period.

These data are not available, so the theoretically inferior measure of accidents per million aircraft miles is used as the basis for comparing the safety records of general aviation aircraft and the air carriers and the way they have changed over time. If an attempt is made to eliminate random factors by taking a three-year average, the result is that, for the period 1958–60, scheduled U.S. air carrier activity resulted in 0.0104 fatal accident per million aircraft miles, falling to 0.0042 (a drop of 63 percent) by 1967–69. For general aviation there was a fall of 25 percent from 0.24 to 0.18 fatal accident per million miles. (These figures hide significant differences in accident rates among various categories of general aviation.)

What then are the costs that result from general aviation accidents? Fromm has dealt with this subject at length, showing that the total depends almost entirely on the value placed upon human life.[23] Estimating the average cost of a general aviation fatality at $502,000, he calculated the total cost of general aviation accidents in 1966 as follows:

| | |
|---|---|
| Aircraft damage | $44 million |
| Other property damage | $2 million |
| Nonfatal injuries | $21 million |
| Fatal injuries | $578 million |

Although there is considerable scope for debate over these figures, the costs "external" to general aviation operators and passengers in that year were apparently very small—of the order of $2 million only. However, this figure could have been swamped entirely by just one midair collision with an air carrier. A collision with a Boeing 747 carrying 300 passengers could cause external costs of $155 million, if the aircraft is valued at $20 million and each life at $450,000, which is the figure Fromm used for airline passengers.

Since private aviation insurance is as yet not very well developed, an event such as this—quite apart from the human tragedy involved—would be a further net social cost imposed on the rest of society by general aviation, which bears no liability for it. If details of accidents of this nature could be predicted with confidence, there would be grounds for levying charges on the general aviation community to cover the costs involved. However, in view of the stochastic nature of such an event, no attempt is made here to predict the number of midair collisions that will occur in future years. Past data have also become less valuable for predictive purposes as a result of the proposed rapid modernization of the airways and associated regulatory changes.

23. Fromm, "Aviation Safety," pp. 598–605.

# Index

Accident investigation: costs, 67–68; National Transportation Safety Board, 67–68; responsibility for, 67–68. *See also* Safety requirements

Aeronautics Branch (Department of Commerce), 45–46

Aerospace Industries Association, 13*n*, 168

Aerostar Corporation, market share, 12

Air carriers: cost studies, 53, 57; data on, 6–7; delay costs to, 146–50; fuel tax, 89–91, 125–26; growth estimates, 9–10; landing and renting fees, 128–30; mileage tax, 85; peak pricing effect, 142–44; registration fee, 85–87; types of, 5; usage projection, 62, 66. *See also* Airports

Air Commerce Act of *1926*, 45

Aircraft: manufacturers, 5–6, 10–12; number projection, 9–10, 163; owner income data, 100–03, 150; types and usage, 14

Aircraft Owners and Pilots Association (AOPA): on external benefits of general aviation, 103; functions, 24; on landing fees, 126; membership, 16, 167; owners' income data, 100–02, 150; on peak pricing, 142–43, 146, 150; on safety regulations, 181–84; on taxation of nonusers, 95–96; on treatment compared to air carriers, 97*n*, 106*n*, 114*n*

Airline Pilots Association (ALPA), automation demands, 51

Airmail contracts, 46

Air navigation subsystem: aids to, 48–49; expenditures for, 50; Federal Aviation Act of *1958*, 63

Airport and Airway Development and Revenue Acts of *1970*, 47, 61–63, 112, 115–21, 162

Airport and Airway Trust Fund, 60–63, 116

Airport development program (ADP), 115–21, 124, 162

Airports: air carrier, 111–19, 127–30; Airport and Airway Development Act of *1970*, 115–21; Airport Development Program (ADP), 115–21, 124, 162; density ranking, 8–9; federal-air airport program (FAAP), 113; Federal Airport Act of *1946*, 112–15; flight quotas, 80, 145–46; fuel fee, 89–91, 125–26; general aviation, 11–19, 122–26, 130–34, 137, 145, 162; "hubs," 112, 119; intermediate, 55; landing and renting fees, 126, 128–30, 157–58; local versus itinerant operations, 8–9; ownership, 25; peak pricing, 138–46, 159–61; pricing policies, 38, 121–30, 141–46; reliever, 112, 116, 118–19, 124, 127, 162; STOL runways, 148; subsidies, 112–15, 127–30, 162–69; types and numbers, 88, 111–12. *See also* Congestion

Air taxi, 16–17; feeder service, 17–18; licensing, 16–17; subsidy for, 106–07; user charges, 84–85

Air traffic control system: air route traffic control centers (ARTCC), 49, 52, 55, 65; automation demands, 49–52; control towers, 9, 48; Project Beacon, 51–52; usage estimates, 8–9; weather and, 55. *See also* Safety requirements

American Airlines, 137*n*

American Association of Airport Executives (AAAE), and direct charging, 119–20

Appalachian Regional Development Act of *1965*, 121*n*

Automation, demands for, 51, 78

Average incremental cost (AIC) pricing. *See* Pricing policy

Average incremental social cost (AISC) pricing. *See* Pricing policy

189